SEX LIVES
OF THE
GREAT DICTATORS

D1250062

SEX LIVES
OF THE
GREAT DICTATORS

An irreverent exposé of despots, tyrants and
other monsters

Nigel Cawthorne

PRION

First published in Great Britain in 1996
This revised edition published 2004 by

Prion
an imprint of the
Carlton Publishing Group
20 Mortimer Street
London W1T 3JW

A catalogue record for this book is available from the British Library

ISBN 1 85375 545 1

Printed in Great Britain
by Mackays

Contents

	Introduction	1
1	Not Tonight, Joséphine	6
2	Ten Days that Shook the Bed	46
3	More Revolting Red Ravers	59
4	Hanging Out With Mussolini	76
5	Hitler Having a Ball	92
6	The Thoughts of Chairman Mao	124
7	The Pleasure Peninsular	144
8	Cuba's Casanova	151
9	Going Down South of the Border	166
10	Don't Cry for Me, Argentina	181
11	Shoe Fetishism in the Philippines	193
12	Eating Out in Africa	206
13	Atatürk – Father of a New Turkey	222
14	Playboy of the Western World	228
15	The Peacock Throne	249
16	The Bawdy Saudis	263
17	The Mother of All Mothers	268
	Index	279

Introduction

Seventies shuttle-diplomat Henry Kissinger, explaining his success with women, once said: 'Power is the ultimate aphrodisiac.'

In a letter to a bishop, Liberal historian Lord Acton penned the aphorism: 'Power tends to corrupt and absolute power corrupts absolutely.'

Between the two, there is a great deal of scope for your average dictator to indulge himself. Some, of course, don't bother. General Pinochet of Chile was a man of the highest repute – apart, of course, from the obvious human shortcomings. You may say that he headed a ruthless regime that raised the murder, torture and false imprisonment of political opponents to an artform, but, a married man, he never even looked at another woman.

And Egypt's rogue president Gamal Abel Nasser? Wonderful family man.

Look at Generalissimo Franco, dictator of Spain from 1939 to his death in 1975. As a youth he took a normal

1

interest in girls, favouring slim brunettes mainly from among his sister's schoolfriends. He wrote them poems and was mortified when they were shown to his sister.

After he joined the army and was posted to Morocco, he assiduously courted Sofía Subirán, the beautiful daughter of the High Commissioner, General Luis Aizpuru. For nearly a year, he bombarded her with love letters. But his inability to dance and his elaborate formality put her off.

During the Moroccan war, he was injured by a bullet in the lower abdomen. Some people have speculated that this was the reason he showed little interest in sex.

Posted home to Oviedo, he met a slender, dark-eyed local girl called María del Carmen Polo y Martínez Valdés. She was fifteen; he was twenty-four. Despite the opposition of her family, he began writing to her at her convent. When she came of age in 1923, they married. For Carmen, it was a dream come true. Five years later she said: 'I thought I was dreaming or reading a novel about me.'

It was a stable, if not passionate, marriage. They had one child, a daughter, Nenuca, born in 1926. There have been persistent rumours that Nenuca was not their child, but the daughter of Franco's notoriously promiscuous brother, Ramón. Anyway, Franco did not have the usual latin desire for a son, so when he died there was, thankfully, no one to step into his shoes.

In 1936, he was mocked as 'Miss Canary Islands' – but this was because of his hesitation in backing the military coup against the government, rather than a reflection of his sexual proclivities.

Franco and his wife gradually grew apart. After El Caudillo – the leader – came to power, he seemed morose and inhibited in the company of Doña Carmen. Neither of them seems to have taken any other lovers. He preferred playing cards and fishing. They were still married when Franco died fifty-two years later. The life of a dictator can be positively boring.

And who wants to know what a monster like Pol Pot – totalitarian leader of Cambodia who caused the deaths of three million of his own people – got up to in bed?

Well, actually, not a lot. Pol Pot's first wife was a teacher, eight years older than himself. Her students called her 'the old virgin' behind her back. They met when they were both studying in France. The marriage took friends by surprise. Few Cambodian men marry older women. She was a revolutionary and encouraged him in his murderous scheme to turn Cambodia back to 'Year Zero'. After he was forced from power by the Vietnamese, she had a nervous breakdown. With her permission, he took a second wife – this time, true to his ideological commitments, he chose not an intellectual but a peasant. In 1988, she gave birth to his first child. Pol Pot, you will be delighted to hear, is a very affectionate father and was often seen carrying his baby daughter in his arms to cadre training sessions – which only goes to prove, never trust a politician who espouses family values.

However, the boring ones are the exception. Think about it. You are a dictator. You rule over millions of people. What you say goes. The temptation to use your unlimited power must be overwhelming.

Look at President Sukarno of Indonesia, the authoritarian president who believed in 'guided democracy'. Like many anti-colonial leaders of his era, he spent much of his youth in jail where, presumably, he was sexually deprived. But once in power, he loosened up. Well into his sixties, he was an extraordinary womanizer, making up for lost time. American magazines called him a 'skirtchaser' and a 'lecher'. French newspapers referred to him as 'le grand seducteur' and British reporters claimed that, over and above his eight legitimate children, he had sired a hundred more.

During his childhood, Sukarno had found security in the bed of Sarinah, the family servant, and spent the rest of his life trying to regain it in the beds of others.

Much of his early political education came from courting Dutch girls. In his twenties, he married his first wife, Inggit. She was eleven years his senior and had to divorce her first husband to marry Sukarno. She supported him and gave him confidence during his years of struggle. But after seventeen years of marriage, he decided that she was barren and married a young model named Fatmawati.

After the revolution, he married Hartini. Once he had consolidated power, his interest in sex became more excessive. He married twice more – Dewi, a highly talented Japanese bar-girl he had met in Tokyo in 1959, and Yurike Sanger, whom he could not formally marry because he had already fulfilled his four-wife Islamic quota.

His sexual athleticism won him admiration as well as notoriety. In his fifties, he was a playboy. In his sixties he was a philanderer of the worst kind. However, this brought with it the censure of more conservative elements and helped hasten his downfall. When he finally fell from power, his wives deserted him too.

Even essentially boring dictators such as the Ceausescus come to life under the sexual microscope. Elena

Ceausescu worked in a bar-cum-brothel when she first arrived in Bucharest from the countryside as a teenager. Nicholae Ceausescu's brother, Nicholae-Andruta, testified that one day in 1943 he had found his wife and Elena naked with two German officers. Nicholae was in prison at the time.

Elena does seem to have been hotter all round than Nicholae, who never had a girlfriend before he was married. Once they were in power, palace spies say she always initiated sex.

Nicholae was not above instructing his spies to use sexual entrapment; Nicholae and Elena watched blue movies together – special ones made by the Romanian intelligence service showing Western diplomats in compromising positions. Nicholae was embarrassed, though. He preferred watching Kojak.

Elena was also obsessed with the sexual peccadilloes of the Politburo wives. She had the Romanian intelligence service bug them so she could listen to the sounds they made when they made love.

Their son Nicu was a sexual monster. Nicholae Ceausescu praised him for attaining his manhood at fourteen by raping a classmate. Nicu casually raped his way around Bucharest and no one did anything about it.

The collapse of Communism put paid to the Ceausescus and the dictators of Eastern Europe. Even in South America, democracy is on the march. In the Middle East though, secular dictators like the Shah of Iran have fallen, only to be replaced by theocratic dictators like the Ayatollah Khomeini. Sadly, they lie beyond the scope of this book; and I can guarantee you now that there will be no Sex Lives of the Mullahs in this series. I don't like the company of Special Branch that much.

1

Not Tonight, Joséphine

Sexual love is 'harmful to society and to the individual happiness of men', wrote the young Napoleon – but then he was kind of mixed up. His first sexual fumblings may not even have been heterosexual ones.

At military school in Brienne, the fourteen-year-old Napoleon was well known for his inability to make friends. He did, however, become very close to one boy named Pierre François Laugier de Bellecour, a pretty aristocrat from Nancy. It was rumoured that Pierre François was, in Brienne slang, a 'nymph' and Napoleon got rather jealous when Pierre François widened his circle. He demanded that Pierre François assure him that he was still his best friend.

The two of them went together to the Ecole Militaire in Paris. As Pierre François was quickly sucked into overtly homosexual circles, Napoleon renounced his friendship and told Pierre François never to speak to him again. Napoleon wrote to the Minister of War suggesting that the 'rigours of Spartan youth' be introduced into military academies, but he was advised to drop the matter.

During his first posting, to Valence in 1785, the sixteen-year-old Second Lieutenant Bonaparte grew close to a Madame du Colombier. A long way from home, the middle-aged Madame du Colombier provided a comforting mother-figure for him. She also had a pretty daughter named Caroline and, during the summer of 1786, romance blossomed.

Napoleon recalled the affair from exile in St Helena thirty years later: 'no one could have been more innocent than we were. We often used to arrange little assignations and I recollect one in particular, which took place at daybreak one morning in the middle of summer. You may not believe it, but our sole delight on that occasion consisted of eating cherries together.'

Twenty years after that summer of young love, he wrote to Caroline and they met in Lyons. She could scarcely believe that her lanky boy soldier was now Emperor.

'She watched his every movement with an attention that seemed to emanate from her very soul,' a courtier recorded.

But in his eyes, his pretty young love had turned into a fat and boring housewife. He regretted arranging the meeting. Nevertheless, he gave her husband a government post, made her brother a lieutenant and appointed her lady-in-waiting to his mother, or Madame Mère, as she was officially known.

Napoleon did not lose his virginity until he was eighteen, with a prostitute he picked up in the Palais Royal in Paris. It was a deliberate act – 'une expérience philosophique' as he wrote in his notebook. The Palais Royal was a well-known centre for prostitution throughout the Revolution. The more expensive prostitutes took rooms on the mezzanine. From the half-moon windows, they would lean out and shout to passersby, or strike suggestive poses. Better-known harlots sent out runners who would hand out leaflets describing their specialities and their prices to the crowd below, while the cheap whores would work the garden outside.

The young Napoleon had just collected his back pay. As he walked in the Palais Royal gardens he noted that he was 'agitated by the vigorous sentiments which characterize it, and it made me forget the cold'. He recorded that he was stopped by a frail young girl to whom he explained the nature of his philosophical quest. Apparently she was used to earnest young men undertaking such arduous research assignments. He asked her how she lost her virginity and why she had turned to prostitution. She told him the usual story – she had been seduced by an officer, kicked out of the house by an angry mother, taken to Paris by a second officer and abandoned there to fend for herself. She then suggested that they go back to his hotel.

'What shall we do there?' he asked naively.

'Come on,' she said. 'We'll get warm and you'll have your fill of pleasure.'

Napoleon found the experience disappointing and he remained shy around women.

It is widely rumoured that Napoleon had a tiny penis. The evidence comes from the autopsy report performed by the British and was probably largely propaganda. His pubis was described as feminine in appearance, resembling 'the Mons Veneris in women'; his body completely hairless; his skin soft and white; and his breasts plump and round such that 'many amongst the fair sex would be proud of it.' The penis was removed and preserved at the time and came to auction at Christie's in 1969. His member, referred to genteelly by the auctioneers at Christie's as 'Napoleon's tendon', was small and unsightly. But who would be at their best after 150 years in brine?

At twenty-five, he fell in love for the first time. The object of his affections was Désirée Clary, a renowned beauty. He called her Eugénie, finding Désirée too vulgar. She was dark-haired and slender, and had the characteristics that Napoleon most craved in a woman – small hands and feet, and a large dowry. His brother had married Eugénie's older sister and Napoleon hoped this would smooth the way. But when the question of marriage was broached, Eugénie's wealthy parents said that one penniless Bonaparte in the family was quite enough.

Napoleon did not give up. He continued the affair, largely through correspondence. She was in Marseilles with her parents, while he was making his way in Paris. His letters were passionate. He even wrote her a flowery love story called Clisson et Eugénie to indicate the depth of his feelings for her. It is the tale of a brilliant young warrior, Clisson, who dies gloriously in battle after learning that his wife, the gentle Eugénie, has fallen in love with his best friend.

'Sometimes on the banks silvered by the star of love, Clisson would give himself up to the desires and throbbings of his heart,' Napoleon wrote. 'He could not tear himself away from the sweet and melancholy spectacle of the night, lit by moonlight. He would remain there until she disappeared, till darkness effaced his reverie.

9

He would spend entire hours meditating in the depths of a wood, and in the evening he would remain until midnight, lost in reveries by the light of the silver star of love.'

Who says tyrants have no heart. Even from the distance of his exile in St Helena, he recalled Eugénie as his 'first love'. However, he suddenly withdrew his offer of marriage. The brush-off was delicately delivered. Napoleon wrote that one day, he knew, her feelings towards him would change. That being the case, he could not hold her to her vow of eternal love. The very day she no longer loved him, she must tell him. And if she fell in love with someone else, she must give way to her emotions. He would understand.

Eugénie was heartbroken.

'All that is left to me now is to wish for death,' she wrote.

But after a while her heart mended and she married another up-and-coming soldier, Jean Baptiste Bernadotte. He went on to become a Marshal of France and, in 1810, ascended to the Swedish throne. Eugénie became the Queen of Sweden and her descendants sit on the Swedish throne to this day.

Eager to marry, Napoleon shifted his attention to more mature women. He proposed at least five times – one of the women, Mademoiselle de Montansier, was sixty – but, shabby and badly dressed, the young Napoleon was not a very savoury prospect. He wore his battered round hat crammed down over his ears while his lank, ill-powdered hair hung down over the collar of his greatcoat. His boots were cheap, shoddy and unpolished, and he never wore gloves, condemning them as a 'useless luxury'. In truth, he could not afford any.

What's worse, he was a bore, making frequent outbursts against the iniquities of the rich.

Madame Permon was one of the few women who allowed Napoleon to attend her salon, and this was largely because she was a fellow Corsican. There he would dance with Madame Permon's daughter, Laure.

'At that time,' Laure wrote, 'Bonaparte had a heart capable of devotion.'

Napoleon's fortunes improved out of all recognition when he led a detachment that shot down a column of royalists who were marching on the National Assembly. Overnight, Napoleon became the 'saviour of the Republic'. He was made a full general with command of the Army of the Interior. He had a brand new uniform and moved out of his shabby hotel and into a house on the Rue des Capucines. He even had his own carriage.

When Monsieur Permon died, Napoleon visited the house regularly to comfort the widow. On one occasion, finding himself alone with her, he suggested that they united their two families. Her son Albert, Napoleon suggested, should marry his pretty young sister Pauline. But Albert might have plans of his own, Madame Permon said.

Then her daughter Laure should marry his brother Jerome, Napoleon suggested. They were too young, said Madame Permon. In that case, the two of them should marry, Napoleon proposed. They would, of course, have to wait until a decent period of mourning had been observed.

Madame Permon took this proposal as a joke. She was forty and much too old for him. But it was no joke and after he was refused, Napoleon never visited the house again.

Soon after that he met Joséphine Tascher-Beauharnais. A thirty-two-year-old former vicomtesse from Martinique, she had been imprisoned and her husband guillotined during the Terror. When she was released, like the rest of Paris, she was determined to have some fun.

The city was in the grip of a dance craze. Over six hundred dance halls opened. Determined to put the excesses of the Revolution behind them, women wore their hair à la guillotine, cropped or pinned up, leaving the neck exposed. To enhance the macabre effect, the fashion was to wear a thin, blood-red ribbon around their necks. There was even a Bal à la Victime, a dance to which only the relatives of those who had been guillotined were invited.

Joséphine fostered out her thirteen-year-old son, Eugène, to General Hoche, a fellow prisoner and former lover. Then she began borrowing money to fund an extravagant lifestyle, squandering it on carriages, furniture, exotic food, flowers and fashionable clothes.

With her slender build, topped by a riot of chestnut curls, Joséphine had the perfect seductive figure for the new Directoire style. Although she did not go quite as far as her friend Madame Hamelin who walked down the Champs-Elysées naked to the waist, she could be seen bare-armed and practically bare-breasted in flimsy gowns over flesh-coloured body stockings.

She used her well-displayed charms to persuade those in authority to give back the property that had been confiscated from her during the Terror. Her Paris apartment was unsealed and her clothes, jewels and furnishings returned. She was granted access to her late husband's château and was richly compensated for the furniture, silver-ware and books that had already been sold. She was also reimbursed for the horses and equipment her husband had lost when he was stripped of his command of the Army of the Rhine. This exercise gave her all sorts of important contacts. Joséphine made such a habit of sleeping with the important men in post-revolutionary France that the security services paid her for the pillow talk she garnered. It was truly amazing, a contemporary wit remarked of Joséphine, that bountiful nature had the foresight to put 'the wherewithal to pay her bills beneath her navel'.

One of Joséphine's closest friends was another fellow prisoner, Thérèse de Fontenay. She was the daughter of a Spanish banker who distributed her favours so liberally around high government circles that she was said to have been stamped 'government property'. She was the mistress of financier Gabriel Ouvard, government minister Jean Tallien, to whom she was later briefly married, and the Director himself, Paul Barras.

Barras was a former nobleman who had joined the Revolution when he saw which way the wind was blowing. He supported the Terror; then, when the time was right, engineered Robespierre's downfall. He became the most important man in post-revolutionary Paris and he lived in the Luxembourg Palace in a style as lavish as any pre-revolutionary salon. His taste for pleasure, a contemporary remarked, was like that of 'an opulent, extravagant, magnificent and dissipated prince'.

Thérèse introduced Joséphine to Barras – indeed, the two of them had danced naked before him. When Barras grew tired of Thérèse, Joséphine took her place in his bed. Some of her acquaintances were shocked, but to Joséphine this was perfectly natural. Both her husband and father had been tireless adulterers and she had an aunt who slept with her father-in-law. Besides, Barras was a very handsome man.

Joséphine was definitely not the type of woman Napoleon was looking for. He was quite dismayed by the way powerful men seemed to be controlled by feckless and immoral women.

'Women are everywhere,' he wrote to his brother, disapprovingly, 'applauding in the theatre, strolling in the parks, reading in the bookshops. You will find these lovely creatures even in the wise man's study. This is the only place in the world where they deserve to steer the ship of state. The men are mad about them, think of nothing else, and live only for them.'

As commander of the Army of the Interior, Napoleon was now invited to all the important salons. Although there was still some debate about his charms, some young women were impressed by his classical 'Grecian' features and his large eyes that seemed to light up when he spoke.

'You would never have guessed that he was a military man,' wrote one. 'There was nothing dashing about him, no swagger, no bluster, nothing rough.' Most agreed that he looked painfully thin.

He met Joséphine after an order had been issued that all weapons in private hands were to be handed in to the authorities. Joséphine's son, Eugène, had a sword that had belonged to his father. Eugène did not want to hand this memento in, so he approached the General commanding the Army of the Interior to ask if he could keep it. Impressed by the child's filial devotion, Napoleon gave his consent.

The next day, Joséphine came to thank General Bonaparte in person. Napoleon admitted later that he was bowled over by her 'extraordinary grace and her irresistibly sweet manner'. He asked if he could call on her.

Joséphine can hardly have been impressed with what she saw. This short, skinny man, with gaunt, angular features and lank hair, was hardly the sort to turn a girl's head. But she spotted that Bonaparte was the coming man and invited him to one of her regular Thursday receptions.

Napoleon was not comfortable in such surroundings. He was appalled that the money she spent on flowers and food for one of these soirées would have been enough to keep his family for a week. Joséphine's house, a neighbour noted, was stacked with luxuries – 'only the essentials are missing'.

Joséphine's salon was full of actors and playwrights, leaving Napoleon tongue-tied; and the beautiful women intimidated him.

'I was not indifferent to the charms of women, but up to this time they had not spoiled me,' he said, 'and my disposition made me shy in their company.'

But with Joséphine, it was different. Her attentiveness reassured him. A friend noted later that there was 'a certain intriguing air of languorousness about her – a Creole characteristic – apparent in her attitudes of repose as well as in her movements; all these qualities lent her a charm which more than offset the dazzling beauty of her rivals'. Before long, Napoleon was hopelessly in love.

He must have known about her relationship with Barras – all of Paris did. They were hardly discreet.

15

When she entertained him at her house in Croissy – which he paid for – the neighbours would see baskets of luxuries turning up from early in the morning. Then a detachment of mounted police would arrive, followed by Barras and a huge party of friends.

Barras himself said: 'Bonaparte was as well acquainted with all of the lady's adventures as we were; I knew he knew, because he heard the stories in my presence. And Madame de Beauharnais was generally recognized as one of my early liaisons. With Bonaparte a frequent visitor to my apartment, he could not have remained ignorant of such a state of affairs, nor could he have believed that everything was over between her and me.'

Napoleon also knew of her affair with General Hoche. One evening at a party given by Thérèse Tallien, in a playful mood, Napoleon pretended to read palms, but when he got to General Hoche's hand, his mood changed.

'General, you will die in your bed,' he said darkly. This was an insult, coming from one soldier to another. Only Joséphine's speedy intervention prevented it developing into a full-scale row.

Plainly, Napoleon could not handle his feelings and he stopped seeing her. Joséphine wrote to him: 'You no longer come to see a friend who is fond of you. You have completely deserted her, which is a great mistake, for she is tenderly devoted to you. Come to lunch tomorrow. I must talk to you about things that will be of advantage to you. Goodnight, my friend. A fond embrace.'

Napoleon replied immediately.

16

'I cannot imagine the reason for the tone of your letter,' he wrote. 'I beg you to believe me when I say that no one so yearns for your friendship as I do, that no one can be more eager for the opportunity to prove it. If my duties had permitted, I would have come to deliver this note in person.'

Soon he was visiting her more than ever.

'One day, when I was sitting next to her at table,' he recalled later, 'she began to pay me all manner of compliments on my military expertise. Her praise intoxicated me. From that moment I confined my conversation to her and never left her side.'

Joséphine's thirteen-year-old daughter Hortense confirmed his puppy-like devotion. One evening she accompanied her mother to a dinner party being held by Barras at the Luxembourg Palace.

'I found myself placed between my mother and a general who, in order to talk to her, kept leaning forward so often and with so much vivacity that he wearied me and obliged me to lean back,' she wrote. 'In spite of myself, I looked attentively at his face, which was handsome and expressive, but remarkably pale. He spoke ardently and seemed to devote all his attention to my mother.'

Soon after that they became lovers. For Joséphine, making love was a pleasant way to round off a memorable evening together. For Napoleon, it was transcendent. At seven o'clock the next morning, he wrote breathlessly: 'I wake full of you. Between your portrait and the memory of our intoxicating night, my senses have no respite. Sweet and incomparable Joséphine, what is this strange effect you have on my heart? What if you were to be angry? What if I were to see you sad or troubled? Then my soul would be shattered by distress. Then your lover would find no peace, no rest. But I find none, either, when I succumb to the profound emotion that overwhelms me, when I draw from your lips, from your heart, a flame that consumes me... I shall see you in three hours. Until then, mio dolce amor, I send you a thousand kisses – but send me none in return, for they set my blood on fire.'

Napoleon's aide-de-camp Auguste Marmont witnessed the effect this consummation had: 'He was madly in love, in the full sense of the word, in its widest possible meaning. It was, apparently, his first real passion, a primordial passion, and he responded to it with all the vigour of nature. A love so pure, so true, so exclusive had never before possessed a man. Although she no longer had the freshness of youth, she knew how to please him, and we know that to lovers the question of 'why' is superfluous. One loves because one loves and nothing is less susceptible to explanation and analysis than this emotion.'

Long after they divorced, Napoleon embittered by defeat and exile, stood on St Helena and admitted still: 'I was passionately in love with her, and our friends were aware of this long before I ever dared to say a word about it.'

Many were shocked at his love for Joséphine who, they considered, had 'lost all her bloom'. Napoleon was twenty-six. She was thirty-two, though she thoughtfully shaved four years off her age for the marriage certificate while he, gallantly, added two years to his.

Full of the optimism of young love, Napoleon wrote to Joséphine: 'You could not have inspired in me so infinite a love unless you felt it too.'

She did not. He was deluding himself. She was amusing herself with what she called her 'funny little Corsican'.

But Barras was eager to shed the spendthrift Joséphine and Joséphine needed a new sugar daddy – all the better if he was young and naive.

Napoleon later admitted that it was Barras who advised him to marry Joséphine. He made it clear that Napoleon would gain both socially and financially. Barras also encouraged Napoleon's mistaken idea that Joséphine was rich. In fact, her dowry would be a stack of unpaid bills. But she was from an aristocratic family and Napoleon was an incurable snob.

Joséphine was quite taken aback when Napoleon proposed. She had expected to be his mistress for a while, not his wife. She admitted to a friend that she did not love him, feeling only 'indifference, tepidness'. Frightened by his ardour, she accused him of having some ulterior reason for marrying her. He was mortified:

For you even to think that I do not love you for yourself alone!!! For whom, then? For what? I am astonished at you, but still more astonished at myself – back at your feet this morning without the will-power to resent or resist. The height of weakness and abjection! What is this strange power you have over me, my incomparable Joséphine, that a mere thought of yours has the power to poison my life and rend my heart, when at the same time another emotion stronger still and another less sombre mood lead me back to grovel before you?

Eventually, the force of his passion overwhelmed her.

'I don't know why,' she said to a friend, 'but sometimes his absurd self-confidence impresses me to the point of believing anything is possible to this singular

19

man – anything that might come to his mind to undertake. With his imagination, who can guess what he might undertake?'

Later, on St Helena, Napoleon gave a more objective account of his reasons for marrying Joséphine: 'I really loved Joséphine, but I had no respect for her... Actually, I married her only because I thought she had a large fortune. She said she had, but it was not true.'

Napoleon's family opposed the match. They disapproved of Joséphine's frivolous ways and her outré clothes. Joséphine's children were also against it.

'Mama won't love us so much,' Hortense told her brother. But they were eventually persuaded that having a General as a stepfather would be a help to Eugène, who was planning to be a soldier. Even so, Hortense never quite reconciled herself to the marriage. Later, when her headmistress – and the rest of France – were lauding his victories, Hortense said: 'Madame, I will give him credit for all his other conquests, but I will never forgive him for having conquered my mother.'

When they went to draw up the marriage contract, the homme d'affaires who dealt with the property settlement advised Joséphine against tying herself to a penniless young soldier who might get killed in battle leaving her nothing but 'his cloak and his sword'. Nevertheless, she went ahead.

Barras gave her away. Napoleon was two hours late for the ceremony – the mayor had gone home – but at ten o'clock on 9 March, 1796, Napoleon and Joséphine were married by a minor official who did not even have the proper authority to conduct the two-minute ceremony.

Barras was as good as his word. The marriage did advance Napoleon. A week before the ceremony, Barras had made him commander of the Army of Italy.

After the wedding Napoleon moved into Joséphine's new house at 6 Rue Chanterine. It was a secluded house set in a wooded garden. The walls and ceiling of her boudoir were mirrored, but the gilded swans gliding through a sea of pink roses on the ceiling of her bedroom had to go. In honour of Napoleon, Joséphine had her bedroom redecorated like a soldier's tent.

On their wedding night, while they were consummating the marriage, Joséphine's pug dog Fortuné, fearing that his mistress was being attacked, bit Napoleon on the leg. The dog and his insatiable mistress were all too much for Napoleon. After the necessary deed had been done, he refused further enticement and retreated to his books of strategy and tactics. After thirty-six hours, he cut the honeymoon short and went to take up his posting in Italy. It was definitely a case of 'Not tonight, Joséphine'.

While Napoleon threw himself into war, the voracious Joséphine amused herself with a score of generous lovers. Among them was a handsome young cavalry officer, Lieutenant Hippolyte Charles. He was tall, dashing and handsome, and she immediately fell head-over-heels in love with him.

But Napoleon was missing his darling Joséphine and summoned her to Milan.

'Come and join me as soon as you can,' he wrote, 'so that at least before we die we can say we were happy for a few days.'

He assured her that 'never was a woman loved with more devotion, more fire or more tenderness. Never has

21

a woman been in such complete mastery of another's heart.'

She was busy with Charles and did not respond. When he returned one day to find that, yet again, she had not arrived 'sorrow crushed my soul', he wrote. He begged her to write to him and told her: 'I love you with a love beyond the limits of imagination, that every minute of my life is consecrated to you, that never an hour passes without my thinking of you, that I have never thought of another woman.'

Joséphine eventually arrived, but was bored. Napoleon was occupied with the siege of Mantua at the time and she wrote home, saying how much she missed her other lovers. Napoleon, on the other hand, could hardly concentrate on the battle for kissing, teasing, fondling and caressing her 'beautiful body', even in front of a room full of people.

He did not mind going even further. The French diplomat, Miot de Melito, wrote an account of a carriage ride around Lake Maggiore. He and General Berthier sat in a state of shock, he said, while on the seat opposite, Napoleon took 'conjugal liberties' with his wife. The visit made him the happiest man in the world.

'A few days ago, I thought I loved you,' he wrote afterwards, 'but now since I have seen you again I love you a thousand times more. Everyday since I met you I have loved you more. Thousands of kisses – even one for Fortuné, wicked beast that he is.'

This was precious little comfort for Joséphine.

'My husband does not love me,' she wrote. 'He worships me. I think he will go mad.'

When Napoleon and his army advanced, he wrote to her begging her to come to Brescia where 'the tenderest of lovers awaits you'. She went immediately, but only because her lover, Lieutenant Charles was now attached to Napoleon's command.

When the campaign turned disastrously against the French, Joséphine, back in Milan, feared for the lives of her husband and her lover. Things may have been going badly because, instead of concentrating on the battle, Napoleon was taking the time to write long, passionate love letters to Joséphine once or twice a day. There was just one thing on his mind.

'A kiss upon your heart, another a little lower, another lower still, far lower!' he wrote. On another occasion, he wrote: 'I kiss your breasts, and lower down, much lower down.' It is hard to strike out decisively against the enemy when all you can think of is oral sex.

Despite the passion of his letters, Joséphine rarely wrote back. When she did, she would address him as 'vous' rather than the familiar 'tu'. However, in her letters to Lieutenant Charles, she expresses an ardour that matches anything Napoleon came up with.

Joséphine was happy to share her husband's intimate thoughts with others. One friend she showed his letters to noted:

> They were extraordinary letters; the handwriting almost indecipherable, the spelling shaky, the style bizarre and confused, but marked by a tone so impassioned, by emotions so turbulent, by expressions so vibrant and at the same time so poetic, by a love so apart from all other loves that no woman in the world could fail to take pride in having been their inspiration. Besides, what a position for a woman to find herself in – being the motivating force behind the triumphal march of an entire army.

Napoleon finally turned the tide at Rivoli; and his passion for her did seem to spur him on.

'My every action is designed with the sole purpose of reuniting with you,' he wrote. 'I am driving myself to death to reach you again.'

Two days after the battle, he wrote to her in relief:

> *I am going to bed with my heart full of your adorable image. I cannot wait to give you proof of my ardent love. How happy I would be if I could assist at your undressing, the little firm white breasts, the adorable face, the hair tied up in a scarf à la créole. You know that I never forget the little visits to, you know, the little black forest. I kiss it a thousand times and wait impatiently for the moment I will be in it. To live with Joséphine is to live in the Elysian fields. Kisses on your mouth, your eyes, your breast, everywhere, everywhere.*

Six days later he was back in Milan. He ran up the staircase of the Serbelloni Palace to find her bedroom – empty. She was in Genoa with Lieutenant Charles.

For nine days he waited for her, writing her tortured, passionate, pitiful letters:

> *I left everything to see you, to hold you in my arms. The pain I feel is incalculable. I don't want you to change any plans for parties, or to be interested in the happiness of a man who lives only for you. I am not worth it. When I beg you to equal a love like mine, I am wrong. Why should I expect lace to weigh as much as gold? May the fates concentrate in me all sorrows and all grief, but give Joséphine only happy days. When I am sure that she can no longer love me, I will be silent and content only to be useful to her.*

After he sealed the envelope, he re-opened it and added desperately: 'Oh Joséphine, Joséphine!'

Napoleon still did not understand his wife's depth of feeling for Lieutenant Charles. Although he had heard that they spent a lot of time together, he considered Charles a fop – hardly a rival for a victorious general like himself. Back in Paris, his brother and sister told Napoleon that Joséphine was using her influence to secure lucrative army contracts for her lover.

When Napoleon confronted Joséphine, she burst into tears and denied everything. If he wanted a divorce, he should just say so, she said. Napoleon was all too eager to believe his wife innocent. He even believed her when she said that she would break off all communication with Charles. But directly after the confrontation, she wrote to Charles, saying: 'No matter how they torment me, they will never separate me from my Hippolyte. My last sigh will be for him. Goodbye my Hippolyte, a thousand kisses as fiery as my heart, and as loving.'

A few days later they were back together again in a secret assignation because 'only you can restore me to happiness. Tell me that you love me, that you love me alone. That will make me the happiest of women. I am yours, all yours.'

The two lovers were separated when Napoleon took Joséphine to Toulon, where he was embarking his army for Egypt. Before leaving, Napoleon summoned General Dumas to his bedroom where Napoleon and Joséphine were lying naked under a sheet. Once they had conquered Egypt, Napoleon said, they would send for their wives and do their utmost to impregnate them with sons. Dumas would stand godfather to the young Bonaparte.

During his Egyptian campaign in 1798, Napoleon was again told of Joséphine's unfaithfulness – and that he was the laughing-stock of Paris. To get his own back, he got his secretary to round up all the women he could find, but they were all too fat and ugly for his tastes.

Then nineteen-year-old Pauline Fourès came to his attention. She had dressed in a man's uniform to accompany her husband to Egypt. The skin-tight pantaloon that the French army wore at the time pandered to Napoleon's tastes. According to a contemporary, she had a 'rose-petal complexion, beautiful teeth and a good geometrical figure'.

Napoleon sent her husband off up the Nile, while he staged a very public seduction. At a dinner party, he deliberately spilt some wine on her dress, then took her upstairs to sponge it off. When Lieutenant Fourès returned to Cairo, Napoleon sent him back to Paris with despatches and installed Pauline in a house near his headquarters in Cairo.

Like many soldiers, Napoleon had a thing about uniforms. Pauline would dress in a plumed hat and gold-braided coat to inflame his passion. She was soon nicknamed 'Madame la Générale' or 'Our Lady of the Orient'.

Poor Lieutenant Fourès finally had to divorce his wife, while she publicly flaunted herself as Napoleon's mistress.

It suited Napoleon for news of the affair to get back to Joséphine. Napoleon ensured this by having Joséphine's son, Eugène, riding escort when Madame Fourès rode around Cairo in her carriage. Napoleon even promised to marry her, if she had a baby. When she did not become pregnant, she complained that the 'little idiot' did not know how to have a child. She said that it was not her fault and pointed out that, in the two years they had been married, Joséphine had not had a baby either, though she had had two by her previous husband.

After the Battle of the Nile, in August 1799, Napoleon left Madame Fourès in Cairo and slipped through the British blockade of Egypt. He never saw Pauline Fourès again, though during the Empire he bought her a house and gave her a liberal allowance. She died at the age of ninety, in 1869, during the reign of Napoleon III.

Joséphine found out about the affair in the most embarrassing possible way. Letters describing the intimate details of the liaison had been captured by the British and published in London, where correspondents for the French papers soon picked them up.

Meanwhile, a scandal over the army contracts she had secured for Lieutenant Charles had brought about an end to their relationship. So Joséphine had no choice but to attempt a reconciliation with her husband. She heard that Napoleon had left Egypt and she raced for the coast, ahead of his brothers.

She got as far as Lyons before hearing that she had missed him on the road and turned back for Paris. Napoleon arrived back at their home in Rue de la Victoire to find the house empty. A few hours later, his brothers turned up. They told him everything and urged a divorce. But Napoleon loved Joséphine so much he still found it hard to deal with the fact that she really had been unfaithful to him. When she finally arrived home, three days later, Napoleon had locked himself in his study. No amount of knocking or pleading would get him to open the door. She remained outside sobbing all night. In the morning, the maid suggested she get Hortense and Eugène. Napoleon loved his stepchildren and eventually he opened the door. His eyes were red with weeping and while he embraced Eugène, Joséphine and Hortense knelt on the floor and hugged his knees. Soon he was unable to resist her. When his brother Lucien dropped round later, he found Napoleon and Joséphine in bed together, totally reconciled.

However, the relationship had been turned on its head. Joséphine now tried desperately to hold on to his love while Napoleon sought pleasure elsewhere – though he never allowed the name of Hippolyte Charles to be mentioned in his presence. After the coup that made Napoleon military dictator in 1800, his chief aide-de-camp, Duroc, would procure young women and take them up to a bedroom next to Napoleon's study. They would be told to strip and get into bed, so that they could attend to le petit général's needs as soon as he had finished working. He even fell in love two or three times.

He made no excuse for his behaviour, telling Joséphine simply: 'You ought to think it perfectly natural that I am allowed amusements of this kind.'

Adultery, he said, was 'a joke behind a mask...not by any means a rare phenomenon but a very ordinary occurrence on the sofa'.

Desperate to secure her position, Joséphine decided that her daughter Hortense should marry his brother Louis. That way, if she could not be mother of Napoleon's heir, she could at least be grandmother. She won Napoleon around to the scheme by 'the influence exerted in the boudoir, by her repeated entreaties and her caresses', one of Napoleon's aides said. However, the marriage foundered when Louis heard the rumour that eighteen-year-old Hortense was having an affair with her stepfather – Napoleon himself.

During Napoleon's second Italian campaign, in the afternoons, Napoleon would regularly send for an Italian girl 'to pass the time agreeably'. He also seduced La Grassini, the prima donna of La Scala, and installed her in a house in Paris. But having a triumphant affair with the conquering hero in Milan was one thing; being the official mistress of a head of state was quite another, and Napoleon was quickly replaced by a violinist named Rhode.

Next came Louise Rolandeau of the Opéra-Comique. While Joséphine was away at the spa town of Plombières, where the waters were supposed to make a woman more fertile, Napoleon invited Louise to entertain the guests at Malmaison, their country home. Joséphine wrote to Hortense, who was official hostess there, to put an end to the visits.

'As if I could do anything about it,' Hortense replied.

Joséphine returned to try to take control of the situation; but things went from bad to worse, when Joséphine began to suspect her husband was having an affair with her young lady-in-waiting and confidante, Claire de Rémusat. Joséphine railed against her husband's sexual depravity. She warned Claire that he was the 'most immoral' of men.

'To hear her tell it, he had no moral principles whatsoever,' wrote Madame de Rémusat. 'And he concealed his vicious inclinations only for fear they would damage his reputation. If he were allowed to follow his inclinations without restraint, he would sink into the most shameful excesses. Had he not seduced his own sisters one about another? Did he consider himself especially privileged to satisfy his sexual inclinations?'

Napoleon responded innocently, asking Claire why Joséphine should get upset over 'these innocuous diversions of mine which in no way involve my affections'.

'I am not like other men,' he would thunder when Joséphine made accusations. 'The laws of morality and society are not applicable to me. I have the right to answer all your objections with the eternal I.'

Nevertheless when Napoleon crowned himself Emperor in 1803, Joséphine was at his side.

Joséphine used the coronation skilfully to her own advantage. When Pope Pius VII travelled to France to anoint the new Emperor, she arranged to see him privately and told him that she was concerned about the legality of her marriage. Indeed, there had only been a civil service, not a religious one. The pope was shocked and refused to play his part in the coronation unless the situation was remedied immediately.

On the evening of 1 December, 1804, in the greatest secrecy, an altar was set up in Napoleon's study. Napoleon's uncle, Cardinal Fesch, performed the ceremony in front of two witnesses. Afterwards, Joséphine asked the Cardinal for a certificate proving that this marriage was legal and binding.

Napoleon's family hated Joséphine and would do anything to get rid of her. They frequently put potential lovers his way. His sister Caroline introduced the ambitious and attractive Marie Antoinette Dûchatel to court. Joséphine soon suspected that Napoleon had taken her as his mistress. One day, she noticed that both her husband and Madame Dûchatel were absent from the salon. She found them in a locked room and began frantically banging on the door. When Napoleon opened it, he and Madame Dûchatel were naked. Madame Dûchatel fled and Joséphine burst into tears, while Napoleon stormed up and down, kicking the furniture and threatening to divorce her if she did not stop her spying.

Joséphine lived in constant fear that one of Napoleon's mistresses would conceive. She was certain that he would divorce her as barren and marry someone who could give him a son.

Next Caroline provided the attractive eighteen-year-old Eléonore Denuelle, whose husband had just been arrested for forgery. Caroline kept Eléonore under constant surveillance and delivered her to the Tuileries for regular meetings with Napoleon. That way Napoleon could be sure that, if she conceived, the child would be his.

In September 1806, she became pregnant. Joséphine said nothing and simply resigned herself to her fate. When Eléonore Denuelle gave birth to a son, Napoleon proudly claimed to be the father. But still he did not drop Joséphine. Later he learned that his sister's attempts to keep Eléonore Denuelle away from other men may not have been as successful as they had hoped. It seems that Caroline's own husband, Joachim Murat, may well have been the father of Eléonore's child.

Many of Napoleon's affairs passed unnoticed, but his liaison with Marguérite Weymer (later called the 'whale' because she became immensely fat) caused quite a scandal. When Napoleon knew her, she was a voluptuous sixteen-year-old actress from the Comédie-Française. In the evenings, Marguérite would be smuggled into a room near his study where, after his day's work was over, he would amuse himself with her before finding his way back to his own bedroom.

Joséphine would sometimes find the waiting unbearable. One night she tried to catch Napoleon and Marguérite together, only to find her way barred by Roustam, Napoleon's fierce Mameluke guard.

On another occasion, just as Napoleon and Marguérite were starting to make love, he blacked out with an epileptic convulsion. Marguérite let out a scream that woke the whole household. Napoleon came round to find Joséphine, Claire de Rémusat and a dozen members of the palace staff crowded around the bed. In bed beside him was a naked Marguérite.

If this was not bad enough, Marguérite Weymer was also known in Parisian society as Mademoiselle Georges. Napoleon finally dropped her when an erotic book was published showing her engaged in homosexual acts with her lesbian lover, Raucort.

Napoleon did nothing to hide his lovers from Joséphine. In front of the court, he would recount the virtues, physical imperfections and anatomical peculiarities of his latest lover 'with the most indecent openness'. Soon the details would be winging their way via diplomats' couriers to the governments of Europe. But Joséphine was so determined to hang on to her position as consort that she tolerated this humiliation. She even helped him get rid of women he had tired of.

Although pamphlets circulated making out that Napoleon was a Hercules among lovers, the truth was far more mundane. In her memoirs, Mademoiselle Georges said it was only at their third meeting that they went to bed together. He was not very physical and never forced himself on her, though he occasionally displayed outbursts of jealousy over former lovers. Once, she recalled, he pranced about the bedroom naked with a wreath of white roses on his head.

The novelist Stendhal knew Napoleon and described the Emperor in the evening, sitting at a small table signing decrees. 'When a lady was announced, he would ask her – without looking up from his work – to go and wait for him in the bed. Later, with a candlestick in his hand, he would show her out of the bedroom and return to his table and his endless decrees. The essential part of the rendezvous had not lasted three minutes.'

One nervous actress was greeted curtly with: 'Come in. Undress. Lie down.'

Sometimes it did not even get that far. Once he sent a servant to get Mademoiselle Duchesnois, another actress from the Comédie-Française. When she arrived at his apartment in the Tuileries she was told to wait. After two hours, the servant went to Napoleon to remind him that Mademoiselle Duchesnois was waiting. He said: 'Tell her to get undressed.'

She stripped off. For another hour, she sat there nude. Then the servant went to Napoleon to remind him again. This time the Emperor said: 'Tell her to go home.' She dressed and left.

Joséphine actually made things easier for him. She liked to be surrounded by pretty young ladies-in-waiting. When Napoleon was in what he called his 'rutting season', he would take his pick.

'Love is a singular passion, turning men into beasts,' he said. 'I come into season like a dog.'

As Napoleon's power increased, his lovemaking became more perfunctory; but it was important for him to keep up his image. In later life, he admitted his 'feebleness in the game of love; it did not amount to much'.

Napoleon's confidant General Louis de Caulaincourt summed up the situation: 'It was rarely that he felt any need of love, or indeed pleasure in it. The Emperor was so eager to recount his amorous successes that one might almost have imagined he only engaged in them for the sake of talking about them.'

In fact, Napoleon did not like women very much. He was candid in his opinions: 'We treat women too well and by doing so have spoilt everything. We have been very wrong indeed to raise them to our own level. The orientals are much more intelligent and sensible making women slaves.'

Men, he thought, should have several wives.

'What do most ladies have to complain of? Don't we acknowledge they have souls... They demand equality! Pure madness! Woman is our property...just as the fruit tree belongs to the gardener.'

Napoleon was also convinced of the 'weakness of the female intellect'. His brother Joseph, he complained, was 'forever shut away with some woman reading Torquato Tasso and Aretino'. No doubt the flames of Napoleon's romanticism had certainly been dampened by Joséphine's affair with Hippolyte Charles.

Not only did Joséphine have to worry about her husband's infidelity at home, he was frequently abroad where she could not keep an eye on him. After a successful campaign against the Prussians in 1806, he moved on into Poland and Joséphine began to fret about 'Polish beauties'.

'Here in the wastes of Poland, one gives little thought to beauties,' he wrote back. 'Besides there is only one woman for me. Do you know her? I could describe her to you but I don't want you to become conceited; yet, in truth, I could say nothing but good about her. The nights are long here, all alone.'

But he was not all alone for long. After a minor victory over the Russians at Pultusk, Napoleon was hailed as the liberator of Poland. At a huge reception given for him in the Palace of the Kings in Warsaw, Napoleon spotted the twenty-year-old Countess Marie Walewska. She looked up to him as her hero. He made it clear that she was the sort of woman that he wanted to see later, in private.

She was married to a seventy-year-old count and was reputed to be chaste, modest and deeply religious. She refused his profuse invitations to share his bed. Expensive gifts did not work. When he sent her a box of jewels, she threw it on the floor.

'He must take me for a prostitute,' she said.

Impassioned letters did not work either; neither did veiled threats.

'Think how much dearer your country would be to me if you take pity on my poor heart,' he wrote.

A delegation begged Count Walewski to force Marie to 'surrender herself' for Poland. He did so and she went unwillingly to Napoleon's private apartments in Warsaw. There, he flung his watch on the floor and crushed it under his heel, saying that he would grind her people into the dust if she did not succumb. Then he 'swooped' on her like 'an eagle on a dove'. She fainted. So he raped the unconscious woman, merely noting that 'she did not struggle overmuch'.

Despite this inauspicious beginning, the affair lasted for three years and contemporaries maintained that the charming and devoted Marie was the only woman he ever really loved.

During his stay in Poland they lived together in Schloss Finckenstein and Napoleon called her his 'Polish wife'. The only problem was that, despite the fact that she had had one child by her seventy-year-old husband, Napoleon did not seem to be able to make her pregnant. But eventually, after he had returned to France, she sent word that she had had a son.

While there had always been some doubt over the paternity of Eléonore Denuelle's child, Napoleon believed that Marie's child was his. Marie's husband gave the child his name and, as Count Alexandre Walewski, he rose to prominence under Napoleon III. However, Countess Walewska's 'sacrifice' was seen to be in vain. Later, Napoleon made a treaty with the Czar, agreeing that the very words 'Poland' and 'Polish' be 'obliterated not only from any transaction, but from history itself'.

Convinced, at last, that he was not sterile, Napoleon decided to divorce Joséphine and marry someone who could give him a legitimate heir. Tired of war, he decided that dynastic alliance was a better policy. He fancied marrying a Russian Grand Duchess. The Dowager Empress was against it, claiming that Napoleon was 'not as other men'. If the Grand Duchess did marry him, she warned, in order to have children she would have to entertain another man in her bed.

Prince Frederick Louis of Mecklenburg-Schwerin was despatched to Paris to investigate. Joséphine, terrified of divorce as ever, lost Napoleon his Romanov bride by telling the Prince that Napoleon was impotent – 'Bonaparte est bon à faire rien [Bonaparte is good for nothing],' she said.

Later, after her divorce, the twenty-nine-year-old Prince Frederick proposed marriage to the forty-seven-year-old Joséphine. She refused.

Joséphine also said publicly that Napoleon's semen was 'no use at all; it's just like so much water'. He may look like other men, she said, but then so did the famous castrato tenors of the time. Napoleon's bouts of impotence were also discussed openly in the family and news of it spread across Europe.

As Joséphine had still failed to produce a son and heir, in 1809 Napoleon had their marriage annulled. Out of political necessity, Napoleon picked Marie Louise of Austria – Marie Antoinette's niece – to be his second wife. Nevertheless, he concluded that the eighteen-year-old virgin was 'the kind of womb I want to marry'.

He told his brother Lucien: 'Naturally I would prefer to have my mistress [meaning Walewska] crowned, but I must be allied with sovereigns.'

The alliance with Austria was a political mistake. It soon led to war with Russia.

Although she had lost the battle over the divorce, Joséphine continued to fight. She backed his marriage to Marie Louise in the hope that the young princess might look to her for advice. The three of them could set up a ménage à trois, she thought. As the older of the two Empresses, she would naturally take precedence. However, two weeks after his marriage by proxy in March 1810, Napoleon banished Joséphine from Paris. They met occasionally at Malmaison when both shed tears of joy.

Marie Louise was over twenty years Napoleon's junior. On the evening they first met, she consented to go to bed with him. His behaviour was described at the time as 'more rape than wooing', but Marie Louise did not seem to mind. In fact, afterwards 'she asked me to do it again,' Napoleon said in a celebrated quote.

Napoleon was very much in love with her and in 1811, she produced a son and heir, though there were rumours that artificial insemination was used. Napoleon was ecstatic. Even Joséphine was pleased. Despite Marie Louise's expressed orders, she managed to see the baby secretly. She also received Countess Walewska when she visited France with her son Alexei.

When Napoleon fell from power, Joséphine wanted to accompany him to Elba, but was prevented 'by his wife'. Marie Louise did not go with him either though. She became Grand Duchess of Parma. Her father sent Count von Neipperg as her aide. He seduced her and she remained his mistress until the day she died. By the time Napoleon returned from Elba, Joséphine was dead. Then, after Waterloo, he was exiled to St Helena and took with him four friends, all men.

There has been a great deal of speculation that Napoleon was gay. He tolerated homosexuality in the army and refused to outlaw homosexual practices in his Napoleonic Code. Many men wrote of his 'seductive charm'. General de Ségur put it most succinctly: 'In moments of sublime power, he no longer commands like a man but seduces like a woman.'

Napoleon himself admitted that his friendships with men usually began with physical attraction. General Caulaincourt said: 'He told me that for him the heart was not the organ of sentiment; that he felt emotions only where men experience feelings of another kind:

nothing in the heart, everything in the loins and in another place, which I leave nameless.'

Napoleon was obsessed with the golden-haired young Czar Alexander I. This obsession eventually brought about Napoleon's downfall after the disastrous Russian expedition in 1812. When they first met on a raft on the River Tilsit, Napoleon exclaimed: 'It is Apollo!'

Afterwards, he wrote to Joséphine, saying: 'If he were a woman I would make him my mistress.'

Joséphine's maid talked about Napoleon's 'predilection for handsome men'. His aides were often young and effeminate, and he would caress them. His secretary Méneval said Napoleon would 'come and sit on the corner of my desk, or on the arm of my armchair, sometimes on my knees. He would put his arm around my neck and amuse himself by gently pulling my ear.'

His aide Louis Marchand was referred to as 'Mademoiselle Marchand' and Chevalier de Sainte-Croix – 'a slightly built, dapper little fellow, with a pretty, smooth face more like a girl's than that of a brave soldier' – was called 'Mademoiselle Sainte-Croix', while Baron Gaspard Gourgard, Napoleon's orderly for six years, referred to the Emperor as 'Her Majesty'.

After his disastrous campaign against Russia, Napoleon became impotent at the age of forty-two, probably due to the failure of his endocrine glands. He was also afflicted by 'burning urine', caused by deposits of calcium in his urethra.

* * *

While Napoleon may have been a little uncertain of his sexuality, his sister Pauline was one of the loveliest women of the age and, by all accounts, sexually insatiable.

'She was an extraordinary combination of perfect beauty and the strangest moral laxity,' said a contemporary. 'She was the loveliest creature I had ever seen; she was also the most frivolous.'

The Countess Anna Potocka agreed:

'She combined the finest and most regular features imaginable with a most shapely figure, admired – alas! – too often.'

In an age when most people rarely washed, Pauline's bath-time was practically a public event. Every morning a bath tub would be filled with twenty litres of fresh milk. She would strip naked, then Paul, her black slave, would carry her to the tub. When people were shocked, she said brazenly: 'Why not? Are you scandalized because he is not married?'

So Pauline married Paul off to one of her maids, but he continued to carry her, naked, to her bath.

At fifteen, Pauline fell in love with forty-year-old Louis Fréron, who was known as the king of the dandies. The family thought that the match was unsuitable, so Napoleon had Fréron removed. To get her own back, Pauline began flirting with his officers.

To reassert control, Napoleon found Pauline a husband – Victor Leclerc, the blond, clean-cut son of a miller. As a wedding present, Napoleon promoted him to Brigadier General. Although it was no great love match, Pauline was happy enough and bore him a son, Dremide, in 1798.

In 1801, the French colony of Saint Domingue – now Haiti – was overrun by the slave rebellion of Toussaint L'Ouverture. Leclerc was sent to put down the uprising.

Pauline did not want to leave Paris and her several lovers. (One of them wrote later: 'Before she left for Saint Domingue, there were no fewer than five of us in the same house sharing Pauline's favours. She was the greatest tramp imaginable and the most desirable.') She locked herself in her bedroom for three days and only consented to go to Saint Domingue when Napoleon promised to send her regular shipments of Paris gowns.

Leclerc successfully put the rebellion down in 1802. Soon after, he caught yellow fever and died. Pauline returned to France, and back in Paris her mourning was shortlived.

Napoleon quickly found her a second husband, Count Camillo Borghese. He was an enormously wealthy Italian, with one of the world's biggest collections of diamonds. Pauline liked his money and his title, but there was one great drawback: sexually he did not measure up. Pauline wrote to an uncle from the Villa Borghese in Rome, saying: 'I would rather have been Leclerc's widow on just 20,000 francs a year than be married to a eunuch.'

Pauline, however, managed to bounce from one extreme to the other. Back in Paris, she fell for Louis Philippe Auguste de Forbin, a society painter. He was reportedly hugely well endowed and Pauline could not get enough of him; but his size caused her acute vaginal distress. A doctor was called in, who found the poor girl on the verge of exhaustion. Her uterus was swollen by constant excitement and her vagina was showing signs of damage due to friction. For the sake of Pauline's health, Forbin was persuaded to join the army and was posted out of harm's way.

Pauline soon found comfort. In Nice she hired a young musician named Félix Blangini to 'conduct her orchestra'. She understudied the leading actor of the day, François Talma, and bedded the twenty-five-year-old aide to Napoleon's chief of staff, Colonel Armand Jules de Canouville. Again, Napoleon stepped in and posted the unfortunate man to Danzig. He died in 1812 during the retreat from Moscow with a locket containing her picture hanging around his neck. Pauline was inconsolable for days.

She shared her brother's exile to Elba and, after the 'Hundred Days', expressed a desire to go with him to St Helena. When the British prevented it, she returned to her husband and died of cancer, mirror in hand, at the Villa Borghese, aged forty-four.

But there is a lasting monument to her beauty. In her heyday, she had been sculpted famously as Venus reclining on a couch by Antonio Canova. Asked how she could have posed nude, she replied: 'It wasn't cold. There was a fire in the studio.'

Her last wish was that, at her funeral, her coffin should be closed. Instead, Canova's nude statue was brought out of storage and displayed in the church.

* * *

Louis Napoleon, the son of Louis Bonaparte, Napoleon's brother, who he installed as King of Holland, and Joséphine's daughter Hortense, became the dictator Napoleon III in 1852.

After the fall of Napoleon, the Bonaparte family was exiled from France and Louis Napoleon was brought up in Switzerland. From an early age, he had a string of lovers and illegitimate children.

Once the Duke of Reichstadt (Napoleon's only legitimate son and consequently considered to be Napoleon II) died, Louis Napoleon headed the family claim to the throne of France. To strengthen his claim, he proposed marriage to his cousin Princess Mathilde Bonaparte. However, his hopes of marriage were dashed by his abortive attempt to overthrow the French government in 1836 and he was exiled to England.

Trying again in 1840, he landed with a small force at Boulogne and was immediately captured. Imprisoned in the fortress of Ham, he begged for female company. The French government allowed him visits from a voluptuous twenty-year-old named Alexandrine Vergeot. She was officially employed to iron the guards' clothes but became known as 'bedmaker to the number one state prisoner'. Louis Napoleon spent six years in prison at Ham, during which time Alexandrine bore him two sons.

In 1846, Louis Napoleon managed to escape and fled back to England. In London, he lived with English beauty Elizabeth Howard, who kept him for the next two years. She also financed his return to France in 1848, where he seized power. He rewarded her with the title Comtesse de Beauregard and five million francs.

In 1853, Louis married the Spanish aristocrat Eugénie de Montijo, but Eugénie was positively the last person he should have married. She thought that sex was disgusting. A devout Catholic, she believed that it should only be tolerated as an act of procreation. Princess Mathilde believed she should have been a nun.

She was a twenty-seven-year-old virgin when they met and married and, two years later, after the birth of their only son, sex between them ceased. Nevertheless, she was jealous of her husband's lovers, accusing him of sleeping with the 'scum of the Earth' just to embarrass her. Indeed, he had a taste for courtesans and prostitutes. He once paid £10,000 for a single night with the English prostitute Cora Pearl. She was notorious. When Bertie, the Prince of Wales, asked to see her, she had herself served up at his dinner table on a silver salver. When the cover was removed, she was naked except for a string of pearls and a sprig of parsley.

Another courtesan Napoleon III shared with the Prince of Wales was 'La Barucci', a beautiful Italian girl called Giulia Beneni. She kept a silver goblet in her salon, engraved with the letter 'N' and the imperial crest. He also had a long-running affair with the famous French actress, Rachael.

Napoleon III did not just sleep with working girls; he had aristocratic lovers too. The Marquise Taisey-Chatenoy reported Napoleon turning up in her bedroom one night, wearing mauve silk pyjamas. With little conversation and no foreplay, they began having sex. After a bit of sweating and grunting, the deed was done and he left. He also seduced Madame Walewska, the wife of his foreign minister.

His last mistress was a sturdy peasant woman, Marguérite Bellanger. Napoleon III was already ill and Eugénie was convinced that a new love affair would kill him, so she persuaded Marguérite to give him up.

Asked why he had so many mistresses, Napoleon III replied: 'I need my little amusements.'

However, his 'little amusements' were a constant political danger. His ministers begged him to be careful and warned him that he might end up in the hands of an adventuress. Indeed he did. The beautiful nineteen-year-old Contessa di Castiglione was sent by the prime minister of Sardinia to enlist his help in the struggle to unify Italy. She accomplished this in bed.

Napoleon III lacked political judgement all round. He embroiled France in several disastrous wars and defeat in the Franco-Prussian War of 1870–71 lost him his throne. He died in exile in England in 1873.

2

Ten Days that Shook the Bed

Uladimir Ilyich Ulynov – better known as Lenin – was a bit of a ladies' man, but he was only attracted to women who were involved in the revolutionary struggle. His first lover was Nadezhda Konstantina Krupskaya. She was a year older than him and already a committed Marxist. When as a young girl she read the first volume of *Das Kapital*, she said she heard 'the knell of capital sound – the expropriators are expropriated' and her 'heart beat so that it could be heard'. Obviously, she was a romantic.

Nadya was dark-haired and attractive, and she was impressed by the ardour of the young Lenin's revolutionary zeal. They would walk along the banks of the Neva and he would talk about the overthrow of capitalism and avenging his brother who had been hanged for attempting to assassinate the Tsar.

Lenin, however, also had eyes for one of Nadya's friends, the quick-witted and adventurous Apollinaria

Yakubova. Lenin proposed to Apollinaria just before he was arrested for subversion. From his prison cell, he wrote to Apollinaria and Nadya, asking them to stand on Shpalernaya Street outside the prison, where he might be able to catch a glimpse of them from a window. Apollinaria did not come and Nadya took up the vigil alone. Lenin took this to mean that his proposal had been rejected.

Apollinaria and Nadya were arrested too. They were exiled to Siberia but, just a few months into her sentence, Apollinaria was rescued by a young law professor named Takhterev. They fled to London where Lenin met them during his stay there in 1902. Apollinaria helped Lenin and Nadya find rooms at 30 Holford Square, off Grays Inn Road.

After a short jail sentence, Lenin was also exiled to Siberia. By that time, he was engaged to Nadya and asked the authorities if they could be together during their exile. The authorities agreed on condition they got married. Lenin's sister Anna was less than thrilled. 'Nadya,' she wrote, 'looks like a herring.'

Although Nadya had been pretty when she was younger, by the time she married Lenin, she was plain and looked older than her years. The writer Ilya Ehrenburg said unkindly: 'One look at Krupskaya, and you can see that Lenin wasn't interested in women.' She suffered from Graves disease, which meant they could not have children. He was no picture either. Nadya's first words to her fiancé, when she eventually arrived in his Siberian village, were: 'My, you've grown awfully fat.' That night they stayed up drinking with the locals and it was nearly dawn before they went to bed.

Whatever chance they had of wedded bliss was shattered when Nadya's mother turned up. A deeply religious woman with a tart tongue, she and Lenin constantly quarrelled.

* * *

Lenin developed a taste for upper-class women. In 1905, when he was living in St Petersburg under an assumed name to protect himself from arrest, he met a divorcée known simply as Elizabeth de K. She was aristocratic and independently wealthy, with a refined taste for the arts, literature and gracious living.

They met in the Restaurant Tartar, where Lenin was dining with his friend Mikhail Rumyantsev. She was dining alone and Lenin could not keep his eyes off her. Rumyantsev, knowing her slightly, went over and invited her to join them.

'You will meet a very interesting man,' Rumyantsev told her. 'He is very famous, but you musn't ask too many details.'

Amused and interested, she came to their table where Mikhail introduced one 'William Frey'. She asked if he was English.

'No, I'm not exactly English,' he said.

They had a pleasant conversation for about an hour. She was conscious that there was an air of danger about him, but she had no idea that he was the N. Lenin who wrote the inflammatory articles in *Novaya Zhizn* that everybody was talking about.

A week later she was visiting the offices of *Novaya Zhizn* when she bumped into the mysterious 'Englishman' again.

'I'm glad to see you,' he said. 'I was worried about you. You don't come to the Restaurant Tartar any more.'

She realized that, in a subtle way, he was inviting her to dinner there again, but she did not know him well enough to accept. She had to find out more. She sought out Rumyantsev and asked him about 'William Frey'.

'You don't understand,' said Rumyantsev. 'My friend Frey is certainly interested in women – but chiefly from a collective, social and political point of view. I doubt very much whether he has any interest in women as individuals. Allow me to add that, after our dinner the other evening, he asked me to vouch for you. He is suspicious of new acquaintances. He is afraid of informers. I had to tell him who you are.'

Elizabeth realized that the mysterious Mr Frey was a dangerous revolutionary. But she had to see him again. Rumyantsev arranged a small dinner party. In the course of the conversation, the question of holding secret meetings in her apartment was raised. Her flat was in a fashionable district and visitors could slip in and out without being seen. The police were unlikely to suspect that revolutionaries were gathering there.

Elizabeth agreed to let them use her flat twice a week. She would send the maid away and prepare a samovar. Lenin would arrive first and give her the password of the day. She would let the other visitors in, once they had given the password. While the discussion was under way, she would retire to her bedroom. Some nights though, Lenin was the only one who turned up.

Their affair was passionate, but they clashed from the beginning. Elizabeth was a woman of broad cultural interests. Lenin cared for nothing except politics. However, she did try to move some way towards him. In June

1906, she attended a secret meeting in a field outside St Petersburg. When Lenin appeared, the crowd went wild. He exalted them to rebel immediately and they set off marching into the city with Vladimir Ilyich at their head.

On their way down Pulostrovsky Prospect, the Cossacks rode the march down, slashing at the crowd with whips. Lenin threw himself in a ditch. He seemed pleased with the outcome, but Elizabeth realized that he was in imminent danger of arrest for inciting a rebellion. She asked him whether he was prepared to put himself totally in her hands and obey her implicitly. He said he was. She led him across the fields and down a series of overgrown pathways to an outlying village, then took him back to the centre of St Petersburg by streetcar.

He was equally protective towards her. Once, when they were alone together in her apartment, a blazing cinder from the samovar fell on her dress, setting it on fire. Lenin hurled himself on her, smothering the flame. When he got up, she noticed he was trembling and as cold as ice. He turned and ran from the house. It was then that she knew he was in love with her.

She followed him when he went to live in Stockholm. Even in Sweden, he was afraid of the secret police. He lived the life of a conspirator – there were secret signs, passwords, meetings in out-of-the-way places.

One day, he phoned and told her to meet him at a certain arcade, but if other Russians were there, she was to pretend not to recognize him. When she arrived, she saw two Georgians hammering away at one of the vending machines. When Lenin turned up, the Georgians shouted, 'Comrade Ilyich, help us with this damn bourgeois machine. We wanted ham sandwiches and all it gives us is pastry.'

The Father of the Revolution then proceeded to use all his dialectical skills to get them their sandwiches, while Elizabeth pointedly looked the other way. Lenin was delighted with her, even though there was no real danger.

'Do you know who those two Georgians were?' he said later. 'They are our delegates from the Caucasus. Splendid boys, but absolute savages.'

Between his wife and party congresses, Lenin had little time to spare for Elizabeth. Sometimes, on Sundays, he would hire a little rowing boat and take her out on the lake. The passion continued though. When she returned to St Petersburg, she got a wild and urgent letter from him.

'Write to me at once,' he wrote, 'and tell me precisely where and how we can meet, otherwise there will be delays and misunderstandings.'

Elizabeth did not like the tone of this letter and decided to break off the affair. But two years later, she was in Geneva when she read in the newspaper that he was giving a speech in Paris. On an impulse, she took a train there. During the intermission, she went to see him in a small room behind the platform. He was surrounded by admirers and she could not get near him. Eventually he spotted her. He looked startled, then his eyes widened.

'What on earth are you doing here?' he asked.

'I came to hear you,' she said, 'and I have a commission to give to you from a certain person.'

She handed him an envelope. In it were the address and phone number of the place where she was staying.

The next morning, she waited by the phone. It never rang. Instead, Lenin came round in person and they threw themselves into each other's arms.

The affair resumed, but without the intensity they had known before. Altogether they met and wrote, on and off, for nine years. Some of his early letters were passionate. The later ones read like a lecture on Marxist dialectics. In the end, they found that they simply lived in different worlds. Though a champion of women's rights, Lenin said that he had never met a woman who had read *Das Kapital* right the way through, could understand a railway timetable or play chess. He gave her a chess set and asked her to prove him wrong.

In response, she sent him a postcard of the Mona Lisa and asked him to study it and tell her his reactions. He wrote back: 'I can make nothing of your Mona Lisa. Neither the face nor the dress tell me anything at all. I believe there is an opera of the same name, and a book by d'Annunzio. I simply don't understand anything about this thing you have sent me.'

The final falling out was over the question of liberty. Elizabeth questioned his belief in rock-solid Marxist dialectics. Surely, she said, there must be a place for personal liberty.

'The people have no need for liberty,' he said. 'Liberty is one of the forms of the bourgeois dictatorship. In a state worthy of the name there is no liberty. The people want to exercise power, but what on earth would they do if it were given to them?'

This was 1914 and Lenin was already a dictator in the making.

During the time he was still seeing Elizabeth de K, Lenin met the great love of his life, another wealthy divorcée named Elisabeth d'Herbenville Armand. A French woman by birth, she was the daughter of a music-hall comedian. When her father died, she went to stay with her grandmother and aunt who were teachers in Moscow. Elisabeth was eighteen and she soon attracted the attention of twenty-year-old Alexander Armand, the second son of a wealthy textile manufacturer. They married, settled down on a nearby estate and had five children. She was happy and life gave her everything she wanted – except for danger and excitement.

Suddenly, she left her husband and moved in with his younger brother, Vladimir. In the name of free love, they had a passionate affair but this did not really satisfy her either, so she went to live with feminist Ellen Key in Stockholm. Soon she was bored with feminism, but at Ellen Key's she read Lenin's essays which promised the challenge and excitement of direct action and she became a Bolshevik.

Returning to Russia to take part in the 1905 revolution, she took the *nom de révolution* Inessa and was arrested within a couple of days. After nine months in prison, she was released, but continued to work as a courier for the Bolsheviks. She was arrested again, this time for the serious charge of suborning the armed forces. Her husband put up the bail, but she continued her subversive work and was arrested a third time. This time she was exiled to Archangel, where the harsh northern winter finished off all but the strongest of political prisoners.

Her brother-in-law Vladimir Armand was still besotted with her and followed her there. He developed tuberculosis and died. She escaped and, with two of her children, fled to France, where she was already something of a legend.

In Paris, Lenin welcomed her with open arms. She was a revolutionary heroine. He had been following her exploits and he arranged for her to live in an apartment next door to the one he lived in with Nadya.

Inessa was thirty. She had enormous eyes, a wide sensitive mouth, finely modelled features and an unruly mass of chestnut hair. She was quick and intelligent. Just having her around inspired the other exiles and she was often seen with Lenin in the cafés on the Avenue d'Orléans.

She was popular, though Angelica Balabanoff – the Bolshevik agitator who went on to become Mussolini's lover – did not like her. Perhaps she was jealous.

'I did not warm to her,' Balabanoff said. 'She was pedantic, a one hundred per cent Bolshevik in the way she dressed, always in the same severe style, in the way she thought and spoke. She spoke a number of languages fluently, and in all of them repeated Lenin verbatim.'

Up until this time, Lenin had been seen as a puritan. Now his fellow revolutionaries saw him addressing an attractive young woman with the familiar *ty* used by educated Russians among intimates. Normally, Lenin only used *ty* with his mother, his two sisters and his wife.

Lenin and Inessa shared a love of Beethoven and a similar interpretation of Marx; and they had both modelled themselves on characters from a novel by Chernyshevsky called *What is to be Done?* – the hero and the

heroine, naturally. Soon they began acting out the parts
Chernyshevsky had written for them.

Nadya had no objection to Lenin's relationship with
Inessa. Indeed, she oiled the wheels. That summer,
Nadya went on holiday with her mother to Pornic, a
village near St Nazaire, leaving the two lovers together in
Paris.

There is evidence that Lenin had an affair with a
French woman before Inessa turned up in Paris. He
wrote a series of letters of an extremely intimate nature
to a woman writer. When they surfaced after Lenin's
death, she agreed not to have them published while
Nadya was still alive and received a handsome pension
from the Soviet government in return.

Perhaps Nadya tolerated his affair with Inessa because
she preferred him to see someone who could at least
speak Russian and was devoted to the cause. Nadya
certainly liked Inessa. She enjoyed being with her and
loved the two children she had brought to Paris with
her. Nadya wrote openly that 'the house grew brighter
when Inessa entered it'. Lenin certainly did nothing to
hide the direction in which his passion lay. However, the
Revolution had to come first.

Lenin and Inessa were separated in 1914, when he
went with Nadya to Cracow on revolutionary business.
Inessa missed him terribly.

'We have parted, you and I, my dear! And it is so
painful,' she wrote from Paris. 'As I gaze at the familiar
places, I realize all too clearly, as never before, what a
large place you occupied in my life, here in Paris. All our
activity here is tied by a thousand threads to the thought
of you. I wasn't at all in love with you then, even though
I did love you. Even now I would manage without the

kisses, if only I could see you. To talk with you occasionally would be such a joy – and couldn't cause pain to
anyone. Why did I have to give that up?'

Her letters also speak eloquently of the stresses and
strains between the three of them.

'You ask me if I'm angry that it was you who "carried
out" the separation. No, I don't think you did it for
yourself. There was much that was good in Paris in my
relations with N.K. [Nadya]. In one of our last chats she
told me I had become dear and close to her only
recently...only at Longjumeau [their revolutionary summer school] and then last autumn over the translations
and so on. I have become rather accustomed to you. I so
loved not just listening to you, but looking at you as you
spoke. First of all, your face is so animated, and secondly
it was easy for me to look at you because you didn't
notice.'

The separation did not last long though and, after
eight months apart, they settled together in Galicia.
Initially, it did not work out and Nadya decided to leave,
so that he could marry Inessa. But Lenin would have
none of it. He depended on Nadya too much for his
revolutionary work. On the other hand, he needed
Inessa too, for other reasons. So the ménage à trois
continued; and there were happy times.

'For hours we would walk along the leaf-strewn forest
lanes,' Nadya recalled. 'Usually we were in a threesome,
Vladimir Ilyich and Inessa and I... Sometimes we would
sit on a sunny slope, covered with shrubs. Ilyich would
sketch outlines of his speeches, getting the text right,
while I learned Italian... Inessa would be sewing a skirt
and enjoying the warmth of the sunshine.'

For years, the three of them travelled and plotted and politicked together. They travelled back to Russia in March 1917 in the famous sealed train. Also on board was Angelica Balabanoff.

It was Lenin, Nadya and Inessa that planned the October Revolution. They formed the inner circle which took over the government, created the Soviet Union, ran the world's first Communist state and lived together in the Kremlin until Inessa's death from typhus in October 1920.

Two weeks before she died, Inessa wrote in her diary: 'For romantics, love occupies the first place in their lives, it comes before everything else.' She was a romantic.

Even as the illness took its toll, she remained devoted to Lenin. In a last scribbled note, she wrote: 'Now I'm indifferent to everyone. The main thing is I'm bored with almost everyone. I only have warm feelings left for the children and V.I. In all other respects, it's as if my heart has died. As if, having given up all my strength, all my passion to V.I. and work, all the springs of love have dried up in me.'

Inessa was laid in state in the House of the Soviets and buried in the Kremlin wall. The message on one wreath read simply: 'To Comrade Inessa from V.I. Lenin.'

Lenin himself was shattered. Angelica Balabanoff, now a Comintern official, wrote: 'Not only his face but his whole body expressed so much sorrow that I dared not greet him, not even with the slightest gesture. It was clear that he wanted to be alone with his grief. He seemed to have shrunk: his cap almost covered his face, his eyes seemed drowned in tears held back with effort. As our circle moved, following the movement of the people, he too moved, without offering resistance, as if he were grateful for being brought nearer to his dead comrade.'

After her death, Lenin and Nadya looked after Inessa's five children. But Lenin never really got over his grief. Without his great love, his health and his political star went into decline. He died of a stroke in January 1924. Nadya survived for another fifteen years, living in their apartment in the Kremlin until her death at the age of seventy in 1939.

3

More Revolting Red Ravers

Communist dictators are not supposed to be concerned with sex. They are supposed to think only of the good of the people. The personal gratification involved in making love is irredeemably bourgeois. Take, for example, Soviet Secretariat member Boris Bazhanov's description of the greatest dictator of them all, Comrade Stalin: 'This passionate politician has no other vices. He loves neither money nor pleasure, neither sport nor women. Women, apart from his own wife, do not exist for him.' This simply was not true.

Stalin's first wife was a Georgian woman named Ekaterina Svanidze. Her brother Aleksandr was at the same theological seminary that Stalin attended before he gave up the priesthood for the Revolution. They married in 1903. Although Stalin was already an atheist, to please Ekaterina's mother the ceremony took place in an Orthodox Church. Ekaterina was also very religious and, while he was away at his revolutionary meetings, she would be on her knees praying that he would turn away from ideas that were displeasing to God and live a life of quietness and contentment. They had one son, Yakov.

Although he saw little of her, Stalin must have loved his wife. He was devastated when she died in 1910. At the gates of the cemetery, he said: 'This creature softened my stony heart. She is dead and with her have died my last warm feelings for human beings.' Then he placed his right hand over his heart and said: 'It is all so desolate here inside, so unspeakably desolate.' Millions died as a consequence.

Although the loss of his first wife hardened his heart, his sexual feelings did not die with her. During the Civil War in 1919, he met Nadya Alliluyeva, the daughter of a railwayman. She was very beautiful, with a distinctly oriental appearance. He was on the run and they met when her parents – who had known him for twenty years – harboured him. She was just sixteen when he took her virginity. He was thirty-nine. Although he was more than twice her age, she found his fanatical revolutionary ideas wildly romantic. Nadya too became a revolutionary and, despite her mother's opposition, married Stalin as a revolutionary act.

Stalin fulfilled her girlish fantasies by taking her to Moscow in an armoured car. They honeymooned in Tsaritsyn, where Stalin organized the defences against the White Russian Army. He re-organized the police force, uncovered counter-revolutionary plots and had the plotters executed. The city was renamed Stalingrad. It was there that Nadya lost her political virginity. Stalin's ruthless suppression of anyone who opposed him was her first exposure to the naked use of power.

Nadya became one of Lenin's secretaries and she lived with Stalin in an apartment in the Kremlin, which she hated. Their first child, a son, Vasily, was born in 1920; their daughter, Svetlana, in 1926.

When Stalin took over the reins of power after Lenin's death, Nadya became disturbed by the power and privileges that went with his position. It offended her Communist principles. She decided to go to college. There, from other students, she began to learn about what was happening in the Ukraine, where her husband's policy of forced collectivization had caused a famine which cost five million lives.

Raising such issues at home was not a recipe for domestic bliss. Stalin would respond with the crudest of insults. He also swore at Lenin's wife, greatly upsetting her. Even his own mother was called an 'old whore' to her face.

Stalin would complain to others that Nadya had never been much to his taste, she was 'a woman with ideas...a herring with ideas – skin and bones'. Much more to his taste was the former waitress – 'a young one with a snub nose and a gay, ringing laugh' – who he employed as a housekeeper at his dacha. Svetlana summed up her virtues in her father's eyes: 'Plump, neat, served softly at table and never joined in the conversation.'

By the time the waitress joined the household, Svetlana believed that her parents' sexual relationship had come to an end. Nadya had her own bedroom, while Stalin slept in his office or in a small room with a telephone in it, next to the dining-room. It was rumoured that he was having an affair with a ballerina.

There was also a rumour that it was Stalin who had made the sixteen-year-old daughter of Politburo member Lazar Kaganovich pregnant. Trotsky believed that

Stalin had another daughter besides Svetlana, whose mother was not Nadya.

Matters came to a head between Stalin and Nadya on the night of 8 November, 1932. There was a party in the Kremlin celebrating the fifteenth anniversary of the Revolution. Stalin insisted that she drink, though he knew she was teetotal. There was a row and Stalin threw a lighted cigarette at her. Nadya ran from the room, humiliated. She walked around the grounds of the Kremlin for a long time, trying to compose herself. When she returned to their apartment, she found Stalin in bed with the wife of a party official. Nadya went to her room and shot herself.

Stalin was unconcerned about her death. At her open coffin, he was heard to say: 'She left me as an enemy.'

He did not attend her funeral or her memorial service and took his anger out on her family. Nadya's sister Anna was sentenced to ten years' solitary confinement. Her brother Pavel died of a heart attack in 1938 during the purges. Pavel's wife, Eugenia, was imprisoned on the trumped-up charge of having poisoned him. Anna's husband, Stanislav Redens, was arrested and shot the same year. Many said that Nadya was lucky she committed suicide when she did, otherwise she would have fallen victim to the purges too.

Only his daughter Svetlana enjoyed the love of her father, but she became a prisoner of the Kremlin. He would call her his 'housekeeper' and she would have to sit on his right during working dinners. He had affectionate nicknames for her – 'little sparrow' and 'little fly' – and his letters to her always ended 'I kiss you'. He was always kissing her.

A great distance grew between them when Svetlana learnt, through the *Illustrated London News*, that her mother had not died of appendicitis as she had been told.

Stalin would lose his temper completely if she formed any kind of friendship with a man. He stopped kissing her – she was not his 'clean little girl' any more. When Svetlana defied Stalin, he would talk crudely of her sexual activity in front of her and his male colleagues. He had the NKVD – the forerunner of the KGB – investigate her lovers. While she was still a schoolgirl, Stalin discovered that she was having an affair with a middle-aged Jewish film-maker named Aleksei Kapler. He confronted her.

'I know the whole story,' he said, brandishing the NKVD file. 'I've got all your telephone conversations right here.'

'But I love him,' she protested.

'Love!' he said, slapping her across the face. 'Your Kapler is a British spy. He's under arrest.'

Kapler served five years in the mining camps at Vorkuta, in the Arctic Circle.

Stalin was delighted when Svetlana's first marriage broke up, but when she married again soon after, they became estranged. After Stalin died, Svetlana defected to the West. She lived in Britain, America and Switzerland, and after four broken marriages, at the age of 70, she became a nun 'to atone for the sins of my father', she said.

While, at the beginning, there were kisses for his daughter, his sons were handled brutally from the outset. Yakov, his son from his first marriage, was treated with contempt, perhaps because he reminded Stalin of his own Georgian origins. He only came to live with his father in the Kremlin at Nadya's insistence. He probably wished he hadn't.

'The boy Yakov was subjected to frequent and severe punishments by his father,' Trotsky related.

When Yakov tried unsuccessfully to commit suicide in 1928 or 1929, Stalin said callously: 'Ha, he couldn't even shoot straight.' When he was captured during World War II, Stalin denounced him as a traitor as 'no true Russian would ever surrender'. He refused a German offer to exchange him and had Yakov's wife imprisoned.

His younger son, Vasily, was also beaten.

'At home, he would knock the boy down and let him have it with his boots,' Svetlana said.

After a disastrous career in the Red Air Force, Vasily died an alcoholic wreck at the age of forty-one. One of his sons died of a heroin overdose. One daughter was an alcoholic; another was confined to a mental asylum.

Stalin loved to be photographed with young children and the party machine trumpeted his love for them. A story frequently told at the time is of a three-year-old child coming home from his first day at school and telling his father: 'You are not my father any more.'

'What do you mean I am not your father?' the man would exclaim, horrified.

'You are not my father,' the child would say. 'Stalin is my father. He gives me everything I have.'

In fact, Stalin turned his brutality towards his own sons into public policy. In 1935, Stalin changed the law so that children could be hanged. Children as young as ten were arrested and tortured into informing on their parents or confessing that they were 'counter-revolutionary, Fascist terrorists'. The children of adults who had been arrested were also vulnerable to arrest. When asked why, Stalin replied: 'For being freethinkers, that's what.'

During the famine of 1932, Stalin personally issued orders to shoot the hungry children who were stealing food from railway trucks and who, for some reason, Stalin thought had contracted venereal diseases. In all, it is estimated, that 'Uncle Joe' was directly responsible for the deaths of hundreds of thousands of children – plus two or three million children who starved to death during the famines of the 1930s.

There was a joke in the old Soviet Union that ran this way:

> *A schoolteacher asked one of her pupils: 'Who is your father?'*
> *The child answered: 'Comrade Stalin.'*
> *'And who's your mother?'*
> *The child said: 'The Soviet motherland.'*
> *'And what do you want to become?' the teacher asked.*
> *The child said: 'An orphan.'*

Stalin had a thing about boots. Not only were they useful for kicking his son, his own father was a cobbler. When drunk, he had kicked the young Stalin with his boots. He also beat Stalin's mother, leaving Stalin with a deep misogyny.

The Soviets even had some jokes about his boots:

Question: Why did Lenin wear botinki [ankle-high boots], while Stalin wore sapogi [high boots]?
Answer: Because during Lenin's time, in Russia, the shit was only up to the ankles.

Official photographs always show Stalin in high boots, usually with his trousers tucked in them, peasant style. He rarely took his own boots off, and he always slept with his socks on, but this may have been to hide his deformed left foot. According to Tsarist police records, the second and third toes of his left foot were joined together.

Stalin even had one of his bodyguards sent to the gulag for abandoning his boots. The man wore slippers instead so as not to wake Stalin when he was sleeping. Stalin accused the man of planning to sneak up and assassinate him.

Stalin wore boots on even the most inappropriate occasions. On holiday in Georgia in the late twenties, he was in the garden with his guests, showing off his prize roses. He was wearing a lightweight tussore silk suit and heavy black riding boots which were quite out of keeping.

'Joseph Vissarionvich,' asked one of his guests, 'it's so hot, but you are still wearing boots. How can you stand it?'

'What can I say?' said Stalin. 'Boots are really comfortable things. And useful. You can kick someone in the head with them – so hard he'll never find all this teeth.' And he burst out laughing.

This was typical of Stalin's sadistic fantasies. He always identified with the aggressor – even his own father. In power, he modelled himself on the Tsars, particularly Ivan the Terrible and Alexander I who defeated Napoleon. Stalin even compared himself to Nicholas II, who had imprisoned and exiled him.

Stalin's all-time favourite aggressor was Hitler. He used Hitler's Night of the Long Knives as a model for his own purges. Even when Hitler attacked Russia in June 1941, he ordered frontline troops not to fight back, thinking there had been some mistake. He simply could not believe Hitler was attacking, even though everyone else saw it coming.

Many political commentators had remarked on a homosexual element in the Nazi–Soviet pact, but Stalin had strong feelings about homosexuality. In 1933, he made all homosexual acts illegal, giving no clear reason. For propaganda purposes, a 'homosexual conspiracy' was dreamt up. Gays were ganging up to overthrow the state.

In January 1934, mass arrests of homosexuals began and Maxim Gorky published an article in *Pravda*, saying: 'Destroy homosexuals and fascism will disappear.' Stalin often referred to his enemies as 'prostitutka' – male prostitutes.

There were rumours that Stalin had a homosexual relationship in the mid-1930s with his chief bodyguard, the Hungarian Jew, K.V. Pauker. Pauker would have been the submissive partner in the relationship. He certainly knew what Stalin liked. His party piece was an imitation of Grigori Zinoviev who, when about to be executed, fell to his knees and embraced the boots of his executioner.

'Stalin watched every move of "Zinoviev" and roared with laughter,' an eyewitness reported. 'When they saw how much Stalin enjoyed the scene, his guests demanded that Pauker repeat the performance. Pauker obliged. This time Stalin laughed so much that he bent down and held his belly with both hands. And when Pauker introduced a new improvisation and, instead of kneeling, raised his hands to heaven and screamed,

"Hear Israel, our God is the only God!" Stalin could bear it no longer and, choking with laughter, began to make signs to Pauker to stop the performance.'

There were also some homosexual overtones to Stalin's all-male drinking parties after the war. Polish government official Jakub Berman attended one of these parties in 1948 and recalled dancing with Molotov.

'Don't you mean Mrs Molotov?' he was asked.

'No, she wasn't there,' he said. 'She'd been sent to a labour camp. I danced with Molotov – it must have been a waltz, or at any rate something simple, because I haven't a clue about how to dance and I just moved my feet to the rhythm.'

'As the woman?'

'Yes, Molotov led,' said Berman. 'I wouldn't know how. He wasn't a bad dancer, actually.'

Stalin wound the gramophone and watched. Berman said that Stalin really had fun.

This is not an isolated incident. Stalin often forced men to dance with each other at his parties. Indeed, there were fewer and fewer women around the Kremlin. Like Mrs Molotov, Stalin was arresting them all.

Stalin only joined in on one occasion. After drinking Bruderschaft with Tito, he grabbed the Yugoslav dictator and span him around the floor to a Russian folk melody. Stalin danced so exuberantly that he lifted the bemused Yugoslav up in his arms several times.

William Bullitt, U.S. ambassador to the Soviet Union in the 1930s, reported a far more overt incident: 'Stalin was very affectionate toward me. At one time when he had had a little too much to drink, he kissed me full on the mouth – what a horrible experience that was!'

* * *

Stalin's heir apparent was Lavrenty Beria. He was head of Stalin's secret police and notorious for his sexual attacks on young women and girls. When Stalin died he was waiting in the wings.

Like most would-be dictators, on the surface, his sex life seemed normal enough. He met his wife in 1920 in Georgia. At that time Stalin's home state was not yet Communist and Beria was in jail. The wife of one of his Bolshevik colleagues came to visit him and brought her niece, fifteen-year-old Nino Gegechkori. Beria was immediately struck by her beauty.

The following year, when the Communists had taken over and Beria was released, he met her in the street in Georgia's capital, Tbilisi. She was on her way to school and he asked her if he could meet her later for a talk. She agreed.

'We sat on a bench,' Nino said. 'Lavrenty was wearing a black topcoat and a student's service cap. He told me that for a long time he had been very taken with me. What's more, he said that he loved me and wanted to marry me. I was sixteen years old at the time.'

Beria explained that the Soviet government wanted to send him to Belgium to learn about oil processing, but he could only go if he had a wife. She thought about his proposal and agreed to marry him.

They married quickly, fearing objections from her family. But the Belgian trip never materialized. As a loyal Communist, Beria was to head the Cheka (a forerunner of the KGB). They had one son, Sergo.

Well, that's the official version of the story at least, but in a book called *Commissar* by Thaddeus Whittlin, himself a former inmate of the gulag at Vorkuta, another, more harrowing, version is told. Whittlin maintains that Beria met Nino when he was already head of the secret police in Georgia. He had a luxurious train at his disposal, which he used as his travelling headquarters. One day at the station, he was approached by a young girl, who asked him to intercede for her brother who had been arrested. It was Nino. She was extremely beautiful – medium height with black eyes and a creamy white complexion.

Beria was taken with her and asked her to board the train so he could take more details of the case. He took her to his bedroom compartment and ordered her to undress. When she tried to leave, he locked the door and slapped her face. Then he grabbed her arms, twisted them behind her back, pushed her down onto the bed and raped her.

When it was all over, he went to call the guard to have her taken to jail. But he looked at her tear-streaked face and decided that she was, indeed, very attractive. In half-an-hour or so, he might want her again. So he locked her in his compartment and went down to the restaurant car for dinner and some vodka.

He kept the girl all night, raping her repeatedly. In the morning, he ordered breakfast for two. When he left the train to perform official duties, he left her locked in the compartment. Despite the show of brutality, Beria was completely spellbound. Nino was the type of woman that appealed to him. She had small breasts, big eyes and a full ripe mouth. Although she was young and innocent, her body was full and mature.

He kept her on board the train with him for several days, while he travelled around supervising the progress of a Five-Year Plan in the Sukhumi region of Abkhazia. During that time, Beria started thinking how stupid it would be to throw away such a find. All his comrades and his superiors were married, while he spent his time seducing young girls. Despite its ideological commitment to free love, the party, he knew, had a puritanical streak in it. If he was to get on, it would be best if he got married. So he did. Nino, his captive, had no say in the matter.

Whittlin's story seems to be more in keeping with Beria's character. An ugly child, girls had teased him at school. As an adolescent, they snubbed him and he hated them. He did not have enough money to pay good-looking prostitutes and had to make do with the older, uglier ones.

But, with the Revolution, everything changed. As head of the Cheka, he was charged with seeking out anti-Bolshevik elements. He did this largely in schools, where he would interrogate pupils personally, slapping their faces or beating their hands with a reed cane until they gave him the names of reactionary elements. He particularly liked interrogating girls – the pretty ones, the sort who had teased him when he was younger and turned him down. The more helpless and innocent the girl the better. It was the violation of innocence that he liked and he would not stop even at murder to get it.

In 1935, the People's Commissar of Foreign Trade, Arkaday Rosengoltz, made the mistake of taking his beautiful young daughter, Yelena, on a trip to Sukhumi in Georgia. They were the guests of Nestor Lakoba, the Secretary of the Executive Committee of Abkhazia, and Lakoba arranged for his two cousins Basil and Michael to show Yelena around.

When Beria saw Yelena he was smitten. A few days later, Lakoba invited Beria to his country house, intimating it was for a stag party. When Beria arrived, Lakoba was nowhere to be seen, but Basil and Michael were there, along with Yelena. They played some records and Yelena danced with each of them in turn. Turkish delight, tea and wine were served.

When Yelena excused herself to go to the lavatory, one of the boys poured pure alcohol into her wine glass. When she returned, Beria proposed a toast 'to the Queen of Beauty' and urged her to down her wine in one gulp.

Soon after, she felt dizzy and hot, and went outside to get some air. The three men followed. Out on the lawn, she collapsed. When she came to, they were fiddling with her clothes. To start with, she thought they were loosening her clothing, so that she could breathe more easily. The three of them raped her in turn.

Afterwards they began to panic. What if she told her father? He was a highly respected Bolshevik with a lot of influence in Moscow. So one of them put his hands round her throat and strangled her.

Beria telephoned the investigating magistrate. When he arrived, Beria explained that he was the Chief of the Secret Police in Georgia and informed the magistrate that the girl had had a few glasses of wine. A little drunk, she had become hysterical and run out into the garden where she had committed suicide. No autopsy was necessary. A statement signed by the First Secretary of the Transcaucasian Committee of the Communist Party, Lavrenty Pavlovich Beria, corroborated by the Secretary of the Executive Committee of Abkhazia, Nestor Lakoba, would do. All the magistrate had to do was inform the dead girl's father about the unfortunate accident.

Next day, Beria went back to Tbilisi.

* * *

As a fellow Georgian, Beria was one of the few people Stalin could trust, so his rise through the ranks of the Communist Party was effortless. In 1938, he moved to Moscow to head the People's Commissariat of Internal Affairs – the NKVD – and ran the huge chain of labour camps that spread across the Soviet Union.

As deputy premier in charge of both internal security and war production, it is hard to work out when Beria could have had time for all his womanizing. Nevertheless, Moscow was abuzz with rumours of him seducing – or raping – young girls, but the truth was not widely known until after Stalin's death in 1953, when Beria lost out in a power-struggle to Nikita Khrushchev.

When Beria was finally arrested during the struggle for power, one of his bodyguards produced a list of thirty-nine women with whom Beria had had sexual relations. He also claimed, rightly, that Beria had contracted syphilis in 1943. At Beria's trial another bodyguard said that he had been employed to pick up women in the street and transport them to Beria's home, where Beria raped them. U.S. embassy staff corroborated this. Their residence was in the same street as Beria's home and they saw girls brought there late at night in a limousine.

Beria did not confine his activities to his office. At night, he would often risk taking girls back to his villa, despite the presence of his wife. To keep them quiet, his victims would be plied with wine until they fell asleep. Then Beria would rape them.

Outside Moscow, he was no better. The Minister of Culture for Georgia told of going for a ride in Beria's cherished speedboat. Out in the lake, they came across a young woman swimmer, a member of a local sports club. Beria stopped the boat and insisted that she climb aboard. Then he began making lewd remarks and indicated his desire to seduce her, though she was plainly terrified of him. He turned to the Minister and told him to jump overboard and swim to the shore. When the poor man said he could not swim, Beria pushed him overboard. He would have drowned if he had not been spotted by one of Beria's bodyguards who was watching from the shore and sent out a boat to rescue him.

Beria had a proclivity for sportswomen. He insisted on having the pick of the female athletes who travelled from Georgia to Moscow for the annual Day of Physical Culture.

The NKVD kept a special watch on the intelligentsia, while Beria himself kept a close eye on young actresses. He had an affair with Nina Alekseeka, a member of the Ensemble of Song and Dance that was sent to Finland in 1940 to entertain the troops.

After Beria's arrest, his office was searched. Love letters and items of women's clothing were found. Beria's son, Sergo, leapt to his father's defence, but even he was forced to admit that Beria had a secret love child.

Stalin, of course, knew all along what Beria was getting up to. The Soviet historian Dimitri Volkogonov said: 'Even though he professed to value asceticism and puritanism, the General Secretary must have known that Beria was a notorious profligate.'

It is said that Stalin laughed when he heard of some of Beria's escapades. Beria even tried it on with a close friend of Stalin's, Eugenia Aleksandrovna, in front of Uncle Joe himself. One evening, at dinner, he put his hand on her knee under the table.

'Joseph, he's trying to squeeze my knee!' she said loudly. The whole table looked at Beria. That didn't mean he didn't try again.

Nadya, Stalin's wife, hated Beria and warned her husband against him, but he took no notice. There is even a picture of Beria with Svetlana sitting on his lap. He has his arms around her and she is looking very uncomfortable.

During his trial Beria was accused of being an 'imperialist agent' and conducting 'anti-party and anti-state activities', along with four counts of rape. The indictment cited orgies with teenaged girls incarcerated in his villa in Georgia as well as the girls he abducted and raped in Moscow. He was found guilty of all charges in December 1953 and immediately executed.

4

Hanging Out With Mussolini

There was nothing furtive about Italian dictator Benito Mussolini's sex life. In fact, he could have been a Democrat. He had all the wham, bam thank you ma'am of a JFK or a Lyndon Johnson.

During his teens, he admitted to undressing every girl with his eyes. Even before he was eighteen, when he was at school in Forlimpopoli, he would visit the local brothel. In an early fragment of an autobiography written during one of his frequent periods of imprisonment, he described having sex with a whore whose 'flaccid body exuded sweat from every pore'.

It also told how he seduced his cousin and a number of her friends, but these encounters were usually quick and unpleasant. He described his first brutal sexual encounter with a country girl named Virginia. She was 'poor...but she had a nice complexion' and 'was reasonably good-looking'.

'One day I took her upstairs, threw her onto the floor behind the door, and made her mine. She got up, crying and insulting me between her sobs. She said that I had violated her honour. I probably had. But what sort of honour can she have meant?'

These passages are, of course, omitted from his official autobiography published in 1939.

His first steady sexual partner was the Russian socialist agitator Angelica Balabanoff. She was fourteen years his senior and soon got tired of the violent, egotistical youth.

When he was nineteen, Mussolini spent four months working as a schoolteacher in Gualtieri. There he met a woman named Luiga. She was the wife of a soldier, a beautiful girl of twenty and he treated her ruthlessly.

'I accustomed her to my exclusive and tyrannical love,' he said. 'She obeyed me blindly, and I did what I liked with her.'

He bullied and abused her, and once stabbed her in the thigh. He always made love to her savagely and selfishly in a way that characterized all his affairs.

Mussolini saw himself primarily as a man of action. He could not hang around in a small Italian town, teaching a class of forty children. He had to get out and make his mark on the world. In June 1902, he travelled to Switzerland without a penny. He slept under bridges, in public lavatories and, occasionally, with a medical student, a Polish refugee whose love-making he said was 'unforgettable'. Around this time he contracted venereal disease from a married woman who was 'fortunately older and less strong than I was' and who, as always, 'loved me madly'.

He returned to Italy to become a journalist and political agitator, getting himself arrested regularly. During a brief period of freedom in 1909, he was living at his father's house when he fell in love with Augusta Guidi, the older of the two daughters of his father's sullen mistress, Anna. He decided that he would marry her, but she thought he was much too unstable. She married a man with regular work as a gravedigger instead. So Mussolini turned his attention to Augusta's younger sister, Rachele, who gossips referred to as his half-sister.

Mussolini had just finished his one and only published novel, *The Cardinal's Mistress*, which was serialized in *Il Popolo d'Italia*. It was not well received, but Rachele liked it. One of the most sympathetic characters, the maid who gives her life to save her mistress, was called Rachele.

One night, after they returned home to his father's house from an outing to the theatre, Mussolini demanded that Rachele be allowed to live with him. Anna, her mother, would not countenance it, so Mussolini produced a pistol and said: 'You see this revolver, Signora Guidi? It holds six bullets. If Rachele turns me down, there will be a bullet in it for her and five for me. It's for you to choose.'

Anna gave the couple her blessing. A few days later, Mussolini rented two cramped damp rooms in Forli.

'We moved into the place one night,' Rachele recalled. 'I remember how tired and happy he was – perhaps a little uncertain of my reaction because the marriage papers were not yet ready. But I understood I saw the man of my heart there before me, eagerly awaiting the only gift life could give him – my love. His young face was already lined by his daily struggle. There was no hesitation. I went with him.'

Life together was hard. Mussolini was offered a job as editor of a newspaper in Brazil which he was tempted to take; but Rachele's pregnancy, with the first of their five children, prevented him from accepting it.

Rachele, Mussolini and their growing brood lived together in the two rooms for three years. He became the Secretary of the Forli Socialist Federation, and used his wages to fund his own weekly paper *La Lotta di Classe* – 'The Class Struggle'. He wrote all four pages of it himself, drank wine with his friends and, occasionally, pinched the bottom of a pretty girl. But for the time being he remained faithful.

He also wrote another novel, this time about the Archduke Ferdinand who committed suicide with his seventeen-year-old mistress at Mayerling. It remained unpublished. Like *The Cardinal's Mistress*, it was practically soft porn. Throughout his life Mussolini had a taste for cheap and erotic novels.

Gradually, *La Lotta di Classe* became influential. As his message spread, Mussolini began to spend more time away from home. The temptation this put in his way proved irresistible.

By the time Mussolini came to power, he was insatiable. He compulsively sexually confronted any women who came up to his hotel room, or the flat he had in the palazzo in the Via Rasella. There were no ifs or buts and no niceties. He simply took them with a frantic passion. He rarely bothered with a bed, preferring to do it on the floor or against the edge of his desk. The act was perfunctory. He would not bother to take off his trousers or his shoes. The whole thing would be over in a minute or two.

As a young man he had preferred intellectual women, especially schoolteachers, but as he grew older, anyone would do provided they were not too skinny. He liked his lovers to smell a lot. He particularly liked the smell of sweat, though a strong scent was good too. He was not that clean himself, often dabbing himself with Cologne rather than washing with soap and water. He often did not bother to shave; once he even turned up unshaven at an official reception for the King and Queen of Spain.

The sexual act was always performed purely for his own gratification. He thought of neither the woman's pleasure nor her comfort. But the women did not seem to mind. Without the tiniest preamble, he would launch himself on female journalists, the wives of party members, actresses, maids, countesses and foreign visitors. Afterwards, they would speak of their sexual encounter with him with pride. Many said they enjoyed his no-nonsense approach. They liked the brutal carnality of it. As he reached a climax, he would curse violently; then, for a moment, he would be tender. Sometimes, when he lifted himself from a woman's body, he would take up his violin and play something beautiful. The whole experience of sex was unself-conscious and animal – though, once he was satisfied, women seemed to perceive in him a deep affection.

One of his casual lovers said that, at first, she was repelled by his clumsy attempt at foreplay, which amounted to roughly squeezing her breasts before he forced himself upon her. But afterwards, she found herself going back to him because she was unable to resist 'a man of such importance'.

Mussolini had a free hand because Rachele did not want to come to live in Rome. She was conscious that she looked and talked like a peasant. In Rome, she felt gauche and out of place. She also knew of his many mistresses. Often, when he said he was visiting his family, he was staying with one of them, Margherita Sarfatti. But it did not bother her. He loved his family and the marriage was a happy one. Hard-working and long-suffering, she was the perfect Fascist wife.

His love of sex and children was soon turned into public policy. He urged a doubling of the birth-rate. Italy needed large families, he said, to have more soldiers. He imposed a tax on 'unjustified celibacy', while employers were told to discriminate in favour of family men.

Hypocritically, he imposed severe punishment for adultery – harsher for women than for men. Closer to his heart, he made it an offence to infect anyone with syphilis. He was also against modern dancing, which he complained was 'immoral and improper' and he tried to regulate Rome's decadent night life. The pope applauded, but complained that there were still nude shows in defiance of the law.

Il Duce was deeply devoted to his five children and the Italian press portrayed him as uomo casalingo – the perfect family man. But it was hard to hush up some of his not-so-homeloving activities and scandalous stories about his sexual activities leaked to the foreign press.

One of his early mistresses was a neurotic woman named Ida Dalser. They had lived together on and off until 1915, when he abandoned her. She had a physically deformed and mentally retarded son, Benito

Albino, whom Mussolini acknowledged as his own although he had a horror of deformity and illness.

When Mussolini broke off the affair with her, she had to be confined to a mental hospital. From as early as 1913, she began claiming that he had promised to marry her. Sometimes she changed her story and claimed that she had actually married him – and she was not going to be bought off with maintenance money for the child. When he was still a journalist on *Il Popolo d'Italia* in Milan, she stood outside the offices with her son and shouted up to Mussolini to come down if he dared. His response was simple and direct. He came to the window with a pistol.

Later, she set fire to a room in the Hotel Bristol in Trento, screaming hysterically that she was the wife of Il Duce. She died in a mental hospital in Venice in 1935. Their son Benito was confined to an asylum in Milan, where he died in 1942.

* * *

Mussolini seduced the anarchist intellectual Leda Rafanelli in 1913. Only later did she discover that he was married. He explained that Rachele did not mind his infidelity. He wanted to continue the affair, claiming that every good newspaper editor needed a talented woman as an official mistress.

Another woman who Mussolini said 'loved me madly' was Margherita Sarfatti, the art critic of *Avanti!* She became the editor of the Fascist magazine *Gerarchia*, ghosted articles in American magazines for him and wrote his official biography, which ends with a description of 'his eyes shining with an interior fire'. The affair lasted into the 1930s. She was his official mistress, Clara Petacci's only serious rival, but she eventually fell foul of Mussolini's anti-Jewish legislation.

In 1937, the French actress Fontanges, who was also a journalist under her real name Magda Coraboeuf, came to Rome to interview Mussolini for *La Liberté*. After the interview, she refused to return to Paris until he had made love to her. He did so, violently. The first time they had intercourse, he tried to strangle her with a scarf.

'I stayed in Rome for two months and Il Duce had me twenty times,' she told the press.

Desperate to hush up the story, Mussolini made it clear to both the police and the French embassy that Mademoiselle Coraboeuf had outstayed her welcome. Magda reacted violently. She tried to poison herself. When that failed, she shot and wounded the French ambassador, who she blamed for having lost her 'the love of the world's most wonderful man'. She was arrested and sentenced to a year's imprisonment for malicious wounding. In her flat, police found over three hundred photographs of Mussolini.

After the war, she was imprisoned again for having been an agent for the Axis powers. She eventually succeeded in poisoning herself in Geneva in 1960.

Mussolini was not incapable of sustaining a long-term relationship, though. In 1932, he was being driven to Ostia in his official Alfa Romeo when, at the roadside, he saw a pretty young girl waving and shouting 'Duce! Duce!' as he went by. Mussolini told his driver to stop. He got out and walked back to her.

When he spoke to her, she started trembling with excitement. Her name was Clara Petacci. She was the wife of an Italian Air Force officer, whom she later divorced. Mussolini had him posted to Japan to get him out of the way.

Clara was twenty-four (Mussolini was fifty-three). She had green eyes, long, straight legs and heavy breasts – which Mussolini adored. Her voice was husky and her teeth were small, but she learned to smile with her lips only slightly parted. She was a hypochondriac, sentimental, rather stupid and utterly devoted to Il Duce. He felt the same about her, even taking time off from making the trains run on time to be at her bedside when she had her appendix removed after a near-fatal bout of peritonitis.

But when it came to sex, he was no more gentle and considerate with her than he had been with any of his other lovers. Mussolini gave her a flat at the Palazzo Venezia, where he would have sex with her between one meeting and the next. Perversely, the relationship worked. She stayed with him for the next thirteen years and, when escape was possible, she chose to die at his side in 1945.

She knew that he would not leave his wife and family for her, and she knew that he was not faithful to her. Nevertheless she would wait in her apartment, hour after hour, reading love stories, drawing designs for new clothes, painting her nails, or simply staring out of the window or into the mirror. Often he would not turn up until ten o'clock at night. Sometimes not at all, and she would curse the old countesses he was making love to on the black velvet sofa downstairs.

While she tolerated these little peccadilloes, she constantly worried about losing Mussolini's love. She fretted that he might go back to an old mistress or find a new one. Angela Curti or Margherita Sarfatti were two names that constantly cropped up; and she heard that there was another woman called Irma who was trying to take him away from her.

Sometimes she would berate Mussolini about his other lovers. He would grow angry and insult her. She would cry, which would make him more angry still.

She asked Zita Ritossa, her brother's mistress, how she could keep Mussolini's love. Zita advised her not to make herself so readily available to him. Clara said she had already tried that, but it did not seem to bother him.

Indeed, by 1939, Mussolini was trying to get rid of her. He told Princess di Gangi of Sicily that he found Clara 'revolting'. In the spring of 1943, the police guarding the entrance of the Palazzo Venezia were given orders not to let Clara in. She pushed past them, only to find Mussolini cold and unforgiving.

'I consider the affair closed,' he said. It was the kiss-off line he had used a hundred times before with other mistresses.

But Clara cried and he softened. He tried on several other occasions to dismiss her, but the outcome was always the same. The war was going badly, he would say, and his liaison with her made him look weak. It would not matter if he had hundreds of mistresses, but his devotion to just one had led to harmful gossip. One of his officers said that Clara was 'doing Il Duce more harm than the loss of fifteen battles'.

While Mussolini gave Clara practically nothing – a small present now and again, and occasionally 500 lire to buy a dress – the hard-pressed Italian tax-payer thought that Mussolini was using their money to keep his mistress in luxury, while they suffered the deprivations of war. In fact, it was Roman shopkeepers and businessmen who were keeping her in expensive clothes and perfumes in an attempt to ingratiate themselves with Il Duce.

'I won't come in the day any more,' Clara begged. 'Just after dark. For a few minutes, just to see you and to kiss you. I don't want to cause a scandal.'

The real scandal, though, was her family. Before the war they had built a luxurious villa in the fashionable Camilluccia district. It had black marble bathrooms. Knowing which side their bread was buttered, they lavished special attention on Clara's bedroom. The walls were mirrored and the huge silk-covered bed was raised on a dais. But when Mussolini visited and was asked whether he liked the place, he replied: 'Not much.'

Clara's mother suggested that she ask Mussolini to pay for the villa, but Clara refused even to suggest it. However, everyone assumed that he had picked up the tab.

Even if they did not receive direct patronage from Il Duce, the Petacci family were clever enough to use their position to their advantage. Clara's brother Marcello, a naval doctor, for example, made a fortune smuggling gold through the diplomatic bag.

In July 1943, when the Allies landed in Sicily, Mussolini was voted out of office by the Fascist Grand Council. The next day he was arrested by order of King Victor Emmanuel III. Clara was arrested too and imprisoned in the Visconti Castle at Novara. There she spent her time writing love letters to her beloved Benito – who she addressed as 'Ben' – and filling her diaries with memories of the wonderful times she had had with him.

'I wonder if you'll get this letter of mine,' she wrote, 'or will they read it. I don't know and I don't care if they do. Because although I used to be too shy to tell you that I loved you, today I'm telling all the world and shouting it from the roof-tops. I love you more than ever.' The letters never reached him. They were intercepted by the censors

Mussolini was rescued by the Germans and set up a puppet state in Northern Italy. Clara, determined to rejoin him, persuaded the nuns who were looking after her to smuggle a letter out to the German headquarters in Novara. They sent a staff car to fetch her.

Although the Germans did not trust her, they thought they could use her. They found her a villa on Lake Garda where Mussolini could visit her every day. Her guard at the villa was the young and charming Major Franz Spögler, who reported directly to Gestapo headquarters in Vienna.

However, the Germans' plans fell a little flat because Rachele learned that Clara was around. Her jealous outbursts meant that Mussolini could see little of his mistress. But occasionally, in the evenings, he would leave his official Alfa Romeo outside his office to allay suspicion and drive over to see her in a small Fiat. Their meetings were cold and sad. Twice he told her that he did not want to see her any more. On both occasions, she began to cry and, yet again, he relented.

Eventually Rachele could take no more and went to see Clara herself. Clara sat in silence while Rachele berated her. Then, when Rachele's ranting finished, Clara said quietly: 'Il Duce loves you, Signora. I have never been allowed to say a word against you.'

This placated Rachele for a moment. Then Clara offered to give her typed copies of the letters Mussolini had sent her.

'I don't want typed copies. That's not why I came,' Rachele shouted and flew into a rage again. She hurled abuse at Clara. With her face growing redder and redder, Clara phoned Mussolini.

'Ben, your wife is here,' she said. 'What shall I do?'

Rachele grabbed the phone and forced Mussolini to tell Clara that he had known beforehand that Rachele had been planning to come to see her. Rachele told Clara that the Fascists hated her almost as much as the partisans did.

Both women ended up crying. When Rachele eventually left, her parting curse was: 'They'll take you to the Piazzale Loreto' – Milan's haunt for down-and-out prostitutes. This is exactly what happened.

As the Allies fought their way up the Italian peninsula, Mussolini left Rachele to make a last stand at Valtellina. When they parted in the garden of their villa, he said he was ready to 'enter into the grand silence of death'.

His advisers told him that he should fly to safety in Switzerland or Spain. A former mistress, Francesca Lavagnini, invited him to join her in Argentina, while Clara suggested that they stage a car accident and announce that he had been killed.

Mussolini rejected all these proposals. Once he had made sure Rachele and his family were safe, he urged Clara to flee to Spain. The Petacci family went, but Clara herself refused to go.

'I am following my destiny,' she wrote to a friend. 'What will happen to me I don't know, but I cannot question my fate.'

Together Mussolini and Clara fled north to Como. There, Elena Curti Cucciate, the pretty, fair-haired daughter of his former mistress Angela Curti, joined them. Mussolini went for a walk with her, which sent Clara into paroxysms of jealousy.

'What is that woman doing here?' she screamed hysterically. 'You must get rid of her at once. You must! You must!'

He didn't. Instead, Elena and Mussolini travelled on in a German convoy, but Clara caught up with them when they were stopped by a partisan road block on the road to Switzerland. The partisans said that, to prevent unnecessary bloodshed, they would allow the Germans through – but not any Italian Fascists. Clara urged Mussolini to disguise himself as a German and make his escape. Then she burst into tears. He donned a German greatcoat and helmet and climbed on board a German lorry. As it pulled away, Clara ran after it and tried to clamber on, but one of Mussolini's ministers grabbed her. It took all his strength to pull her off the tailboard.

Someone, however, had spotted Mussolini at the road block. In the next town, the convoy was searched and he was found. The redoubtable Clara caught them up again, only to be arrested herself. At first, she pretended that she was not Clara Petacci but a Spaniard. She even asked the partisans what they would do to Clara Petacci if they caught her. But soon she confessed.

'You all hate me,' she told her interrogators. 'You think I went after him for his money and his power. It isn't true. My love has not been selfish. I have sacrificed myself for him.' She begged to be locked up in the same jail as him.

'If you kill him, kill me too,' she said.

Orders were given to take Mussolini and Clara to Milan. When the two cars carrying them met up on the road, they were allowed a few moments to talk. Clara was absurdly formal.

'Good evening, Your Excellency,' she said.

Mussolini was angry to see her.

'Signora, why are you here?' he demanded.

'Because I want to be with you,' she replied.

The prisoners and their escorts arrived at Azzano at a quarter past three in the morning. They were to stay at the home of a partisan family called the De Marias.

At about four o'clock the next night, a man in a brown mackintosh named Audisio turned up, saying that he had come to rescue them. They were driven to a nearby villa where they were ordered out of the car. Their 'rescuers' were Communist partisans who had been ordered to execute Mussolini, along with fifteen other leading Fascists.

Clara threw her arms around Mussolini and screamed: 'No! No! You mustn't do it. You mustn't.'

'Leave him alone,' Audisio said, 'or you'll be shot too.'

But this threat meant nothing to Clara. If Mussolini must die, then she wanted to die too and she clung on to him.

Audisio raised his gun and pulled the trigger but missed his target. Clara rushed at him and grabbed the barrel of the gun with both hands. As they wrestled, Audisio pulled the trigger again.

'You cannot kill us like this,' Clara screamed.

Audisio pulled the trigger a third time, but the gun was well and truly jammed. So he borrowed a machine gun from a fellow partisan and sprayed them with bullets. The first shot killed Clara. The second hit Mussolini and knocked him down. The third killed him.

Their two bodies were thrown onto the back of a lorry, on top of the corpses of the other Fascists who had been executed. They were driven to Milan. In the Piazzale Loreto, they were strung up from a lamp-post by the feet. Clara's skirt fell down over her face, leaving her lower half naked. A partisan stood on a box and tied the torn hem of her skirt up between her legs to preserve some of her modesty. Curiously, though Mussolini's mistress was widely hated, many men who were there that day remarked on Clara's face. Even beneath the dirt and smears of blood, they said, she was remarkably beautiful.

5

Hitler Having a Ball

Adolf Hitler was the most evil man of modern times; but, although he has been dead for over fifty years, he still has a growing band of followers across Europe, America, Russia, India, Africa, Asia, Latin America and the Far East. Racists, anti-semites, religious fundamentalists, authoritarians and just plain nutcases are mesmerized by his demagoguery, his totalitarian vision and his simple, bloodthirsty solution to any political problem. But if his followers knew about his pitiful, pathetic, perverted sex life, they would find it hard to hold him in such awe. It is difficult to have any respect for a man who likes to cower naked on the floor while being kicked by a woman or gets the ultimate sexual satisfaction from being urinated or defecated upon. Several of his lovers committed suicide, they were so appalled at his depravity.

There is no doubt that Hitler was a very strange man. That was plain long before he came to power. His ranting, hypnotic speeches often excited women to orgasm. A man who worked as a cleaner in Munich said that they would sometimes lose control of their bladders too and the whole of the front row would have be to sponged dry. Hitler would have loved that.

Homosexual men were convinced that Hitler was a homosexual too. Almost all of his bodyguards were homosexual. So were many of the inner circle of the Nazi Party. Reichsmarschall Herman Göring was a transvestite. Deputy Führer Rudolf Hess was known as 'Fraulein Anna' and Ernst Röhm, the homosexual head of the Nazi storm troopers and Hitler's long-time friend, said: 'He is one of us.'

Soon after the Night of the Long Knives, when Röhm and his friends were killed, there were mass arrests of homosexuals in Germany. The following year, the law was revised to make it illegal for a man even 'to touch another man in a suggestive way'. Homosexuals were given pink stars to wear and sent to the concentration camps. It is estimated that over half a million homosexuals died during Hitler's Reich. What was he trying to prove?

Early newsreels show that his gestures and walk were very effeminate – until Leni Riefenstahl, the great film actress, film-maker and possible lover of Hitler, began shooting him from a low camera angle to emphasize his power and encourage his mythic status. American generals would joke that he would never have gotten through West Point with his camp little mincing walk.

Another characteristic was his habit of clasping his hands protectively in front of his genitals. This prompted the joke that he was 'hiding the last unemployed member of the Third Reich'.

When war broke out, the Allies needed to know what made the Nazi dictator tick. If they could get inside the mind of the man, perhaps they would be able to predict what he was going to do next. In America, General William 'Wild Bill' Donovan, head of the OSS – the Office of Strategic Services, the forerunner of the CIA – put Boston psychologist Dr Walter C. Langer on the case. Assisted by Dr Gertrud Kurth, a refugee from Hitler's persecution, and Professor Henry A. Murray of the Harvard Psychological Clinic, he collected all the material he could from published sources and interviewed as many people as he could find who had known Hitler personally. Langer and his team made a particular effort to understand Hitler's sex life. In the psychoanalytical theories that were fashionable at that time, this was thought to be crucial.

Although Langer's report was sent to propaganda departments, it was not itself a tool of propaganda. Langer tried, as objectively as possible, to distil everything that was known about Hitler and his sexual proclivities. General Donovan expressed his satisfaction with the report. It was circulated widely. British foreign secretary Lord Halifax personally congratulated Langer; and it was read by Churchill and Roosevelt with evident satisfaction.

Given his psycho-analytic background, Langer, naturally, traced the roots of Hitler's behaviour back to his childhood. Hitler's father, Alois Hitler, was an Austrian customs official on the German border, a good-looking man and an insatiable womanizer. He was the illegitimate son of Anna Maria Schicklgrüber, a housemaid who had worked in the home of a wealthy Jew named Frankenberger. Frankenberger was probably Alois's father. Later, Anna Maria married Johann Georg Heidler, whose name could be spelt in a number of ways, including the way Alois chose to spell it – Hitler. But Alois Schicklgrüber did not change his name to Hitler until the age of forty, long after his step-father was dead and only then because he thought it would help his career in the customs service.

Hitler's mother, Klara Polzl, first came to work for her uncle, Alois Hitler, when she was sixteen and, by all accounts, very beautiful. She was nanny to Therese, Alois's illegitimate daughter by a former lover in Vienna. A relative of Johann Heidler, she was not a blood relative of Alois's.

Alois lived in a tavern in Linz and Klara had been warned about his drunken, womanizing ways. He was married to Anna Glassl, fourteen years his senior. She had brought with her a considerable dowry, which Alois soon squandered while satisfying his sexual lust with a serving maid, seventeen-year-old Franziska 'Fanni' Matzelberger.

Klara's supple young body scarcely escaped the attention of the lecherous Alois, and soon the atmosphere became so heated that Anna could stand no more and she fled.

With Anna out of the way, Alois's young lover Fanni took her place. She was clever enough to spot that Klara could, in turn, step into her former place as Alois's mistress. So she refused to go on living with Alois unless he sent Klara away.

Fanni and Alois married. They had two children, Alois Junior and Angela, but soon after the birth of Angela, Fanni became ill and Alois sent for Klara to nurse her on her deathbed. When Fanni finally succumbed, Alois consoled himself with Klara. At the same time, he was having an incestuous affair with his daughter Therese, who had an illegitimate son by him. Klara, too, became pregnant.

Alois and Klara married. Their first son, Gustav, was born a few days after the ceremony, but died within a few days. Klara lost two more children in a diphtheria epidemic. Then on the morning of 7 January, 1885, she had a son, Adolf, who survived.

Having lost three children already, Klara lavished all her love on Adolf. She continued breast-feeding him long after the age when he should have been weaned.

The morbid bond between mother and son was further strengthened by the death of another child, Adolf's brother Edmund, at the age of six. Klara's sixth and final child, Paula, survived but was feeble-minded. Hitler, alone of Klara's six children, was sound. Her love for all of them was focused on him. He described himself throughout his life as a 'mother's boy', even writing about his mother in his political treatise, *Mein Kampf.*

The cloying love between Klara and her only sound child left little room for Alois. A promotion meant that he was away from home a lot, but when he returned he expected sex from her. Once when Klara would not oblige him, he went to visit his former lover in Vienna, Therese's mother. But she was in the advanced stages of pregnancy and could not help him out. Alois returned to Linz full of sexual craving and, on a hot August night, he brutally raped Klara in front of her son who was, at the time, too young to go to her assistance.

For the first seventeen years of his life, the young Hitler witnessed the total sexual subjugation of his beloved mother by his brutal and drunken father, until January 1903, when Alois collapsed and died. It was a relief to all concerned. His epitaph read: 'The sharp word that fell occasionally from his lips could not belie the warm heart that beat beneath the rough exterior.'

That epitaph certainly belied Hitler's feeling for him. After the Anschluss, which unified Austria with Germany, the cemetery where Alois was buried became part of an artillery firing range, destroying his grave for ever.

With Alois dead, mother and son were alone together, but not for long. Four years later, Klara Hitler contracted breast cancer. The doctor who treated her, Eduard Bloch, was Jewish. Hitler was also one of his patients, having caught syphilis in Vienna.

Despite the fact that his mother had already had one breast removed and was plainly dying of cancer, Hitler had decided to enrol at the General School of Painting at the Academy of Fine Arts in Vienna. As the capital of the decaying Austro-Hungarian Empire, Vienna was a cesspit of vice. Its infamous red-light district was Spittelberggasse, where girls sat semi-naked behind lace curtains.

Due to the virulent anti-semitism of the time, many young Jewish girls were forced to eke out a living there, where sexual diseases were almost unavoidable. Prostitutes with syphilis had to work all the harder to pay the increasingly extortionate bribes for a medical certificate, and eager young men paid little attention to the risks.

After many visits to the Spittelberggasse, Hitler had already contracted syphilis – then an incurable disease – when he was summoned back to Linz, where his mother was dying in great pain. At Hitler's insistence, Dr Bloch administered iodoform, which very occasionally, and for reasons then unknown to medical science, halted the growth of tumours. Hitler insisted: 'My mother must be treated by all possible means. A poison must be used to kill a worse poison.'

In Klara's case, iodoform had no effect on the cancer. It simply produced hallucinations and increased her pain and she finally died in agony. Hitler was devastated by the loss.

Around this time, Hitler had a strange fantasy love affair. One evening he was walking down the main street of Linz with his friend Gustl Kubizek, when he pointed out a beautiful young woman named Stefanie Jantsen. Hitler said that he was in love with her. Although he never spoke to her, this infatuation lasted for four years. Somehow Hitler imagined he was going to marry her and have children. For him, she was the very ideal of German womanhood. He wrote poetry dedicated to Stefanie and once, when he imagined she was angry with him for some reason, he threatened to kill himself. When Kubizek enquired further, he discovered that Hitler had devised an entire fantasy suicide plot. Every aspect had been planned in detail, including the fact that Kubizek should witness the event.

When Kubizek related the tale later, he insinuated that Hitler made up the fantasy as an aid to masturbation. For much of the time when this 'affair' went on, Stefanie does not even seem to have been in Linz.

Returning to Vienna, Hitler would lecture friends about the dangers of prostitution. He took Kubizek, now his room-mate, to the Spittelberggasse to see for himself 'what imbeciles men become in the grip of their lowest desires'. They walked the entire length of the quarter and back again, while Hitler ranted about the evils of prostitution and the foolishness of men who succumb. Kubizek sensed that Hitler derived some voyeuristic pleasure from their visit.

In the chronology of Hitler's life, there is a year during the period when he lived in Vienna that is unaccounted for. It is thought that he may have been undergoing some form of hospital treatment, possibly for syphilis. If he was, it was unsuccessful. During that entire period in Vienna, he seems to have had no female company.

'For two years,' he wrote, 'my only girlfriends were Sorrow and Need, and I had no other companions except constant unsatisfied hunger. I never learned to know the beautiful word "youth".'

This is not surprising, given the description of him at the time. He wore the Bavarian mountain costume of leather shorts, which showed off his short, spindly legs, a white shirt and braces. His hips were wide, his shoulders narrow and chest so puny that, later, he had to have his uniforms padded. His muscles were flabby. His clothes were none too clean, his fingernails dirty and he had a mouth full of rotten, brown teeth.

There were stories that Hitler had several homosexual liaisons during this period. They may have been put about later by political enemies but one, in particular, stands out. During World War I, Hitler was brave and fanatically patriotic. He received two Iron Crosses for courage, but was never promoted beyond the rank of lance-corporal. The widely circulated story was that Hitler was kept in the ranks because he had been court-martialed on a charge of indecency which implicated a senior officer. When he came to power, the story was suppressed by the Gestapo, who destroyed his military records. Comrades in the trenches also noted that Hitler 'was a peculiar fellow – he never asked for leave; he did not have even a combat soldier's interest in women; and he never grumbled, as did the bravest of men, about the filth, the lice, the mud, the stench of the front line'.

During World War I, Hitler was gassed by the British. While he recuperated in a crowded ward in a hospital in Pasewalk in northern Germany, he suffered blindness and hallucinations. The doctor who treated him, Edmund Forster, believed that these symptoms were brought on by a psychopathic hysteria. This may have been related to his syphilis, which would now have been well into its secondary phase.

Again, when Hitler came to power, Forster's records were located and suppressed by the Gestapo. Forster, by then a professor, was forced to resign. Living in constant fear of being hauled off by the Gestapo, he eventually shot himself. Gestapo head Heinrich Himmler would have seen those files and he confirmed that Hitler had syphilis.

After World War I, Hitler settled in Munich, a recognized centre of venereology. During his early days there, Hitler's main sexual outlet was solitary. According to friends, the bookshelves of his room were stuffed with pornography, including well-thumbed volumes of the *History of Erotic Art* and *An Illustrated History of Morals*. He continued his interest in art and would go to life classes to ogle the nude models.

But Hitler was not without sexual attraction and he rose to power thanks partly to the women of Germany. The first to take him up was Helene Bechstein. She and her husband were immensely wealthy. They supported his fledgling Nazi Party financially and introduced him to their wealthy friends, whose wives encouraged their husbands to contribute too.

Hitler was an unlikely sex symbol. Though he now hid his spindly legs under a blue suit, it was shabby to say the least. He had a facial tic that caused the corner of his lip to curl upwards. When he walked, he would cock his right shoulder every few steps. At the same time, his left leg would snap up. Those who got close to him, talked of his terrible body odour. Throughout his life, he suffered from chronic flatulence. He dosed himself with anti-gas pills and gave up eating meat in an attempt to minimize the smell.

Hitler made an odd dinner guest. He ate little and drank nothing – he had got drunk once in his teens and had promised his mother he would be a teetotaller. But once the conversation turned to politics, he would grow excited and flushed. Making wild gestures, he would brook no interruption, his shrill voice swelling higher and higher as if in verbal orgasm. Older women, particularly, were quickly won over and would donate their jewels on the spot. At public meetings, middle-aged women would get so agitated they would have to be given medical attention. On one occasion, a woman bent down, picked up a handful of gravel that he had trodden on and tried to swallow it. To women like these, Hitler was a god. They handed over their money and many claimed to have gone to bed with him, though it is unlikely that he would have risked giving any of his backers syphilis.

While Hitler knew how to woo women his mother's age, he was less successful with younger women. In Munich, Hitler used to go chasing girls with his first chauffeur, Emil Maurice, who was half Jewish. Although Maurice was much more successful than him, Hitler adopted the alias 'Herr Wolf'. The sexually predatory wolf is an image that is repeated in Hitler's fantasy life. He even persuaded his weak-minded sister Paula to change her name to Wolf when he came to power, as she failed to live up to his Aryan ideals.

Hitler described Helene Bechstein as the greatest lady in Germany, but she thought of him more as a son than a lover. After his failed putsch in 1923, it was Helene who persuaded Hitler to end his jail-cell hunger strike; and she urged him to continue the fight when he said all was lost.

When he was released, he threw himself at her feet. Acutely embarrassed, she begged him to get up.

'It would have been awful if somebody had come in, humiliating for him,' she said.

Helene did not want him for herself. She was grooming her daughter, Lotte, to be his bride. But Hitler had no intention of getting married to her, he said. He was already wedded to Germany.

Hitler also flirted with English-born Winifred Wagner, the widowed daughter-in-law of the composer Richard Wagner. She organized the Wagner festivals at Bayreuth. Hitler's whole Nazi ethos was shot through with Wagnerian myth and he suggested, not entirely in jest, that she was his rightful bride.

Many of the women who were besotted by Hitler found openly supporting such a dangerous organization as the Nazi Party difficult. So they made their contributions direct to Hitler himself. These gifts became the foundation of his personal wealth. He bought a country home in Berchtesgaden. There he met Elisabeth Büchner, the wife of a racing driver who ran a local hotel. She was tall and Hitler saw her as his Brunhilde. She made him so excited that he would march up and down, striking his thigh with his rhinoceros-hide whip.

Although he seems to have been circumspect about women at this time, Hitler was particularly attracted to girls who were young, naive and easily influenced. He met a girl named Mitzi Reiter while out walking his dog in Berchtesgaden. She was more than twenty years his junior. He took her to a concert – their next date was a Nazi rally.

At first, the affair was innocent enough. Hitler would go for walks in the park with her and bombard her with flattery. He idolized her, he said. Then he suddenly grabbed her by the shoulders and kissed her.

'I want to crush you,' he said.

At one time, they considered finding an apartment and living together in Munich. A year later, Mitzi attempted suicide. She tried to throttle herself with a clothesline, but was found by her brother who resuscitated her. She was clearly terrified of Hitler. Once, she said, he had whipped his dog so savagely that she was 'overwhelmed by his brutality'.

Another lover, Susi Liptauer, hanged herself after an overnight engagement with the Führer.

Next, Hitler had an affair with his own niece, Geli Raubal. Hitler's widowed half-sister Angela came to Munich to keep house for him in 1927 and brought her twenty-year-old daughter Geli with her. She was fair-haired and well developed.

When she first moved into the Brown House, Hitler's headquarters on Brienner Strasse, Geli could barely disguise her admiration for her 'big, famous uncle'. He promptly appointed himself her guardian and protector and moved her into a room next to his. But things became difficult.

Geli was bored by politics and wanted to go out dancing. Hitler forbade her the company of people her own age and once, when he met her in the street with a fellow student, he threatened to beat her with the whip he carried. He constantly gave her ranting lectures, in hideously graphic detail, on the dangers of sexual intercourse.

Otto Strasser, younger brother of Gregor Strasser, one of the leading figures in Hitler's Munich 'Beer Hall' putsch of 1923, arranged to take her out to a masked ball. While Otto was dressing, his brother burst into the room with the news that Hitler had forbidden him to go out with Geli.

The phone rang. It was Hitler himself.

'I understand that you are going out with Geli this evening,' Hitler bellowed. 'I won't allow her to go out with a married man. I'm not going to have any of your filthy Berlin tricks here in Munich.'

Later, when Otto saw Geli, he said she had the look of a hunted beast.

'He locked me up,' she sobbed. 'He locks me up every time I say no.'

During another jealous tantrum, Hitler accused Geli of being a whore and forced his half-sister to take her to the gynaecologist. He strutted up and down outside the doctor's surgery while Geli was examined. When it was found that she was, indeed, still a virgin, Hitler bought her an expensive ring; but he still locked her in her room at night.

By this time, Angela was becoming concerned about Hitler's intentions towards her daughter. She asked him to promise that he would not seduce her. Hitler replied that he was not the problem. Geli was a cunning hussy and, the gynaecological tests notwithstanding, a demi-vierge.

Otto Strasser, who escaped to Canada after his brother was purged in the Night of the Long Knives, learned the full depravity of the affair between Geli and Hitler, that had left her virgo-intacta but no longer innocent.

'Hitler made her undress,' he told Dr Langer's interviewer. 'He would then lie on the floor. She would have to squat over his face where he could examine her at close quarters and this made him very excited.' It was of the utmost importance to Hitler that Geli squat over him in just such a way that he could see everything. 'When the excitement reached its peak, he demanded that she urinate on him and that gave him his sexual pleasure. Geli said the whole performance was extremely disgusting to her and it gave her no gratification.'

Strasser had heard such things before, from Henriette Hoffman, the daughter of Hitler's official photographer, but he had dismissed them as hysterical ravings.

The chambermaids who had to clean up Geli's bedroom also complained of the 'very strange and unspeakable' things that had been going on there.

Geli also told a girlfriend that Hitler was 'a monster-...you would never believe the things he makes me do'. Others did. They saw the evidence with their own eyes. In 1929, a portfolio of pornographic sketches Hitler had made of Geli fell into the hands of the landlady's son, Dr

Randolf. They showed her in every sort of indecent and obscene pose and outlined in detail the depth of his coprophiliac cravings.

Father Stempfle, a rabid anti-semite, had organized for Hitler to buy them back via a collector of political memorabilia named Rehse. However, Rehse double-crossed Stempfle and upped the price when the Party Treasurer, Franz Xavier Schwartz, went to collect the portfolio. Stempfle was another of those who perished in the Night of the Long Knives. Schwartz was told not to destroy the drawings, but to return them to Hitler at Nazi headquarters.

While Geli was locked up at night, Hitler claimed the right to visit other lovers. He spent time at the studios of official photographer Heinrich Hoffmann, which was a meeting place for homosexuals of both sexes. Hoffmann made erotic films which Hitler watched there while taking an unhealthy interest in Hoffmann's daughter Henriette, who was then sixteen. He later encouraged her to marry Baldur von Schirach, the reputedly homosexual leader of the Hitler Youth and Gauleiter of Vienna.

Hitler still spent time with the Wagners. Winifred became so fanatically attached to him that she threatened her own daughter with extermination when, sickened by what was happening to the Jews, she fled to Switzerland.

Emil Maurice took advantage of Hitler's absences and started seeing Geli. When Hitler caught them together, Emil was sacked on the spot and Hitler cursed him as a 'filthy Jew'.

In 1931, Geli was determined to leave Hitler and move to Vienna were she could study music. Angela was also determined to get her daughter out of Uncle Adolf's grasp. The situation was urgent; Geli was pregnant. The child may have been Emil Maurice's, though she had also slept with the young Nazi assigned to guard her. Reports that the baby may have been Hitler's have been discounted. One of his last letters to her includes pornographic images indicating that he was impotent. Worse – Hitler's nephew, his half-brother Alois's son, Patrick Hitler, suggested that the father was 'a young Jewish art teacher in Linz'.

One night that autumn, Geli and Hitler had a terrible row. She insisted that she was leaving him and going to Vienna. He forbade it. Hitler was due in Hamburg and a car was waiting downstairs for him. She called down to him from the window, begging one more time to be allowed to leave for Vienna. He refused and gave orders that she was to see no one until he returned. The next morning she was found dead.

The coroner's report said that the cause of death was a bullet which had entered below the chest and penetrated the heart vertically. Geli Raubal was just twenty-three.

A number of other stories circulated at the time. One was that Himmler had murdered Geli on Hitler's orders; another, that Hitler himself had pulled the trigger during a violent struggle with Geli over a gun. It was said that they had a 'major row over breakfast' when Geli told Hitler that she was engaged to be married to a man in Austria in order to escape his domination.

Otto Strasser said that Hitler had shot Geli during a quarrel. His brother Gregor had to spend three days and nights with Hitler after her death, in case he committed suicide. Pre-empting the inquest, the Nazi Party issued a communiqué saying that Hitler had gone into deep mourning following the 'suicide' of his niece. According to Strasser, the public prosecutor wanted to charge Hitler with murder, but the Bavarian Minister of Justice, Wilhelm Gürtner, quashed the case and a verdict of suicide was recorded. Gürtner went on to become Reich Minister of Justice and the hapless prosecutor fled Germany when Hitler came to power.

However Geli died, the Nazis went to considerable lengths to hush things up. Her body was taken down the backstairs of the flats and sealed in a lead coffin in a Munich mortuary. Then it was smuggled out of the country. Himmler and Röhm attended the funeral. Hitler remained in Munich, prostrate with grief, though he managed to issue a libel writ against the *Münchener Post* which had dared to suggest that Geli's body had a broken nose and other injuries sustained in a struggle.

A journalist named Gerlich investigated Geli's death and was murdered for his pains. Gregor Strasser's lawyer, Voss, who kept Strasser's private papers, was murdered too. Strasser himself was murdered by Hitler's henchmen in 1934.

Despite officially having committed suicide, Geli was given a full Catholic burial in a church cemetery back in her native Austria. Hitler was not allowed to enter Austria without government permission, but he was allowed to visit Geli's grave provided he did not engage in any political activities. Hitler's headquarters in Munich gave Austrian Nazis instructions to ignore his visit. He crossed the border late at night. The cemetery had to be specially opened for him. He walked alone around the grave for some time, and returned to Germany before dawn.

Later he commissioned a life-sized bust of Geli from a photograph. When he was presented with it, he wept. The bust was kept surrounded by flowers and, every year on the anniversary of Geli's death, he would shut himself away with it for hours.

* * *

Soon after Hitler came to power, he invited the beautiful German film star nineteen-year-old Renate Müller to visit him in the Chancellory. He began the evening with gloatingly detailed descriptions of how his Gestapo men wrung confessions from their victims. He boasted that his men were far more brutal and effective than the worst of the medieval torturers.

Even though this sickened her, Renate had resigned herself to the fact that she was expected to go to bed with the Reichschancellor. They went into the bedroom and undressed. Then Hitler threw himself on the floor at her feet and begged her to kick him. 'I am filthy and unclean,' he yelled. 'Beat me! Beat me!'

Renate was horrified. She had never seen such a thing. She pleaded with him to get up, but he just lay there grovelling and moaning. So eventually she had to kick and punish him. The harder she kicked him, the more excited he got. Renate was utterly revolted by this display; but in conversation with film director Alfred Zeisler, she said that this was not even the worst of it. There was something even more unspeakable that she could not bring herself to talk about.

Soon after, Renate Müller jumped to her death out of the window of her hotel in Berlin – though there is some speculation that she may have been pushed out on Gestapo orders after being secretly charged with having a Jewish lover.

Hitler, it seems, had quite a passion for film actresses. Linda Basquette, an American star of the silent movies, claimed to have received a fan letter from him, inviting her to Berchtesgaden. There, he made a vigorous pass at her.

'The man repelled me so much,' she said. 'He had terrible body odour. He was flatulent. But he had strange penetrating eyes.'

Basquette claims that she had to kick the Führer in the groin to dampen his ardour, but this only inflamed him more. To escape his attentions, she claimed that she was part Jewish.

Linda Basquette went on to marry nine times, once to Sam Warner of Warner Brothers. She died in 1994 at the age of 87.

Meanwhile, back at the Reichs chancellery, the party went on. Champagne was consumed by the gallon and fabulous sums were paid to singers and dancers. The Reichsministers indulged their every whim. Josef Goebbels, one of the few heterosexuals among the Nazi élite, was so promiscuous, especially with film actresses employed by his Ministry of Propaganda, that his long-suffering wife Magda told Hitler she was going to divorce him. Hitler pointed out that divorce was impossible. There was not a lawyer in Germany who would handle her case. Magda seems to have tried to get her own back on her husband by attempting to seduce Hitler. She was a considerable beauty, but reported later that the Führer was impotent.

Hitler conceived a short-lived passion for Margaret Slezak, but she was an independent-minded woman. When she would not bend to his will, he banned her from his inner circle.

There was little doubt that Hitler could have his pick of women. One night, Austrian movie-maker Luis Trenker accompanied actress Louise Ulrich to the Chancellory, where the Führer was 'telling stories'. They found him in a room full of dazzling women in evening gowns. His mere presence, it was said, set the décolletages atremble. One woman, the wife of the director of the Nuremberg opera, was half-kneeling, half-lying at his feet in a pose of abject surrender, while Hitler ranted about the need for more tanks, more guns and more bombs.

One of the strangest worshippers at the feet of Hitler was Unity Mitford. The fifth daughter of Lord Redesdale, she came from a distinguished family. Her sister Jessica was a communist, who had a controversial career in journalism in America; Deborah was Duchess of Devonshire; Nancy Mitford became a distinguished novelist; and Diana married Sir Oswald Mosley, blackshirted leader of the British Union of Fascists. Unity thought she could go one better and marry the Führer himself.

It was Diana who introduced Unity to Hitler during a ten-day holiday to Germany in 1935. Unity was immediately besotted. She began to stalk Hitler like a hunter, bleaching her hair blonde to make herself look more Nordic and wearing the swastika pin he had given her prominently on her lapel. Her parents plainly approved. Lord and Lady Redesdale visited Berlin as special guests of the Führer. This caused a split in the family, with Diana and Unity fanatically pro-Hitler and Jessica and Nancy violently against.

It is not known how seriously Hitler took Unity, or whether their affair was consummated – in Hitler's strange way or in any other. However, Hitler did make it a practice to take young innocent girls, like Unity, and manipulate them into fulfilling his desires. He certainly found solace in her company, which seems to have relieved his deepest tensions. But those around Hitler found Unity a bit of a joke. Goebbels and Streicher called her Unity 'Mit-fart'.

With articles like 'I am a Jew-hater' and other pieces of Nazi propaganda that she published, Unity burnt her bridges back in England. The day war was declared, she sat in the English gardens in Munich and shot herself in the head. She did not die immediately. She was taken to Switzerland, then back to Britain. Her mother, Lady Redesdale, nursed her on a remote Scottish island until she died in 1948.

Leni Riefenstahl – who so brilliantly portrayed the puny, effeminate Adolf Hitler as the mythic personification of the Aryan master race in the movies *Triumph of Will* and *Olympia*, the official film of the 1936 Berlin Olympics – claimed after the war that she had never been Hitler's lover, but many people who were around at the time thought she was.

They met when Riefenstahl was a film star rather than a film-maker. Goebbels introduced them. He thought that a marriage between Hitler and Riefenstahl, the athletic heroine of a series of mountaineering movies, would be a propaganda triumph. Herman Göring once remarked: 'She's the crevasse of the Reich' – much to Hitler's displeasure.

Nazi spin doctor Putzi Hanfstaengl, who was present at their first meeting, recalled that Hitler looked awkward and isolated, as if in a panic. Hanfstaengl played the piano while Riefenstahl danced provocatively to the music. She was out to get her man. So Goebbels and Hanfstaengl made their excuses and left.

Riefenstahl had had numerous lovers, including the boxer Max Schmeling, movie producer Ernst Lubitsch and World War I flying ace Ernst Udet. Hanfstaengl believed that if Riefenstahl could not seduce Hitler, no one could.

But apparently, that time at least, Hitler resisted her charms. When Hanfstaengl met Riefenstahl on board a plane a few days later, he asked how it had gone. Riefenstahl's reply was a disappointed little shrug. However, she was not to be put off so easily. Hanfstaengl told Luis Trenker that one morning, about 2 a.m., he and Hitler had gone to Riefenstahl's flat for coffee, when she performed one of her legendary nude dances. Hanfstaengl complained: 'She kept on shaking her navel in front of my nose.'

Riefenstahl, who had all her property confiscated because of her Nazi connections after the war, denies this ever happened. But Luis Trenker thinks it did and that it did the trick. During the filming of *S.O.S. Iceberg!* for Universal Pictures, Riefenstahl was supposed to catch a boat in Hamburg to sail to the Balearic Islands for some location shooting. The whole crew was waiting on the dockside, but there was no sign of her. She had been missing for several days and no one knew where she was. Then the producers got a telephone call. The Führer's plane had just landed in Hamburg. Riefenstahl was on board. She had been a guest at Hitler's country house near Nuremberg.

When Riefenstahl turned up, she was carrying a huge bunch of flowers. 'Her eyes seemed to gaze into the distance,' Luis Trenker said. 'Her whole being was transformed. She wanted everyone to know that she had just been through a wonderful experience.'

Riefenstahl went to great lengths to please Hitler. She stopped using make-up because the Führer disapproved. Parisian lipstick, he believed, was made from pig's urine and he maintained that pure Aryan womanhood needed no cosmetics to improve its beauty.

But the affair did not mature as Goebbels had hoped. The following year, she confided to Jewish reporter Bella Fromm that Hitler 'asks me to dinner a couple of times a week, but always sends me away at quarter to eleven, because he is tired'. However, Hitler continued to take an interest in her. He warned her to be careful when she was filming another climbing movie in the Dolomites. She was needed to make Nazi propaganda films, he said. She proved to be the master of the medium. Although she was only shooting a newsreel, her film of the 1936 Berlin Olympics made it look like a triumph of Hitler's Aryan supermen. Against the demands of Goebbels and other top Nazis, Hitler allowed her to leave in the scenes where the great black American athlete Jesse Owens trounces the best Germany can offer. But the climax of the film is when Hitler greets German javelin thrower Tillie Fleischer, who won two gold medals – surely convincing proof of Nordic superiority.

Hitler was genuinely taken with his vision of Nordic beauty. According to an FBI report, he went to bed with

Danish beauty queen Ingrid Arvad, who fled Europe before the war. In America, she became the lover of a young Naval Intelligence officer called John F. Kennedy, who went on to become President of the United States. Lyndon Johnson found out about it and used the information to get himself onto the 1960 Democratic ticket.

In 1938, when Mussolini visited Munich, Riefenstahl was the only person Hitler personally introduced to Il Duce. The Reich's Ministry of Propaganda was hers to command. After the personal intervention of the Führer, she was allowed to film the Polish campaign including, by accident, several Nazi atrocities. At the front, she wore a field grey uniform, like Hitler.

In gratitude for her propaganda films, Hitler gave Riefenstahl a Mercedes and had a villa built for her with a film studio in the garden. During the war, Hitler added a bombproof shelter so that her 'immortal pictures' would survive the onslaught; but when the Americans marched into Kitzbühel, they found her burning the negatives.

After the war, Riefenstahl denied everything, especially her Salome act in front of Hitler and Hanfstaengl. She told American reporter Budd Schulberg: 'I wasn't his type. I'm too strong, too positive. He liked soft, cowlike women like Eva Braun.'

Hitler met Eva Braun in 1929. She was a laboratory assistant in Heinrich Hoffmann's photographic studio. Hitler was immediately impressed by her pretty ankles and legs. Convent-educated Eva was just seventeen. She was innocent, had few interests, no ambitions and was easily moulded.

Hitler was twenty-three years her senior. From the beginning he kept a very close rein on her. One night at Hoffmann's, not knowing who she was, Luis Trenker danced with her. He was told that he would be shot for trying to steal the Führer's mistress. Later, when they met again, Eva found a way to speak to him privately. She warned him never to mention the evening they danced. Becoming quite hysterical, she said, with unintentional irony: 'You don't know what a terrible tyrant he can be.'

Hitler and Eva Braun first became lovers in the spring of 1932, shortly after Geli Raubal died. Eva's diaries show that she adored Hitler, but at the same time she was tormented by him. She does not go into the details of their sexual relations, only saying obscurely: 'He needs me for special reasons. It can't be otherwise.'

Whatever they got up to, it did not make her happy. On 1 November, 1932, she made the first of several suicide attempts. Shortly after midnight, she shot herself through the neck with her father's service revolver, narrowly missing an artery. She managed to call a doctor, who informed Hitler that she had tried to shoot herself in the heart, but missed and that he had saved her just in time. Hitler immediately crowed to Hoffmann that Eva had tried to kill herself for the love of him.

'Now I must look after her,' he said. 'It must not happen again.'

It did.

After this first suicide attempt, Eva became the exclusive property of Hitler. It made her even more unhappy. On 6 February, 1935, her birthday, she wrote that she had 'just happily reached the age of twenty-three'. Then she ponders whether this 'is really a cause for happiness... At the moment I am very far from feeling that way'. All she craved was a little dog to make her less lonely.

That evening she dined with her friend Herta and despaired that she ended her birthday 'guzzling and boozing'. It was not until five days later that Hitler turned up unexpectedly. She recorded that they had a delightful evening, but he did not bring her the puppy she wanted and there were no cupboards stuffed with pretty dresses.

'He didn't even ask if I wanted anything for my birthday,' she wrote. Nevertheless, she basked in the attention. 'I am infinitely happy that he loves me so much and I pray that it may always remain so. I never want it to be my fault if one day he should cease to love me.'

But by 4 March, less than a month later, she wrote in her diary: 'I am mortally unhappy again and since I haven't permission to write to Him' – like most German women at the time she capitalized the pronoun, putting him on a par with God and Christ – 'this book must record my lamentations.'

She knew that he had been in Munich all that Sunday, but he had not visited her. Nor had he returned the phone calls she had made to the Osteria Bavaria, where he dined. She waited in all day 'like a cat on hot bricks. I imagined every moment that he was about to arrive.' When she decided to do something about it, it was too late. She dashed to the station, only to see the tail-lights of his train as it pulled out. That evening, she turned down an invitation to go out and spent the evening alone in her apartment trying to figure out why he was angry with her.

A week later she still had not heard from him. She longed to fall ill so that he might feel guilty for neglecting her.

'Why do I have to bear all this?' she lamented. 'If only I had never met him.'

She began taking sleeping tablets so that she did not have to think about her plight. From this time on, she became addicted.

'Why doesn't the devil carry me off?' she wrote. 'Hell must be infinitely preferable to this... Why doesn't he stop tormenting me.'

Things got worse. Heinrich Hoffmann told her that Hitler had found a replacement for her. 'She is known as the Walküre and looks the part, including the legs. But these are the dimensions he prefers,' Eva wrote.

This could have been either Winifred Wagner, whose father-in-law wrote 'The Ride of the Valkyrie', or Unity Mitford, whose middle name was Valkyrie. Both were tall, full-breasted women, while Eva was slim with a small bust.

'He'll soon make her lose thirty pounds through worry,' she wrote, 'unless she has a gift for growing fat in adversity.'

Eva wrote that her only concern was that Hitler had not had the courtesy to inform her that he had lost his heart to someone else. It can hardly have been a surprise to her. He was pictured in the newspapers daily with other attractive women.

'What happens to me must be a matter of indifference to him,' she concludes. 'I shall wait until 3 June, in other words a quarter of a year since our last meeting. Let no one say I am not patient. I sit here waiting while the sun mocks me through the window panes. That he should have so little understanding, and allow me to be humiliated in front of strangers. But men's pleasure...'

But she could not wait that long. On 28 May, she sent him another letter and decided that, if he did not reply by ten o'clock that night, she would kill herself. Even if he was not seeing the Walküre, there were so many others.

Eva received no reply – not before ten o'clock, not after. The following morning she took two dozen Phanodorm tablets and, within minutes, was unconscious.

She was discovered by her sister Ilse, who came round to return a dress she had borrowed. Ilse called a doctor and Eva was revived. The whole incident was passed off as an accident, brought on by strain. But, soon after, Hitler found Eva a larger apartment on the outskirts of Munich and, later, the villa she wanted so much.

Around that time, Eva introduced Hitler to Dr Theo Morrell, who was a specialist in venereal diseases. He was Hitler's doctor up to his death in 1945. Morrell never admitted to treating Hitler for VD, but said he had been called in to treat eczema on his leg – a common site for a syphilitic tumour. The drugs he prescribed were also commonly given to patients in the last stage of syphilis.

Later, Eva asked Morrell to give Hitler something to increase his sexual potency. Morrell injected him with Orchikrin (emulsified bulls' testicles). It did not seem to do any good and Hitler never tried it again.

Throughout the war, Eva installed herself at Berghof, Hitler's retreat at Berchtesgaden. There, she played at being the perfect little wife to her Adolf, when he could take time off from the war; but even at Berghof, she was a prisoner.

'His jealousy is peculiar and inhuman,' she wrote in her diary.

He loved to see her naked and encouraged her to swim and sunbathe nude. He constantly hinted that it was 'too hot for clothes', in the hope that she would strip for him. If he had time, he would undress her himself, with fumbling fingers that nearly drove her crazy with frustration.

He also liked to photograph her nude. Often he would take close-ups of her buttocks. When taking intimate shots, he would be careful to photograph her from an obscenely low angle, explaining that he did not want anyone to recognize her if they fell into the wrong hands.

Hitler's commando chief, Otto Skorzeny, reported that Eva told him that Hitler 'doesn't even bother to take his boots off, and sometimes we don't get into bed. We stretch out on the floor. On the floor he is very erotic.'

There was little vaginal sex. Indeed, her medical records indicated that her vagina was too small for normal sex. But she desperately wanted children and had to undergo painful surgery to widen it. After the treatment was successfully completed, her gynaecologist died mysteriously, in a car accident. Despite the operation, their sex life did not become any more normal.

'He only needs me for certain purposes,' she confided to her diary again. 'This is idiotic.'

In February 1945, when it was clear that the war was lost, Hitler ordered her to remain at Berghof. But being separated from her Adolf was more than she could bear.

In April, she disobeyed him and got one of his official cars from Munich to drive her to his bunker in Berlin. She was almost killed by British dive bombers on the way. When she arrived he was so overjoyed that she was safe, that he did not have the heart to scold her.

With the tragedy in its last act, Göring sent an ultimatum, demanding that leadership of the Reich be handed over to him.

'Treachery,' screamed Hitler.

He ridiculed Göring, saying it was well known that a bullet in the groin in World War I had left him impotent. That was why he was so fat. Göring's daughter bore a conspicuous likeness to Mussolini, Hitler said. Mussolini had stayed with Göring and Göring's wife Emmy had become particularly attached to him.

When news came that Himmler had defected, Hitler went into a blood-curdling tirade. His body shook and his face became paralyzed. This rigor is another symptom associated with tertiary syphilis.

Some, mostly women, were still loyal to Hitler. Hanna Reitsch, the test pilot who proved the airworthiness of the V-1 flying bomb by flying it from a strap-on cockpit, made one last dash to be beside Hitler in his hour of need. She landed her plane under Russian gunfire in the avenue that ran down from the Brandenburg Gate. It is said that she had cooked up a plan to fly Hitler to Argentina, only to drop it when she discovered that he had Eva Braun with him in the bunker.

At midnight on 29 April, 1945, Hitler and Eva Braun married. They returned to his suite. Next morning, while the newly-weds slept in late, Eva's brother-in-law, Hermann Fegelein, was shot on Hitler's orders. He had been caught leaving the bunker with a large amount of Swiss francs and a woman who spoke French. Eva had begged Hitler to spare his life – but it had done no good.

Later on 30 April, in Hitler's study, Eva and Hitler bit into vials of poison and shot each other in the head. Goebbels found them. Their bodies were taken out of the bunker, doused with petrol and set alight. They did not burn completely, though; there was enough left for the Russian doctors to carry out a post-mortem. In the autopsy, it was discovered that Hitler did indeed have only one ball, but it could not be determined whether he had been born that way or whether one of his testicles had been removed surgically – not an uncommon practice when syphilis reaches its third and fatal stage.

The great dictator was dead, but that is not quite the end of the story. During the early 1970s, the story circulated that Hitler had had a daughter. It was said that she was the offspring of Tillie Fleischer, the Nordic javelin thrower who had won two gold medals at the 1936 Olympics. After Leni Riefenstahl had filmed a delighted Führer embracing the Nordic beauty they had an eight-month affair. Hitler gave Tillie a white Mercedes and a lakeside villa near Berlin; but when she became pregnant, he dropped her like a stone.

Tillie Fleischer married Dr Fitz Hoser, one of Hitler's aides, and they passed off Hitler's daughter, Gisela, as their own. When Gisela grew up, she married a Jew, the son of a French Rabbi who had died in Hitler's death camps, and she eventually converted to Judaism herself.

HITLER HAVING A BALL

That would have been a rather ironic ending but it seems unlikely – it was Hitler, not Göring, who Magda Goebbels claimed had been rendered impotent by a bullet to the groin in World War I.

6

The Thoughts of Chairman Mao

Although Mao Tse-tung aspired to be an emperor, he remained a peasant. He cared little for his personal appearance or hygiene. He ate smelly food, which tainted his breath, and chain-smoked 555 State Express until his teeth went black. He liked to talk openly about his bowel movements and would unself-consciously remove his trousers in front of guests on a hot day. In later life, he stopped cleaning his teeth altogether and they became covered in a green film. He also stopped washing, considering it a waste of time. Servants would wipe him down with a wet towel each night while he attended to state papers, read or talked.

Also in later life, a medical examination revealed that his foreskin was tight and difficult to pull back. His left testicle was smaller than normal and his right one undescended. It had remained in the abdominal cavity since childhood. When this was pointed out to him, he was sixty. Up until then, he had never realized that most men have two balls.

Born in 1893 in the village of Shaoshan in Hunan province, the son of a peasant farmer, Mao's first sexual experience occurred when he was still a teenager in his hometown. He had a youthful encounter with a twelve-year-old girl. In later years, Mao was fond of recalling this initiation. In 1962, Mao even arranged to meet her again, this woman to whom he had lost his virginity. By then, she was old and grey. He gave her two thousand yuan. When she left, he said wistfully: 'How she's changed.' What did he expect after more than fifty years.

However, the young Mao showed very little interest in sex. He was studious and introverted throughout his youth, and underwent long periods of sexual abstinence while he concentrated on the great political problems of the day. His father was worried about his dreamy, romantic son and decided to shake him out of it. In 1908, he arranged for the fifteen-year-old Mao to marry a woman six years his senior. For the first – and only – time in his life, he went through a full traditional wedding ceremony. Afterwards, although the woman was moved into the Mao family house, he refused to live with his bride. She died in 1910. Later, he maintained that he never laid a hand on her.

During his late teens and early twenties, Mao and his friends were too committed to politics to think about sex. There were women in their circle, such as Tsai Chang who went on to become a Communist leader, but shyness and inhibiting social tradition meant that Mao had little time for romance.

Mao devoted his energies to becoming a full-time revolutionary in Peking and probably remained celibate until he met Tao Szu-yung, a brilliant student. The romance withered when they disagreed about politics and they went their separate ways. Then he met another beautiful revolutionary comrade, Yang Kai-hui. He wrote love poems to her – as he did to his other lovers. She was the daughter of a university professor, white-skinned, with deep-set eyes They entered into a trial marriage before formalizing the situation in 1921, when she gave birth to their first child. This may seem conventional enough to us, but in China at that time for a couple to choose each other, without reference to their parents, was truly revolutionary.

The war against Chiang Kai-shek's Kuomintang nationalist (and vehemently anti-Communist) forces soon separated them. Mao left Yang and their children in Changsha for safety in 1927, while he established himself as a major revolutionary leader. Three years later, the Kuomintang seized Changsha. Yang was captured and executed when she refused to betray her husband. Their two boys fled to Shanghai where they had to fend for themselves on the streets. The younger son, Anqing, suffered from mental illness which was ascribed to the beatings he had suffered as a vagrant at the hands of the Shanghai police.The elder, Anying, was killed in an American air raid during the Korean war.

However, while Yang was sacrificing her life for her husband, Mao was already living with another beautiful revolutionary comrade, Ho Tzu-chen, a girl about half his age. She was eighteen; he was thirty-seven. When he first met his 'revolutionary lovemate', as he called her, he described her as 'attractive and refined'. She spoke in a clear and measured way. Her eyes were a 'pair of crystals'. Meeting her gave him a feeling 'as sweet as honey'.

They married soon after Yang's death – though some reports say that they had already wed in the safety of a Soviet base before Yang gave her life for her husband. When it came to marriage and divorce, Mao was always a bit sloppy about the paperwork.

Rumours were soon circulating, perhaps put about by Mao's enemies, that Ho was sexually dissatisfied with Mao, because he was so much older than her and constantly busy. Mao wrote her a poem showing that he understood her frustration:

> *I am just eighteen, hair not yet white,*
> *Stuck on Well Mountain, waiting for old age...*
> *A messenger comes to the door and says:*
> *'Commander Mao is busy at a meeting'*
> *I have only my pillow, to comfort me in my loneliness,*
> *My grassy bed grows cold as the night wears on*
> *I should have married an elegant man,*
> *and drawn pleasure from the hours.*

Ho was Mao's companion on the Long March, which started in 1934. This was the two-year, 6,000-mile trek from their soviet in South-east China to the Shaanxi province in North-west China which the Communist forces undertook to escape the nationalist Kuomintang. Mao and Ho left their two children behind with a peasant family. They never discovered what happened to them. Ho gave birth to another two children during the Long March and conceived a third. She had six children in all. Only one was male and, as far as they knew, only one, a daughter, Lin Min, survived.

It was during the Long March that Mao began to exhibit his peculiar lavatorial habits. He refused the offer of a commode, preferring to go into the fields with his bodyguards and dig a hole. Mao believed that his bowel movements were an inspiration to his troops.

Lavatories and bowel movements were a big thing for Mao, even after he came to power. While many of his district leaders installed Western-style sit-down lavatories and soft Western mattresses in their residences, Mao preferred to travel with his hard wooden bed and a squat-style Chinese toilet. Even on a visit to Moscow, he would insist on squatting over a bedpan rather than use a decadent Russian sit-down loo.

After the end of the Long March, the Communist set up a base in ancient caves in Yanan and Mao started seeing other women. He had an affair with Ting Ling, a childhood friend of his second wife, Yang Kai-hui. Another lover was Lily Wu, an elegant actress said to be the 'only girl in Yanan with a permanent wave'. He met her one night when he was having dinner in the cave where Agnes Smedley of the *Manchester Guardian* was sheltering. Lily was acting as interpreter and she kept putting her hand on Mao's leg, saying that she had drunk too much.

He was a little startled at first, but then he took her hand and said that he too had drunk too much. Later they arranged a private meeting in another cave. When Ho found out about it, she was furious. She charged Lily formally with alienating her husband's affections.

In 1938, Mao took up with a film actress with a less than savoury reputation, shocking the Communist hierarchy. Her name was Lan Ping – or Blue Apple. She changed it to Chiang Ch'ing – Azure River – though some called her Lang Ping Guo – Rotten Apple – because of her early promiscuity.

Chiang Ch'ing had been born into a troubled family. Her father was violent and her mother's work as a domestic servant bordered on prostitution. Chiang had a string of boyfriends before she married a man called Fei, the son of a merchant from Jinan, in 1930. The marriage lasted only a few months. Chiang fell out with Fei's family who considered her lazy. They divorced.

Soon after, Chiang met Yu Qiwei, the leader of the local Communist underground. They fell in love and began living together in 1931. When the Japanese army seized Manchuria in September 1931, Chiang, already a budding actress, starred in several anti-imperialist plays. When the Nationalist government cracked down on the Communists, Yu Qiwei was arrested and Chiang took up with a student of physical education named Qiao. Soon she finished with him and headed for the bright lights of Shanghai, where she was determined to make it as an actress.

Chiang was poor but ambitious and quickly built herself a career on the casting couch. She was the mistress of movie director and Communist party official Chang Keny. She married actor and movie critic Tang Na, then moved in with leading theatre director, Zhang Min, a married man. Tang was so distraught that he tried to kill himself with an overdose of sleeping pills, but the owner of the inn where he was staying found him in time. Chiang had no pity and continued expanding her career with a series of other liaisons.

'Chiang Ch'ing was a licentious woman,' said the wife of a revolutionary leader in Yanan, where Chiang had gone accompanied by another ex-husband, David Yu. 'She simply does not seem to be able to exist without a man.'

129

At that time, she said, Chiang was seeing an actor named Wang and they would use her husband's office for sex sessions. It was in Yanan that Chiang met Mao.

As soon as Chiang arrived in Yanan, rumours spread about her. Mao immediately sought her out and gave her a ticket to the Marx–Leninist Institute where he was giving a lecture. She sat in the front row and got herself noticed by asking questions. He returned the compliment and went to see her in the theatre. He applauded her performance so loudly that Ho Tzu-chen became jealous. They had a terrible row afterwards.

To Mao, Chiang was just another pretty girl, but Chiang was determined to get her man. She divorced Tang Na and abandoned their two children for Mao, explaining later: 'Sex is engaging the first time around, but what sustains interest is power.'

When Chiang became pregnant, Mao announced that he was going to divorce Ho to marry Chiang. However, this was not just a matter for the individuals concerned. They had to ask permission from the Communist Party.

The party was naturally concerned about Chiang Ch'ing's 'colourful past' and refused Mao permission to divorce and remarry.

'Ho Tzu-chen has always been a good comrade to you,' the Central Committee explained. 'She is a reliable and faithful companion and has shown her true worth in battle and in work. Why are you no longer able to live with a woman like this?'

Mao replied: 'I esteem and respect Comrade Ho. But we should not think along feudalistic lines any more, where divorce is considered an injury to a woman's reputation or position. Without Chiang Ch'ing I cannot go on with this revolution.'

The privations of the Long March had left Ho mentally unbalanced and the rejection by Mao pushed her over the edge. On these grounds, Mao eventually obtained permission to divorce in 1939. Many believed he was callously abandoning a valiant comrade and his divorce cost him a large number of followers. Mao also abandoned Lily Wu, who was despatched home to Szechuan.

Ho was sent to Moscow for psychiatric treatment, but there was no improvement in her condition. She spent the rest of her life in a comfortable house in Shanghai, paid for by the government, but she never fully recovered.

In 1961, Mao received a letter from Ho and decided that he wanted to see her. She was brought to his villa at Lushan. By this time, she was old and grey-haired. She was obviously delighted to see Mao, but her conversation was barely coherent. After she left, Mao sank into a deep depression.

As a condition of their marriage, Mao had to send Chiang Ch'ing to the Party School. The deputy head was Kang Sheng and, despite the fact that he was Mao's right-hand man, Chiang had an affair with him during her four months there.

Chiang and Mao married in 1939. They did not bother with a wedding ceremony or a legal marriage certificate. A simple announcement was enough.

However, malicious gossip still pursued her and Chiang was forced to take a backseat in public. She became the perfect Communist housewife, but her hold on power remained through sex. She told one and all that Mao was a great lover and his whole entourage would know if they had made love the night before.

Mao was not a man to settle for one woman indefinitely and, by 1949, they were becoming distant. In March, he sent Chiang to Moscow while he went to the Fragrant Hills with an actress named Yu Shan. She was the sister of David Yu, Chiang's ex-husband. David did not consider that Chiang Ch'ing had the right qualities to be the wife of Mao, who was by then effectively China's new emperor. His sister was more cultured, more cultivated, superior in every way. However, David Yu had misread the situation. Mao's preference was for earthy peasant girls and, after six months, they broke up. Then, in November, Chiang returned from the Soviet Union and re-established her presence in Mao's household.

It was also in 1949, when Mao was sixty, that his genital abnormalities were discovered, and his prostate was found to be small and soft. The doctor examining him discovered that Mao was infertile. He had fathered several children by three of his wives, but the youngest was now fifteen years old. So Mao must have become sterile after the age of forty-five.

When told, Mao said: 'So I've become a eunuch, haven't I?'

He seemed genuinely concerned. His doctor had to explain that the eunuchs in the old imperial court had their testicles, or often their entire genitals, cut off. Mao, it seemed, had little grasp of the workings of the reproductive system.

By this time, Mao had grown tired of Chiang sexually. He told her that, at sixty, he was too old for sex. But underlings, such as Kang Sheng, moved themselves up the party hierarchy by providing Mao with a constant supply of libidinous young women. Kang Sheng also maintained a library of pornographic material for Mao. No nation on earth had a richer tradition of the erotic arts than China, and Mao's collection far surpassed that of any emperor. During the Cultural Revolution, Kang Sheng looted the official museums to add to Mao's collection.

Mao's favourite topic of conversation was sex and the sex lives of others. In 1954, Mao crushed Gao Gang, who had amassed so much power that Stalin called him the King of Manchuria. Mao accused him of making an 'anti-party alliance' and he committed suicide. But it seemed that Mao was not interested in the details of the political threat Gao Gang represented. It was Gao's sex life that fascinated him. Gao had had sex with more than a hundred different women, it was said.

'He had sex twice on the night he killed himself,' Mao marvelled. 'Can you imagine such lust.'

Mao tried to match these excesses. He was famously interested in swimming and would fill the heated indoor swimming pool in the Forbidden City with hundreds of naked girls, then take a dip.

At first, Mao was discreet about his activities. His confidential secretary, Ye Zilong, would recruit women from the Cultural Work Troupe, the Central Garrison Corps and the Bureau of Confidential Matters. They had to be young, uneducated and fanatically devoted to Chairman Mao. They would stay in Ye's house until Chiang Ch'ing was safely asleep. Then they would be led quietly across the compound, through the dining-room and into Mao's bedchamber. In the morning, before Chiang Ch'ing awoke, they would be led out.

Afterwards, they would be treated generously. Mao could afford to be generous. Millions of copies of his *Little Red Book* had been sold and Mao Tse-tung was one of the richest men in China. He had made over three million yuan (£500,000) from the sale of his *Selected Works* alone.

During high-level party meetings, a special room would be set aside in the Great Hall of the People. The political departments of the army and the Communist Party would supply beautiful girls of impeccable proletarian backgrounds. They were told that they had been recruited as ballroom dancing partners for the Great Leader. In fact, they were fodder for his bed. But many of the party officials saw this as so great an honour, they supplied their daughters and sisters.

Madame Mao was proud of her appearance and her sexual skills and when she heard about his womanizing, it hurt her deeply. She would try and sit in on his dance parties where he tried to pick up girls. She tried to vet his nurses, firing the pretty ones. When Mao's physician questioned her actions, he was told: 'Doctor, you don't understand the Chairman. He is very loose with his love life. His physical pleasure and his mental activity are separate, and there are always women willing to be his prey.'

The doctor was also told that he would have to teach his nurses something about morality: 'They should be polite to their leader, but careful in their contact with him.'

Madame Mao was not wrong. The Great Helmsman was already involved with the railroad nurse on his special train. She did sterling service as they travelled around the country. In Shanghai, he paraded her publicly, taking her to the exclusive Jinjaing Club which was the preserve of top Party officials. The Shanghai authorities knew of the Chairman's passion for female companionship, so they laid on the city's top actresses and singers. But they were too sophisticated and worldly for the proletarian Mao. The Shanghai authorities learnt quickly and began providing young dancers who were more to Mao's taste.

At the time, the Cultural Work Troupe of the Twentieth Army were in the area. The young girls from the troupe would swarm around Mao, vying with each other for the privilege of a dance with the Great Leader. He would stay out dancing until two in the morning, then return to his train with his nurse.

Chiang Ch'ing's suspicion of nurses was confirmed after his sixty-fifth birthday banquet, which was held in Guangzhou. That night, Madame Mao had trouble sleeping. She called for the nurse to get a sleeping pill and got no response. So she got up and went to look for her. When she found the duty room empty, she stormed into Mao's bedroom and found the nurse there. In the ensuing row, Chiang Ch'ing accused Mao of sleeping with a former servant who had visited recently. Mao had encouraged the woman to get her daughter an education and given her three thousand yuan to enrol in school. Madame Mao accused him of sleeping with the daughter too.

Mao's response to these accusations was to head back to Peking, leaving his wife behind. Chiang Ch'ing quickly realized that she risked losing him. As an apology she sent him a quote from the famous Chinese folk story, *Monkey*. In it, a Chinese monk is travelling to

India in search of a Buddhist scripture. But Monkey makes him angry and he leaves him behind in a cave behind a waterfall.

'My body is in the cave behind the waterfall,' Monkey says to the monk, 'but my heart is following you.'

Mao accepted the apology – he realized that it meant he now had his wife's tacit permission to sleep with whoever he chose.

On one trip into Chiangxi province, the director of a new hospital provided four energetic young nurses for one of Mao's dance parties. A musical and dance troupe had also been laid on. Soon Mao was sleeping with a young nurse and a member of the dance troupe. He did little to hide the fact, but he was thoughtful enough to phone Madame Mao and advise her not to meet him there, as arranged. He would join her after his meetings were over.

As time went by, Mao grew careless and she caught him *in flagrante delicto* several times. There was nothing she could do about it. Once, Mao's doctor found her crying on a park bench just outside Mao's compound. She said through her tears that, just as no one, not even Stalin, could win a political battle against him, no one woman would win his heart completely.

Mao and Chiang Ch'ing eventually came to an understanding. In return for playing the public role of his wife, while tolerating his infidelities in private, Mao pledged not to leave her. As Madame Mao was more interested in power than sex, she agreed.

After that Mao made no attempt to hide his infidelities. At the Bureau of Confidential Matters, he met a young, white-skinned clerk, with delicately arched eyebrows and dark eyes. She told Mao that she had stuck up for him at primary school and been beaten up for her pains. Mao began a very public affair with the woman, spending night and day with her in Shanghai. Mao would dance with her until two in the morning, only stopping when his young companion was exhausted. The young woman was so proud of the affair that she tried to befriend Chiang Ch'ing. By this time, Chiang had accepted the situation, and she was warm and friendly in return.

* * *

In the 1960s, Madame Mao emerged as the power behind the Cultural Revolution and a threat to Mao. They became estranged – she even had to apply in writing to see him. Mao's dance parties were stopped and his favourite opera, the decidedly counter-revolutionary *The Emperor Seduces the Barmaid*, was banned.

'I have become a monk,' Mao cried despondently.

But he soon found that even the Cultural Revolution had its perks. As chaos reigned thoughout the country, three of Mao's girlfriends turned up, claiming they had been denounced as imperialists and thrown out of their housing to wander the streets. Mao said: 'If they don't want you, you can stay with me. They say you're imperialists? Well, I am the emperor.'

While the fanatical Red Guards tore China apart, Chairman Mao amused himself with these three pretty young women. One of them even became pregnant. Mao sent her to a hospital reserved for the highest cadres and she gave birth to a baby boy. Everyone was jubilant that Mao had a new son. Neither Mao, nor his doctor, mentioned that Mao was sterile.

His sterility did not bother him. What did concern him was potency. Already he was suffering bouts of impotence and he was determined to remain sexually active until the age of eighty. Like the old emperors of China, he believed that the more sexual partners you had the longer you lived. The first emperor of China, the father of the Han race from whom all the other Chinese are thought to be descended, is said to have made himself immortal by making love to a thousand virgins. The Emperor Qin Shihuangdi, founder of the Qin dynasty, sent a Taoist priest and five hundred virgin children across the sea in search of the elixir of immortality. According to the legend, the Japanese are their descendants. But of all the emperors, Mao thought that Sui Yangdui (AD 604–618), the architect of the Grand Canal, was the best. He lived a decadent, opulent life full of women. He would even have his pleasure boat pulled upstream by beautiful young girls attached by silken cords.

Doctors injected Mao with ground deer antlers – an old Chinese remedy for impotence. It did not work. A Romanian formula called H3 was also pumped into him for three months. That did not work either.

His physician then decided that the problem was more psychological than physical. He noticed that Mao's sexual potency waxed and waned with his political power. During the Great Leap Forward, he was insatiable. One of his bedmates told his doctor: 'He is great at everything – it's simply intoxicating.'

His appetite also seemed to increase with age. So the doctor started giving him a placebo – a concoction of ginseng and glucose which he told Mao was a body-building tonic.

During the late 1960s, when Mao was at the height of his power, although he was in his early seventies, he had no problem with the young women. As he grew older, they grew younger – it was a formula the emperors had used before him.

Mao would spend much of the day in one of the huge beds that he now favoured. He read voraciously and loved exotic literature. His great favourite was *The Dream of the Red Chamber*, a Chinese classic set in feudal times. In it, a young man called Jia Baoyu falls in love with a woman, but his family refuse to let him marry her. Alienated from society, his rebellion takes the form of pleasure seeking and the seduction of young women. Mao saw himself as Jia Baoyu. Even his compound in the Forbidden City, which was called the Garden of Abundant Beneficence, was modelled on Jia's family home.

Mao kept healthy by eating oily food, rinsing his mouth with tea and sleeping, mostly, with country girls. Like the ancient Han emperors, he sought to overcome death with the Taoist method of sex. He would often give new girls a copy of the Taoist sex manual classic of the *Plain Girl's Secret Way*. According to Taoist theory, for good health and longevity, a man must preserve the yang essence found in his semen. At that same time, he must absorb as much yin essence as possible from the yin shui, or virginal secretions of a woman. Consequently, he must have as much sex as possible, with as many partners as possible, without ejaculating.

Mao was happiest when several young women shared his bed simultaneously. He would often sleep with three, four or five women at the same time and encouraged his lovers to introduce him to other women.

Although there was no risk of the young girls who came to his bed getting pregnant, he did give them something to remember him by. With such fervid sexual activity going on, venereal disease was inevitable. One of Mao's girlfriends caught trichomonas vaginalis. This is not strictly a venereal disease as it can be caught from infected underwear – the young girls in Cultural Work Troupes often shared their clothing. But it is an infection of the vagina and causes an unpleasant discharge. Men are not affected, but they act as carriers. So once one of Mao's lovers got it, it spread like wildfire.

Ironically, the author of the problem was Mao himself. During the Great Leap Forward, Mao had decided to increase rice production by deep planting. This meant flooding the paddy fields to waist height, causing an epidemic of gynaecological infections among the women who worked in the fields.

While this condition would normally have been distressing, Mao's young women soon saw it as a badge of honour conferred on them by the Great Leader.

Although he was the carrier of the infection, Mao, naturally, refused to be treated. If it was not hurting him, it did not matter.

'What if Chiang Ch'ing becomes infected?' asked his doctor.

Mao said that would never happen. The doctor insisted that Mao at least wash himself. Normally, he still did not bathe. He was wiped down as usual with damp towels every night and never washed his genitals.

Those around him knew of the problem and were careful with their towels and bedding. At home in Peking, Mao's bedding was sterilized, but when they travelled, no amount of prodding would get the servants in the places Mao stayed to take that same simple precaution. They considered sterilizing his bedding an insult to the Great Leader.

In 1967, Mao contracted genital herpes. He was warned that the disease was highly contagious and passed on by sexual contact, but the Chairman did not think it was so bad and it did not noticeably limit the number of his sexual partners.

Although ballroom dancing had been banned as bourgeois and decadent during the Cultural Revolution, Mao held dance parties once a week, behind the walls of the Forbidden City. Young girls from the Cultural Work Troupe of the Central Garrison Corps would surround him, flirting and begging him to dance. He would waltz, fox-trot or tango with each of the girls in turn.

Mao had one of his beds moved into a room beside the ballroom. He would go in there to 'rest' several times during the evening, often taking one of the girls with him. Peng Dehuai, a member of the politburo, spoke out about this at a meeting. He criticized Chairman Mao, accusing him of behaving like an emperor with a harem of three thousand concubines. The Cultural Work Troupe was disbanded, but Mao continued to find willing young sexual partners from other cultural troupes, the air force, the Bureau of Confidential Matters, the special railway division, the Peking Military Region, the Second Artillery Corps and the provinces of

Hubei and Zhejiang. Meanwhile, Peng Dehuai was purged. He died in prison in 1974.

The dance parties continued. Exposed to so many admiring young women, Mao could not go wrong. In the past, he had depended on underlings to procure for him, but it was better this way. Older women and the better educated often refused his advances, and some nurses thought it would violate their professional ethics to have sex with him. But the young women who came to the dance parties did not. They were from peasant stock, from families who owed their lives to the Communist Party and thought that Chairman Mao was their saviour.

As the cult of personality grew in post-revolutionary China, Mao became a figure of veneration. People would do anything to catch a glimpse of him on top of the Tiananmen addressing a huge crowd. During the Cultural Revolution, Mao would hand out mangoes. These would become hallowed objects, worshipped by all who beheld them. A drop of tea made from the tiniest piece of one of these mangoes was a divine elixir. For a young girl brought up in this ethos, simply being in the same room as Chairman Mao was bliss. To be called to his bedchamber to serve his pleasure was beyond ecstasy itself.

Mao surrounded himself with pretty young women. They would look after him, handle his business and sleep with him. His confidential secretary was Zhang Yufeng. Mao had met her at one of his dance parties when she was eighteen. She had big round eyes and white skin. Soon they were having a tumultuous affair. To keep her close at hand, he made her a stewardess on his official train, and finally his secretary. She stayed with him to the end, but one woman was never enough. During his final illness, Mao was fed and nursed by two young dancers.

When Mao died in 1976, Madame Mao came into her own. She was one of the 'Gang of Four' who tried to take over. But publication of the details of her early promiscuity alienated her followers. She was arrested and expelled from the Communist Party in 1977. Charged with fomenting civil unrest during the Cultural Revolution, she refused to confess and used her trial in 1980–81 to denounce the current leadership. In 1981, she was sentenced to death, suspended for two years to see if she would repent. The sentence was commuted to life imprisonment in 1983. Her death in prison in 1991 was officially reported as suicide.

7

The Pleasure Peninsula

North Korea's 'beloved leader' from the Communist take-over in 1945 to his death in 1995, Kim Il-sung, was a well-known womanizer even during his exile in Manchuria. His first wife was Kim Jong-suk. She had lived with her parents, slash-and-burn farmers in Jiande, China, until 1935. Then, at the age of sixteen, she was picked up by a Chinese Communist guerrilla unit. She was assigned to Kim Il-sung, who kept her barefoot, as a cook and seamstress. She also worked as one of his bodyguards. In 1942, she gave birth to his son and successor, Kim Chong-il, in a military base in Siberia.

When Kim Il-sung took over the Communist paradise of North Korea, he enjoyed intimate relations with innumerable women including movie actresses, dancers, professional models, his own secretaries, good-looking nurses and kisaeng girls – the Korean equivalent of geishas. Having absolute power in this secretive, closed country, he did not have to bother with seduction. He simply had his henchmen kidnap anyone he wanted.

When any North Korean was asked how many children Kim Il-sung had, the answer would always be: 'We are all his children.'

Kim Jong-suk meekly accepted her husband's womanizing. He also mistreated her. She died in 1949, at the age of thirty-two. The rumours at the time were that she shot herself or was poisoned. The official announcement was that she had died of a heart attack. Soon after her death, Kim Il-Sung married Kim Song-ae, a beautiful woman twenty years his junior. She was already pregnant with their child, Kim Pyong-il.

Like father, like son – only more so. Kim Chong-il, who was groomed to take over from his father when he died in the first dynastic succession in the Communist world, inherited his father's taste for women. While working in the General Bodyguard Bureau, Kim Chong-il married Hong Il-chon. She was the daughter of a revolutionary and studied literature at Kimilsung University. They had a daughter.

But Kim Chong-il was not faithful to her; and he beat her. They divorced in 1973. It was also in 1973 that Kim Il-sung named Kim Chong-il as his successor. He appointed his son to the politburo and made him Minister for Propaganda and Art. That same year Kim Chong-il married a typist. They went on to have a son and two daughters. His second wife remains his official consort, but she is far from being the only woman on the scene.

In the early 1970s, Kim Chong-il had sex with a nineteen-year-old movie star called Sun Hye-rim. She was the wife of Li Pyong, the brother of one of Kim Chong-il's school friends. When Sun Hye-rim became pregnant, the Party intervened and Li Pyong was forced to divorce her. The relationship between Kim Chong-il and Sun Hye-rim continued, though Sun Hye-rim and their illegitimate son, Kim Jung-nam, went to live in Moscow. Kim Chong-il has at least seven other illegitimate children from similar encounters.

A singer from the Pyongyang Art Troupe drowned herself in the Daedong River after an affair with Kim Chong-il in the late 1970s. Several other women have committed suicide after he abandoned them.

He had an affair with Son Nui-rim, the sister of the North Korean ambassador to Russia. They had two daughters, but he discarded her when she became mentally ill in 1991. She was moved to Moscow, where she is cared for by her father.

Another long-term lover was Li Sang-jin, who was his classmate at Kimilsung University. She was married to a Foreign Ministry official, according to diplomatic sources.

The famous Korean movie actress Hong Yung-hui was introduced to Kim Chong-il by an aide who knew his boss's tastes. Consenting to become his mistress earned her the leading role in the revolutionary opera *A Flower-selling Maiden* and she was designated 'a people's actress' – the highest accolade that the profession can bestow. She also acted as hostess at his parties and eventually married a man that Kim Chong-il picked out for her.

In 1990, he seduced the nineteen-year-old daughter of the director of the North Korean Judo Association. She was a member of the Mansudae Art Troupe and produced another daughter for Kim Chong-il.

In May 1991, a new actress, a twenty-year-old named Chung Hye-sun, appeared in a leading role in a drama series, *Skylark*, on Pyongyang's Central TV station. She bore an uncanny likeness to Kim Chong-il's mother, Kim Jong-suk. Kim Chong-il had her installed in a luxurious villa near Mount Daesung in an exclusive suburb of Pyongyang. She now drives around in a Mercedes-Benz that he provided.

But Kim Chong-il was not always so kind. He had one lover, pretty young actress Wu In-hui, executed by firing squad in front of a crowd of five thousand. She had been charged with having affairs with other men, against Kim Chong-il's specific instructions.

However, Kim Chong-il's real passion is for foreign relations. In 1991, he invited a number of female Russian singers and bands to North Korea. They were paid large sums of foreign currency to perform for him at his villa. A Russian girl and her vocal group, who were employed to amuse Kim Chong-il at his villa during Kim Il-sung's eightieth birthday celebrations, reportedly had group sex with him and his aides. Scandinavian women have also been offered large sums of money to attend Kim Chong-il at his villa.

But Kim Il-sung and Kim Chong-il's crowning achievement was to turn the entire Korean Communist Party into a huge pimping system. Women were recruited from all over the country and assigned to various 'song and dance', 'happiness' and 'satisfaction' teams. They were housed in secluded villas for the exclusive use of Kim Il-sung and Kim Chong-il.

Each of these different 'pleasure' teams had its own function. As its name suggests, the 'song and dance' teams would sing, play musical instruments and dance for the Kims. The 'happiness' teams relieved their fatigue by means of massage, while the 'satisfaction' teams provided sexual fulfilment. At any one time, there were about two thousand young women in these pleasure teams, housed in villas or special hotels around the country.

The General Bodyguard Bureau was in charge of recruitment. Selection teams, appointed by local branches of the Communist Party, picked out good-looking women around the age of twenty and over the height of 5 feet 3 inches. The girls had to have a 'pure ideological and social background'. Once picked for a pleasure team, a woman had no option but to accept, even if her parents were Party officials; she was not allowed to complain.

Candidates were also selected annually from the students of city and provincial art colleges. One eighteen-year-old student studying music at Kimhyonjik Teachers' College was forcibly 'enrolled' as a member of a pleasure team around 1980. She was sent to Pyongang Music and Dance University to study the violin before being assigned to a 'song and dance' team. Another girl, on her way home from work, was enrolled off the streets by a Party official. Around 1989, the National Sports Commission was instructed to provide ten girls from the gymnastics team to become pleasure-team members. Later foreign women were recruited from Hong Kong, Macao and the Middle East. Some were paid; others were simply kidnapped. They were confined to villas and gave up all hope of returning home.

Once local Party organizations had supplied their annual crop of recruits, Central Party Headquarters sorted out the most promising candidates to send to the Namsan Dispensary, where they underwent rigorous physical and ideological examination.

The selection of 'happiness' teams first began when a special one-year course in massage was organized at the Red Cross hospital in Pyonyang. Thirty young women were enrolled. Later, 'happiness' team members were sent to the Soviet Union for training, before being assigned to one of the Kims' residences.

The 'satisfaction' teams and 'song and dance' teams were given six months' training. They had to perform every Saturday night at parties hosted by Kim Chong-il. Each party had a geographical theme – Tokyo night, Parisian night, Persian night, Indian night – and the teams had to act as if they came from those places.

After six months in the pleasure teams, the women were promoted to the rank of second lieutenant in the General Bodyguard Bureau and sent abroad for two weeks.

Members of pleasure teams lived in luxurious quarters and ate only the best food imported from Japan. Those who had sexual contact with Kim Il-sung or Kim Chong-il were presented with a Swiss watch with their partner's name engraved on it. Special favourites were given cars and were, it was said, treated better than cabinet ministers.

Pleasure-team members had to serve until they were twenty-five, when they were allowed to marry bodyguard officers or holders of national-merit medals. They were, of course, instructed to keep quiet about their pleasure-team activities, but everyone knew what was going on. When pleasure-team members were allowed home visits, Kim Chong-il would alert local Party members who would treat the girl like a princess.

Towards the end of his life, Kim Il-sung made an even more sinister use of this system of recruitment. The

Party were instructed to supply him with young virgins. They were forced to donate blood which would be transfused into Kim Il-sung's body in the hope that it would prolong his life.

When Kim Chong Il succeed his father, he showed no sign of mending his ways. He kept a 10,000-bottle wine cellar and employed top Japanese cook Kenji Fujimoto to become his personal sushi chef. According to Fujimoto, Kim would order the women hired to dance at his all-night banquets to strip naked. On one occasion, Fujimoto recalled women at first 'hesitated, but they had no power to resist. They all took off their clothes and danced.' Then the guests, including Fujimoto, were ordered to dance with them, but were warned to go no further. 'You can dance with them, but you can't touch,' said Kim.

According to Fujimoto, Kim was also an habitual practical joker. The night before his wedding, Fujimoto got drunk and fell asleep, and awoke to find that Kim had shaved off his pubic hair.

Kidnapped South Korean movie director Shin Sang Ok and his ex-wife, actress Che Eun Hui, were kept for eight years and made to produce propaganda films. After escaping, they wrote a book exposing Kim's decadent lifestyle. According to Che Eun Hui, while the rest of the country starved Kim hosted parties where expensive Johnnie Walker Swing and Hennessy's XO were served. Fujimoto talks of serving caviar from Iran and Uzbekistan, along with vintage French wines, while another book describes Kim as an 'illiterate murderer who thinks of nothing but sex'.

But to the world Kim remains a vain and capricious playboy, with a permed pompadour and lifts in his shoes, and a taste for nuclear weapons.

8

Cuba's Casanova

Cuba is a sexy place. Forget baseball, sex is Cuba's national sport. It is the only real escape from the hardships of daily life. Promiscuity and extramarital sex are rife. Partners are swapped so often that few bother to get married. In 1989, 61.2 per cent of babies were born out of wedlock and there are over 160,000 abortions a year, a third of them performed on teenagers.

Posadas – so-called lovers' hotels – are everywhere. For five pesos, the equivalent of fifty U.S. cents, you get three hours of privacy. When your time is up, the phone rings and someone on the other end says: 'Turno.'

Prostitution is widespread, overt and mostly amateur. Women will go to bed for a bottle of shampoo or a new pair of jeans. Businessmen in their sixties can be seen with beautiful brown-skinned girls young enough to be their granddaughters.

Standing high above this sexual maelstrom is a tall bearded figure in a green army uniform. He seems to be the last of the ascetics. Certainly no woman shares the spotlight with him. How different it could all have been. Over the years, there have been one or two prime candidates for the position of First Lady of the Republic of Cuba.

Fidel Castro is the illegitimate son of Angel Castro, a successful sugar planter, and a fifteen-year-old scullery maid, Lina Ruz. Angel had a wife back home in Galicia, so he could not marry Fidel's mother. It was not uncommon for Spanish immigrants to have a second family in Cuba.

Although Fidel was not baptized, he was brought up by priests who instilled in him a fear of sex, masturbation and homosexuality. He never had a girlfriend until he went to university to study law. There, he was dating two sisters when his friend and classmate Rafael Dmaz Balart introduced him to his sister, Mirta. She was a philosophy student. They met in the cafeteria. It was love at first sight.

Castro was still very shy with women and he hated dancing, but he broke off from political meetings to go out on dates with Mirta. They were chaperoned wherever they went. She had green eyes and dark blonde hair, and was his first sweetheart.

Mirta came from one of the wealthiest families on Cuba and were extremely well connected. Her parents were a little worried when they realized that they were about to acquire a son-in-law who had the reputation on the campus of being a gangster. He had led a protest against fare increases that had resulted in the burning of buses and he had twice been accused of murder. But Fidel and Mirta were very much in love and they married in 1948. Castro's father Angel was delighted that his son had made such an advantageous union and paid for a lengthy honeymoon in America. Castro even considered staying on in the U.S. to study at Columbia University, but the politics of Cuba drew him back.

Back in Cuba life was hard, and Castro soon had a new mouth to feed, a son named Fidelito. Mirta was constantly frustrated by Castro's refusal to work. He spent his time politicking; he even slept with a woman with a badly pock-marked face because she controlled key Party votes, casting her aside when her usefulness was over. But Mirta stood by him, intervening to save his life when he was arrested for armed insurrection.

However, he was already having an affair with another woman, Natalia 'Nati' Revuelta. A fellow student at the university, she was a striking green-eyed blonde who moved in aristocratic circles. During her life she had scarcely put a foot wrong. She had studied at a Catholic girls' school in Philadelphia, worked at the U.S. embassy and Esso. She was a member of the Havana Yacht Club and Country Club, and was married to a prominent heart specialist, Orlando Fernandez. Now she wanted some excitement. She first saw Castro when he was addressing a political meeting at the university and found him charismatic and sexy.

After an unsuccessful uprising in 1953, Castro was sentenced to 15 years' imprisonment, but he was released under an amnesty within the year. During his time in jail, Castro wrote passionate love letters to Nati.

'Love is like a diamond,' he wrote, 'the hardest and purest of all minerals, able to scratch anything; it is not perfect until all its edges have been cut and shaped. Then it sparkles from all angles with an incomparable radiance. The metaphor would be perfect if the diamond, once buffed and polished, would grow bigger and bigger. A genuine love is based on many feelings, not just one, and they gradually balance each other off, each reflecting the light of the others.'

While Castro was pouring out his heart to Nati, Mirta was using her influence to have his conditions improved. Then Castro did what every prisoner knew you should not do – he wrote to Nati and Mirta on the same day. To no one's surprise, the two letters got mixed up.

Although Mirta was hurt by Castro's passion for another woman, she tried to woo him back during prison visits, but he divorced her on his release – for political reasons, he said. Her family was too close to the Batista regime he was seeking to bring down. Her brother, his former friend and classmate Rafael, was Minister of the Interior in charge of public order and Mirta herself had taken a botella – a government job which earns pay without any work having to be done – to support herself and their son while Castro was in jail.

Castro's relationship with Nati became very public, but when they had a baby, Alina, they gave her Nati's husband's surname, Fernandez. Back in the 1950s, Cuba's attitude to illegitimacy was not nearly as liberal as it is now.

After spending some time in the U.S., Castro headed for Mexico in 1956 where he assembled a small band of men and a cache of arms ready for the overthrow of Batista; but when the Mexican authorities found out, he was arrested. In jail, he was visited by Teresa Casuso, a Cuban woman who had lived in exile in Mexico for more than a decade. She was a writer. Her husband had been killed, fighting on the Republican side in the Spanish Civil War. She was forty and was attracted to the

young Castro, who she saw as a romantic young rene-
gade. When she met him, she thought that here was a
man who needed someone to look after him.

Although her feelings were in some way reciprocated,
Teresa had made a mistake in bringing with her a young
house guest, sixteen-year-old Isabel Custudio. Her parents, both famous Cuban actors, were touring the
country.

'She looked like an elegant model, with the rims of
her enormous, innocent, greenish-brown eyes darkly
accented in the Italian fashion,' Teresa said. 'On that
day, her hair was its natural colour of dark gold.'

Castro was immediately smitten. After his release
from jail, he visited Teresa Casuso's house regularly.
They talked endlessly about revolution. When she
agreed to keep a few things for him, she found him
stashing guns in her closets. But Teresa suspected the
real reason he was coming around was to see Isabel.

'He sought her out with a youthful effusiveness and
impetuosity that both startled and amused her,' Teresa
said.

Isabel was busy though, studying at the university in
the mornings, working in the afternoons and attending
political meetings in the evenings. When Castro turned
up at Teresa's house, she was often out. In fact, Isabel
was avoiding him. He soon twigged and, one morning,
he turned up really early, before she had left.

'When I started to leave the house, he was there
waiting,' she recalled later. 'We looked at each other
and laughed, because his trick was just as obvious as
mine. It was a very funny encounter, and he offered to
drive me to the university.'

From then on, they were almost never apart. He always wore clean shirts and his suits were freshly pressed, and he made his advances with all the tenacity of a guerrilla leader.

'He treated me like a princess,' Isabel said, 'with a fine and delicate love, just as a man should. I was like a doll, or porcelain. And he was very pre-occupied with the image that I projected. He told me that it was important that I maintain an image equal to his.'

After securing the approval of her parents, he asked her to marry him. She accepted.

Using money that had been donated to the revolution, he bombarded her with expensive presents – new clothes, shoes, French perfume and a modest bathing suit to replace her rather revealing bikini (which infuriated him). He also planned to take her on the reckless assault on Cuba he was organizing. One day, she would be the 'First Lady of Cuba' his men said.

But Isabel wanted romance not danger. Sailing across the Gulf of Mexico with a boat-load of guerrilla fighters was not her idea of a honeymoon. So when a former fiancé returned to Mexico City and asked her again to marry him, she accepted. She left the next day and, for years, Castro could not even bring himself to mention her name.

After Isabel left, he stopped washing. His clothes were no longer kept clean and neat. He did not go out. All he did all day was to aim his favourite rifle at the TV antenna across the way.

Castro wrote to Mirta, asking her to let him see seven-year-old Fidelito. He promised to return him to her custody within two weeks, but he had no intention of doing that. In a letter to the Mexican newspapers he said that he could not return Fidelito 'into the hands of my most ferocious enemies and detractors, who... outraged my home and sacrificed it to the bloody tyranny which they serve'. When Castro and his men set off on their antiquated wooden yacht, the *Granma*, on their historic mission to liberate Cuba, Mirta came to Mexico and snatched Fidelito back.

In December 1956, Castro landed his eighty-two-man expeditionary force on Cuba. They were annihilated in their first attack. The few survivors scattered and Castro took refuge in the Sierra Maestra. From there he got word to Nati, asking her to join him in the mountains. She, too, could become the 'First Lady of the Cuban Revolution'. She refused, saying that she could not leave their baby.

One woman who did join him was Celia Sanchéz. She was the daughter of a doctor from Manzanillo who had helped coordinate the underground movement in eastern Cuba. She came to the Sierra Maestra to organize the camp and control the millions of dollars the guerrillas had collected in 'revolutionary taxes'. She also shared Castro's bed. Their letters are full of affection – though none of the passion that he displayed in his correspondence with Nati. Their time in the Sierra Maestra together was the beginning of a relationship that lasted for twenty years. After the revolution, she took the apartment below his in Havana, but Castro would be found, as often as not, sprawled out on her bed. If anyone deserves to be called 'First Lady of the Cuban Revolution', it is Celia Sanchéz.

After two years in the mountains and a ceaseless guerrilla campaign, Castro successfully launched a full-scale offensive against Batista's police state. He celebrated by having an affair with Gloria Gaitán, known as 'the Dark Rose of Bogotá'. She was the beautiful daughter of the murdered Bolivian revolutionary leader Jorge Eliecer Gaitán. Castro had first met her in Bogotá in 1948. The affair continued for several years, even though she was married to a university professor. One day Castro asked: 'What do you do in bed with this Greek philosopher who is your husband?'

'He is a very intelligent man,' she replied.

'Obviously, but if Karl Marx were a woman, I would not marry him.'

When Castro came to power, Nati's husband left for exile in the United States. Castro would visit Nati and – as he now openly admitted – his daughter in their mansion, or stay with them in their beach house in Varadero. He gave Nati a number of government jobs and a veteran's pension. When the relationship cooled, he sent mother and daughter to Paris to work in the Cuban embassy there. They returned two years later.

Castro continued seeing Alina, though they began to fall out. She married four times and he did not approve of her choice of husbands. Alina wanted to leave Cuba and pursue a career elsewhere, but the authorities would not give her an exit visa.

In power, Castro also made things difficult for Mirta, who had married a Spaniard, Emilio Nuñez. One night in Varadero, he came across them eating in a steakhouse. He ordered the owner to throw them out. He, bravely, refused. Soon after, Mirta and her second husband left to live in Madrid. Thirty years later, there are still some in the Castro family who maintain that Mirta was the only woman he ever really loved.

Soon after the revolution, Castro met a young German woman called Marita Lorenz. She was seventeen and had black hair and green eyes. They met when the *M.S. Berlin*, the ship her father captained, pulled into Havana harbour while Castro was on board the Granma which he was renovating. Castro, always on the look-out for chances to win over foreigners, contacted the *Berlin*. Marita's father invited him on board for dinner.

Castro could hardly take his eyes off the beautiful young Marita. Before dinner, she showed him around the ship. In the elevator down to the engine room, a wave buffered the ship and she fell against him. He took the opportunity to kiss her.

Over dinner, she was impressed by his stories of derring-do in the Sierra Maestra. At one point, her mother recalled, he spread his arms like a messiah, looked to the heavens and said: 'I am Cuba.'

Castro suggested that Marita stay in Havana and work for him, but her father said she had to go to school in New York. Castro made her promise she would come back.

Back in New York, Marita got a phone call from Castro. He said he missed her. Her parents were away for a month and she agreed to go down to Cuba for a week. The next day, three officials from the Cuban embassy turned up and took her to Idlewild – now JFK airport. Once in Havana, she was taken directly to the Hilton Hotel, Suite 2406-8. After an hour, Castro arrived. He put his cigar in the ashtray and grabbed her. He hugged her and kissed her and made her promise that she would stay with him forever.

'Always, always,' the young Marita sighed.

They spent the rest of the day together, making love. She complained that she never saw him completely naked – even when he took all his clothes off, he still wore his beard.

Although Marita was quickly accepted by Celia Sanchéz and Castro's personal guards, she soon grew lonely because she did not speak Spanish very well. He was busy and left her alone for long periods. One night he came in at 4 a.m. with some tropical orchids. She was crying and threatened to leave.

'Don't go, my love,' he said. 'We will get married now.'

Then he knelt on the bed in front of her, made the sign of the cross and said: 'Do you, my Alemanita, Marita Lorenz, want to marry Fidel Castro?'

She said: 'I do marry you, Fidel Castro, forever.'

They laughed and hugged, and Castro said that, in Cuba, he was the law, he was God. So they were now married legally and in the eyes of the Lord. He said that he knew she was lonely and that, from now on, as his wife, he would take her with him, everywhere. A week later he bought her a diamond engagement ring engraved: '3/59, de Fidel para Marita, Siempre.'

Marita went to work for him as a secretary and interpreter. She accompanied him on his fifteen-day visit to the United States but soon found that she was left behind in hotel rooms while he took care of business. Marita was already pregnant and her nerves were frayed. She became jealous when she noticed the effect his charisma was having on attractive female journalists and others. He was bombarded with letters, notes and messages from women who wanted to meet him. One of them was from Ava Gardner.

According to Marita, Ava Gardner turned up at their hotel, drunk. She forced her way into the lift with them, called her 'the little bitch who's hiding Fidel' and slapped her. Captain Pupo, one of Castro's guards, pulled his gun.

Later that night, Castro told her that he had fixed Ava Gardner up with one of his aides, who had orders to satisfy her, compliments of the Republic of Cuba.

Back in Havana, the pregnant Marita became ill. An hallucinogenic drug had been slipped to her by an unknown source. In her delirious state, she remembered her stomach suddenly being flat. The baby had gone and, somewhere in the distance, she heard a baby crying.

Marita had a fever. She was suffering from blood poisoning and the doctors could not stop her bleeding from the womb. Castro gave orders for her to be taken back to America where she would be able to get the best medical attention and her own doctor would be on hand.

Back in New York, Marita was taken into protective custody. She was told that her baby had been born prematurely and died. Castro had killed it, she was told repeatedly.

Confidential magazine broke the story. The front page headline read: 'An American Mother's Terrifying Story – "Fidel Castro Raped My Teenage Daughter".' A smaller headline ran: 'Lured to Cuba by Castro, Marita Lorenz, 18, was kidnapped, raped and then cruelly aborted.'

The story went on to tell the story of the 'rape' in melodramatic detail, right down to Castro tearing the crucifix from the naked girl's neck before he had his evil way with her. Meanwhile, Marita's mother filed a suit against the Cuban government for $11 million. As Marita overcame her trauma, she realized that this was all black propaganda designed to discredit Castro who, having declared himself a Communist, had become a public enemy in the United States.

She was allowed out of hospital, but the FBI kept her under guard. Back home, she received a telegram from Castro, asking her to call him. She went out to a pay phone. When she got through, Castro told her that the child was alive. At that point her FBI bodyguard grabbed the receiver and hung up.

A few weeks later, she received another telegram. This time she gave her bodyguard the slip – rather too easily she thought in retrospect – and went to use the pay phone again. This time she was shot at. *Confidential* magazine ran a story that Castro had sentenced her to death.

The CIA went to work on her. They managed to convince her that her life was in danger and eventually persuaded her to take part in a half-baked assassination attempt on Castro. They wanted her to poison him. On her way to Cuba she hid the poison capsules in a jar of Ponds cream, which partially dissolved them. When she arrived in Havana, she went straight to his suite in the Hilton. First, she checked it for stray blonde hairs. She found stacks of fan mail from lonely women who wanted to meet him. Then she checked the poison capsules, found that they were ruined and tried to flush them down the bidet.

When Castro arrived, they hugged. She asked for news of her baby, but he said he was tired. He lay on the bed and asked her if she had come to kill him. She said she had. He handed her his revolver, the one he had carried with him throughout the revolution.

She pointed it at him and pressed the release, removing the clip of .45 calibre bullets. He tensed, thinking she had retracted the hammer, ready to fire, but he made no attempt to get out of the way, or defend himself.

'It's rusty,' Marita said. 'It needs oiling.'

'Nobody can kill me, Marita,' he said. 'Nobody.'

And he turned his back and went to sleep.

Next morning, they made love. He drank a Coke, without checking to see if she had put anything in it. In the bathroom, she found the remains of the poison capsules still floating in the bidet. She crushed them up and flushed them away, properly this time.

On her knees, she begged for news of her child. It was a boy, he said. He loved the child and she would only be able to see him if she lived with them on Cuba. This was impossible, Marita knew. If she stayed, the CIA would come after her too.

She left the $6,000 the CIA had given her in Castro's room. When she flew back to Florida, her bosses were furious. Not only had she blown two chances to kill Castro – once with the poison, once with the gun – she had paid him $6,000. It was government money, too. On the other hand, they had proved he was vulnerable. They now knew they could get a potential assassin right to the target. Marita never returned to Cuba and never discovered the truth about her child.

This was not the end of Marita's association with dictators. As part of her CIA duties, Marita went on to become the mistress of General Marcos Peréz Jiménez, the failed dictator of Venezuela and sworn enemy of

Castro. From his comfortable exile in Miami, he would phone Castro and taunt him about Marita. But soon after Marita gave birth to the General's daughter, Monica, Jiménez was extradited back to Venezuela to stand trial.

Since Marita, Castro's love life has been a series of one-night stands. His security guards were charged with finding him bed partners. He was not the most considerate of lovers – a dancer from the Tropicana complained that he read while he was making love to her.; a French actress, that he smoked the whole time; another woman, that he never took his boots off.

A Cuban actress said: 'You can't imagine what a brute he is, what a selfish monster. He just pulled down his pants, and was quick.'

The most common complaint, though, was that he talked incessantly, on such romantic topics as the future of the revolution or agricultural reform.

Castro's affairs are widely known about in Cuba. Those who he slept with could expect flowers on their birthdays and valuable gifts – a rare paella or a lobster, all despatched with cold-hearted efficiency by Celia Sanchéz, who was never very far from the leader.

Only one other women has occupied Castro for any length of time. She was another green-eyed, black-haired aristocrat, Dalia Soto Del Valle Jorge, known as 'la mujer de Trinidad' – the woman from the city of Trinidad. Her father, Enrique, was the owner of a large cigar factory and she worked as a secretary at the sugar workers' union, where Castro met her in 1962 or 1963. She had been primed for the affair by a fortune-teller who told her: 'You will have the love of a great man.'

When she took up with him, her family considered her to be Castro's prisoner and her father told friends that he had 'lost a daughter'. But the affair endured and Dalia had five sons by Castro. All of them bear his middle name, Alejandro, and he sent them to be educated in the Soviet Union, along with his other, legitimate son, Fidelito.

9

Going Down South of the Border

Latin America has seen its fair share of dictators. One of the most unpleasant was Francisco Solano López of Paraguay. Far from liberating his country, he almost destroyed it by going to war simultaneously with three powerful neighbours – Brazil, Argentina and Uruguay.

Born in 1827, Francisco López was the son of the Paraguayan dictator, Carlos Antonio López. The United States Minister to Paraguay, Charles Ames Washburn, once described Francisco:

> *Short and stout, always inclining to corpulence. He dressed grotesquely, but his costumes were always expensive and elaborately finished. His eyes, when he was pleased, had a mild expression; but when he was enraged the pupil seemed to dilate till it did not appear to be that of a human being, but rather a wild beast goaded to madness. He had, however, a gross animal look that was repulsive when his face was in repose. His forehead was narrow and his head small, with the rear organs*

166

largely developed. His teeth were very much decayed, and so many of the front ones were gone as to render his articulation somewhat difficult and indistinct. He apparently took no pains to keep them clean, and those which remained were unwholesome in appearance, and nearly as dark as the cigar that he had almost constantly between them. His face was rather flat, and his nose and his hair indicated more of the negro than the Indian. His cheeks had a fullness that extended to the jowl, giving him a sort of bulldog expression.

This repulsive creature was the terror of the first families of Asunción and their daughters. He had a predilection for aristocratic virgins and any who resisted would find their fathers jailed on Carlos López's orders.

One woman he particularly liked was Pancha Garmendia, known as 'the pride and jewel of Asunción'. Every young man in Paraguay desired her, but Lopez scared them all off. Nevertheless she rejected him, threatening to commit suicide if he laid a finger on her.

Unfortunately, Francisco could not have Pancha's father jailed as he was already dead. He had been executed as an enemy of the state by Carlos López's predecessor, El Supremo, the first Perpetual Dictator for Life of Paraguay. Instead, he had her brothers charged with being enemies of the state and executed. With his father's permission, Francisco confiscated their property and had Pancha arrested. She spent the rest of her life in chains. Even when Francisco López was forced to withdraw from Asunción by the Allied armies twenty years later, he dragged Pancha along with him into the jungle where she died soon after.

After dealing with Pancha, Francisco fell for Carmencita Cordal and was determined to make her his concubine. She was about to be married to her cousin, Carlos Decoud, the son of one of Paraguay's leading families. Decoud had the temerity to pick a fight with Francisco and thrash him humiliatingly. It was a foolish move. Carlos López had Decoud arrested on trumped-up charges of plotting a coup d'état.

The night before he was to be wed to Carmencita, Decoud was executed and his bloodstained corpse was flung into the street in front of her house – some say it was actually delivered to her living-room. Carmencita spent the rest of her life dressed in black, praying in desert shrines and gathering flowers by moonlight.

The daughters of all the leading families began applying for passports and Francisco's behaviour became so outrageous that Carlos López thought it best that he leave the country while the situation cooled down. So Francisco headed off to Europe with an unlimited bank account. His mission was to buy a navy – just what a landlocked country like Paraguay needed.

On arriving in Paris, young López left the tedious business of state to his secretary and, as the American ambassador put it, 'gave loose rein to his natural licentious propensities, and plunged into the vices of that gay capital'.

A great fan of Napoleon, Francisco was eager to be presented at the court of Napoleon III. He squeezed himself into one of his smallest uniforms – he thought, mistakenly, that tight clothing would disguise his corpulent form.

When he was presented to the Emperor, he kissed the Empress's hand. She turned away and promptly vomited over an ormolu desk, later excusing herself on the grounds that she was pregnant.

Francisco López made a flying visit to London, but Queen Victoria discovered that she was 'quite too busy' to entertain her Paraguayan guest.

Back in Paris, Francisco met a young woman who managed to overlook his repulsive appearance. It was said that, where others saw only rotting teeth, she saw jewels. Her name was Eliza Lynch.

Born in County Cork in 1835, she was said to have too much imagination, too many brains and too much libido. She was married at the age of fifteen, divorced at seventeen, and had taken a string of lovers by eighteen. Her family had fled to France to escape the 1845 famine. Her first husband was Xavier Quatrefages, a career officer in the French Army. He was old enough to be her father, but the marriage was an escape from the poverty her family had sunk into.

Her husband was posted to Algiers where Eliza was raped by his commanding officer. Quatrefages took no action to defend his wife's honour, but she had met a dashing young Russian cavalry officer who did. He killed the colonel and took Eliza off to Paris where he established her in a house in the fashionable Boulevard Saint Germain. But her dashing young cavalry officer soon abandoned her for the excitement of the Crimean War.

Pictures of her from that time show that she was an extraordinarily beautiful woman and she decided to pursue a career as a courtesan. Argentinian journalist Héctor Varela described her:

She was tall with a flexible and delicate figure with beautiful and seductive curves. Her skin was alabaster. Her eyes were of a blue that seems borrowed from the very hues of heaven and had an expression of ineffable sweetness in whose depths the light of Cupid was enthroned. Her beautiful lips were indescribably expressive of the voluptuous, moistened by an ethereal dew that God must have provided to lull the fires within her, a mouth that was like a cup of delight at the banquet table of ardent passion. Her hands were small with long fingers, the nails perfectly formed and delicately polished. She was, evidently, one of those women who make the care of their appearance a religion.

She had a flair for language and a quick wit, and was soon entertaining numerous gentlemen callers. Her reputation grew and no man of substance would leave Paris without having paid a visit to Chez Lynch.

Eliza was still only nineteen when she entertained a man named Brizuela, who was one of Francisco's retinue. He boasted of his dalliance to the young López, who decided to see this jewel with his own eyes. Eliza was equally eager to entertain this savage who all Paris knew was spraying money around like buckshot.

Within hours of entering Madame Lynch's salon, Francisco entered her boudoir. The next day he told her of the riches of his country. The day after that, she gave notice to her landlord.

There is no doubt that López was desperately in love with Eliza. He had met beautiful women before, but Eliza was the first woman to go to bed with him without putting up a struggle first.

Eliza, for her part, must have felt some physical revulsion for the loathsome creature. But, although she had no real idea where Paraguay was, she had a shrewd sense of money and power. She was quick-witted enough to know that, while she was a sought-after beauty at nine-teen, all too soon she would loose her power to charm, and here was a man who could keep her in clover for the rest of her life. He told her that, one day, he would become the emperor of South America. Could she not be his empress?

Neglecting the tiresome formalities of marriage, they set off on a honeymoon around Europe. On the way, Eliza picked up trunkloads of gowns and jewels. They dined with the notorious Queen Isabella of Spain, who suggested that Paraguay hold a referendum to see if the people wanted to return to the Spanish fold. Francisco said he would think about it. He didn't.

In Rome, it was said, Eliza held a 'wickedly obscene' dinner party for the pope. Then, after a tour of the Crimean battlefront, the happy couple headed for Paraguay.

Francisco's brother Benigno, who had been with Francisco in Paris, had already returned to Paraguay and told Carlos López that Francisco was involved with 'una ramera irlandesa' – an Irish prostitute. Fearing his father's wrath, Francisco and Eliza stopped off in Buenos Aires. Doña Juana and Francisco's two sisters said that they refused to accept 'La Irlandesa', but Carlos realized that he was getting old and needed his son and heir back in the country. Reassured by a message from his father, Francisco and an apprehensive Eliza began the slow thousand-mile voyage up river to Asunción.

When they arrived, Eliza was heavily pregnant. The women of the López family were good to their word. They refused to accept Eliza. She responded by strutting around Asunción in the latest Paris fashions, showing off her magnificent figure. This quite outshone any-thing the López sisters had to offer.

Eliza soon found that she did not have a free hand with Francisco. He still maintained his former lover, Juana Pesoa, and their two children in his town house in Asunción. He also took other lovers. Eliza took control by selecting his concubines for him. She took great pains over this task. Although she would not marry Francisco herself – fearing that, as his wife rather than his mistress, she would lose all power over him – she had to make sure that no one else did either.

Francisco López also persisted in his brutal seduction techniques. When he fell in love with the daughter of Pedro Burgos, a magistrate from the small provincial city of Luque, he threatened to confiscate her father's prop-erty if she did not submit. However, Pedro Burgos was not without some influence with Carlos López. Eliza stepped in. Once she had ascertained that Pedro's daughter had no desire whatsoever to marry Francisco, she encouraged Pedro to accept Francisco as his daugh-ter's lover – on the promise that he would be amply rewarded when Francisco came to power. His daughter submitted, but Pedro Burgos was later executed by Francisco in the belief that he was plotting against him.

Eliza's skilful manipulation of Francisco's sex life put her in a position of considerable power. She still had ambitions to be the Empress of South America, as he had promised. As part of that plan, she decided that the ramshackle town of Asunción must be transformed into an imperial city. She persuaded Francisco to begin an extensive building programme, which included the con-struction of a replica of Napoleon's mausoleum at Les Invalides, to be used as Francisco's own tomb.

Eliza also wanted to secure the position of her son, Juan Francisco. Although he was Francisco's favourite, she feared that he might one day fall from his father's favour. The answer was to have him baptized.

Francisco liked the idea. Belatedly he announced his son's birth with a hundred-and-one-gun salute. This caused eleven buildings in downtown Asunción to collapse, five of which were newly built under Francisco's modernization plan. One of the guns, an English field piece, had not been cleaned properly and backfired, killing half the battery and putting the other half in hospital.

The López ladies got themselves into a flap over this, and Carlos banned the planned baptism in Asunción's Catedral de la Encarnacion. The Bishop of Paraguay, who was Carlos's brother, threatened to excommunicate any priest who performed the baptism.

But Eliza was not to be put off. She found a priest, Father Palacios, and promised him that, if he would baptize Juan Francisco, he would succeed as Bishop of Paraguay when Francisco came to power.

Francisco was loathe to go against his father's wishes, but Eliza talked him round. If Francisco did not consent to the baptism, she said she would take the child to Europe and have him baptized an Anglican! Francisco blustered that he could prevent her leaving Paraguay if he wanted. She replied that if she told Carlos López that she intended to leave, he would provide her with an armed guard, and probably a considerable sum of money too.

Francisco had no choice. The baptism went ahead in Eliza's country house, though no one from Asunción society or the diplomatic corps turned out. They were still more afraid of Carlos than of Francisco.

Although she had won this battle, the war between Eliza and the López family continued. Eliza neatly upstaged them at the opening of the National Theatre, built as part of Francisco's reconstruction plan. She got Francisco to designate a small box to the left of the stage the 'Royal Box'. Carlos López, his wife and daughters were directed there, while the prominent box at the centre of the auditorium was reserved for Francisco and Eliza.

Eliza also made her presence felt in Asunción society by holding a regular salon. Although the ladies of Asunción shunned it, their husbands all turned up and vied for the opportunity to flirt with the hostess.

Francisco was still determined to have his consort accepted by the ladies, not least his mother and sisters. When he opened the disastrous agricultural colony upstream in the Rio de la Plata region of Paraguay, he organized a tour for high-ranking Paraguayans and the entire diplomatic corps. The men would ride up to the colony, while the women would travel by boat. Madame Lynch would be Official Hostess on board, he announced.

This was an occasion that everyone had to attend. Even Doña Juana and her two daughters puffed up the gang plank. But everyone pointedly ignored the Official Hostess. Soon after they had cast off, the boat was moored in the middle of the stream and a huge feast was laid out – suckling pigs, roast turkey, baby lambs, fresh fruit and vegetables, the best imported wines. The ladies crowded around, but would not allow Eliza near the table. When she asked to be allowed through so that she could preside, they huddled more closely together, blocking her path. So Eliza summoned the waiters and said: 'Throw it all over the side.'

The ladies fell silent. The waiters hesitated and Eliza repeated the order.

'Throw it all over the side.'

They picked up the food and the wine and pitched it overboard. Eliza then sat in silence, staring at the ladies who had snubbed her. They waited, famished, parched and sweaty for the next ten hours, before Eliza gave the captain permission to return to the quay.

By the time of his death, Carlos López probably did not want Francisco to succeed him. Despite his unsavoury dictatorial ways, Carlos was essentially a man of peace, and he feared Francisco's belligerent intentions towards their neighbours. On his father's death, Francisco called a National Congress which confirmed him as president for the next ten years. Francisco López also took the opportunity to announce that Eliza was about to present him with another son, her fifth. As the Congress erupted in spontaneous applause, he added: 'I would like it to be known that it is our pleasure and desire that from this day forward Madame Eliza Lynch should enjoy the same privileges as those usually accorded to the wife of a head of State.'

The López ladies and half the female population of Asunción fainted.

Within a month of Francisco López's coming to power, a thousand of the most prominent citizens of Paraguay were either in exile, in prison or on the run. Their crime? Opposing Francisco.

Next, he decided to bring the church under his dominion. Father Palacios, as promised, became Bishop

175

of Paraguay. Not only had he baptized Juan Francisco, he had gone on to provide Francisco with useful intelligence, gleaned in the confessional box.

Formerly derided as 'the Irish concubine', the British Minister in Asunción now called Eliza 'the Paraguayan Pompadour'. López still maintained a separate house where he entertained prostitutes, but he lived openly with Eliza. She was now 'First Lady of Paraguay'. The ladies of Asunción had to swallow their pride and call on her. Eliza organized huge balls and dictated exactly what the other women should wear. She, of course, outshone them all.

López suddenly announced that he intended to marry the beautiful young Princess Isabella of Brazil. This was for strictly political reasons, he explained. Eliza would remain his favourite. As always, Eliza turned the situation to her own advantage. She demanded co-equal status and forced López to legitimize her children, making Juan Francisco his undeniable heir. When Princess Isabella got wind of this, she decided to marry one of the French royal family instead.

To celebrate the first anniversary of Francisco López's accession to power, Eliza arranged a great circus, with bullfighting, dancing and plays, in a hippodrome built down on the waterfront. Wine and caña, the local rum, flowed freely and, according to one observer, the crowds 'actively engaged in raising the birth rate'.

Francisco López still had international political ambitions. He tried to intervene in a squabble Brazil and Argentina were having over Uruguay, but he mishandled the situation so badly that all three countries declared war on Paraguay. López went on the offensive, disastrously. Nevertheless, Madame Lynch organized a

Victory Ball, where all the ladies of Asunción were to wear their baubles – which Eliza promptly impounded as a contribution towards the war effort. She further humiliated them by inviting all the city's prostitutes, personally opening the door to them and bidding them welcome. Her excuse was that 'all classes should mingle on so festive an occasion'.

López himself went to the front to direct operations, leaving Eliza in Asunción as regent. Her first act was to announce that the women of Paraguay would donate the rest of their jewellery to the state in its hour of need. She also had a good line in uncovering plots – accused plotters had to pay up in gold coin to prove their loyalty.

Soon the war was going so badly that López was running short of able-bodied men. All males between the ages of eleven and sixty were drafted, including the aristocrats. Women were left to plough the fields and the only men seen in Asunción were the police.

The armies of the Triple Alliance began to invade Paraguay. They defeated the Paraguayan army at the battle of Estero Bellaco on 24 May, 1866 and the Paraguayans were so emaciated that their bodies would not burn. Seemingly determined to turn this rout into an even greater disaster, López had every tenth officer and man among the survivors executed for 'cowardice under fire'.

A truce was offered, but a precondition was that López go into exile in Europe. He refused. Instead, he began imprisoning, flogging, torturing and executing as many of his own people as he could get his hands on. Not content with having three powerful neighbours aligned against him, López turned his tender mercies on foreign residents and the U.S., Great Britain, France and Italy all sent gunboats.

Madame Lynch tried to keep things going by using her not inconsiderable charm to woo envoys and to reassure López that the disasters that had befallen him were not his fault. They were the fault of the conspirators who surrounded him, and who López mercilessly sought out.

After another military fiasco, López was forced to evacuate Asunción. He had already tortured and executed his two brothers and his sisters were imprisoned in covered bullock carts. Occasionally, they were let out to crawl into their brother's presence, make fresh confession and submit themselves to be flogged. He also sentenced his mother to floggings, although she was over seventy.

Madame Lynch tried to carry as much of her booty with her as she could, but she had to abandon her piano in what is now the village of Piano, Paraguay.

López withdrew into the jungle when he signed treaties with the Indians, but the Brazilian army pursued him relentlessly. Hours before the last attack, López condemned his mother and sisters to death, though the sentence was not carried out.

While his men made a human shield against the enemy, López tried to escape on horseback, but his horse got stuck in the mud of a river bed. When the Brazilians caught up with him, they were ordered to take him alive, but he pulled a gun and they had no choice.

'I die with my country,' he said as he expired.

Madame Lynch tried to escape in her carriage with her children, but they were caught by a Brazilian cavalry detachment. Juan Francisco tried to fight them off and was run through with a lance. Eliza was taken to see López's body. She and her remaining sons dug a grave for him and Juan Francisco with their bare hands.

When news of López's death reached Asunción, there were scenes of wild joy. A celebration ball, which matched anything that Eliza had put on, was organized.

Madame Lynch and the López ladies travelled back to Asunción together on board a Brazilian gunboat. There, Doña Juana and her two daughters were allowed to return home. Madame Lynch was kept on board, under guard, for her own safety. The Provisional Government charged her with extorting money and jewellery for her own use, on the pretext that it was going towards the war effort, and wantonly conspiring in the murder of tens of thousands of Paraguayans in an unwinnable war.

The Brazilians rejected the petition and Madame Lynch and her four surviving sons were taken to Buenos Aires where they were put aboard a ship for Europe.

During her time in Paraguay, Madame Lynch had managed to deposit four thousand ounces of gold in the Bank of England, taken there by the Italian consul and an American minister who had taken her fancy. The Brazilians were similarly kind to the fair Eliza, allowing her to take a vast inventory of booty with her into exile.

She sent her children to school in England and began litigation to try to recover more of her loot. When the Paraguayan government seized her assets, she returned to Paraguay to pursue the matter in the courts there. Her presence was so divisive that the government asked her to leave.

She went to live in Paris again, dying there in 1886. She was buried in Père Lachaise cemetery but, seventy-five years later, she was disinterred and her remains were shipped back to Paraguay where she now lies, an unlikely national heroine.

10

Don't Cry for Me, Argentina

Argentina's most famous dictator of modern times was Juan Domingo Perón. He was born on 8 October, 1895 in Lobos, a small town in the Pampas about sixty miles south-west of Buenos Aires. His parents were Creole and unmarried. At the age of fifteen, he went to military school. Far from the warmth of his family, his first sexual experiences were with prostitutes. He recalled later: 'In the era when we were boys, we weren't accustomed to going to social parties, and it would not have occurred to us to go to a home and make love to a family girl.'

In 1928, at the age of thirty-three, he married schoolteacher Aurelia Tizon. She was a modest soul. Her only contribution to his career was her translation of some English military textbooks for him. Though it seems to have been a loving marriage, he seldom mentioned her in later years. She died in 1938, leaving no children.

In 1939, just months before the outbreak of the war in Europe, Perón was appointed military attaché in Rome, where he witnessed Mussolini's methods at first-hand.

Perón travelled through Hungary, Austria, Germany, Spain and Portugal, observing Fascism at work. In Spain, he had an affair with an Italian woman. After they parted, he discovered she was pregnant, but was never able to find her or the child again.

While Juan Perón learnt his Fascism from the European master, he would never have been able to put it into practice if it had not been for his second wife, the redoubtable Evita. A second-rate actress and right-wing ideologue, she was South America's Ronald Reagan.

Born Marma Eva Duarte in Los Toldos on 7 May, 1919, she was the fourth child of Juanita Ibarguren, the mistress of the local landowner, Juan Duarte. At the time, any man with wealth or station in Argentina was expected to keep a mistress. Wives accepted it, provided the husband did not flaunt his mistress in their social circles.

Men would maintain a garçonnière, or bachelor apartment, where they would entertain women and even the smallest town would have its amoblados, or love hotels, where rooms could be rented by the hour.

The best a peasant girl like Evita's mother could expect was to become the mistress of a man wealthy enough to keep her. She and Duarte were together for fifteen years until suddenly, when Evita was seven, Juan Duarte died. After that, to support her children, Evita's mother ran what was said to be a boarding house, but was probably a brothel.

Los Toldos was a poor town in the middle of the Pampas, 150 miles from Buenos Aires. Prospects there were bleak for a girl like Evita. At fourteen, she agreed to sleep with tango singer José Armani if he would take her to Buenos Aires. Later, she claimed that the better-known singer Agustin Magaldi was her first lover.

Although it is popularly supposed that she worked as a prostitute when she first arrived in Buenos Aires, she probably never walked the streets. She certainly worked as a photographic model and posed for pornographic pictures; and she picked up rich and powerful men who could help raise her status.

At fifteen, she became the mistress of Emilio Kartulovic, publisher of the movie magazine *Sintonia*. His contacts gave her the perfect springboard into society.

She was fairly tall for a latino – 5 feet 5 inches – with brown eyes and dyed blonde hair, and she longed to become an actress. Using her charms on Rafael Firtuso, the owner of the Liceo theatre, she was cast in one of his productions. Ironically, her first provincial tour was in a play called *The Mortal Kiss*. It was about the evils of sexual promiscuity, financed by the Argentine Prophylactic League who thought that a rousing melodrama would cut down Argentina's soaring illegitimacy rate.

Her first film part, obtained through one of Kartulovic's contacts, was in a boxing movie called *Seconds Out of the Ring* and she had a brief affair with the star of the film, Pedro Quartucci. She appeared in small parts in a number of other dreadful Argentine films – *The Charge of the Brave* (1939), *The Unhappiest Man in Town* (1940) and *A Sweetheart in Trouble* (1941) – which, together with the occasional modelling assignment, was barely enough to keep her afloat.

To make ends meet, she would spend her nights in clubs like the Tabaris, the Embassy or the Gong, where wealthy businessmen would spend more in a night than she would have earned in a year. It was not done for couples to leave together at closing times, so they made assignations to meet at one of the nearby bachelor apartments or love hotels. A girl could expect to ride home in a taxi with an extra fifty pesos in her handbag, though Evita would probably have saved the cabfare and walked. She was safe in the rough streets of Buenos Aires even unchaperoned. It was said: 'She had a tongue that could skin a donkey.'

Evita's career began to take off. Soon she became radio's queen of the soaps, appearing on Radio Argentina and Radio El Mundo on shows like *Love Was Born When I Met You* and *Love Promises*. But the show that brought her national stardom was *My Kingdom of Love*. It was a series of historical love stories written by a philosophy student. In it, Evita played the female leads – Queen Elizabeth I, Lady Hamilton, the Empress Joséphine, Tsarina Alexandra of Russia and Madame Chiang Kai-shek. Twice she appeared on the cover of *Antenna*, the weekly radio listings magazine which had the largest sale of any magazine in Argentina.

In June 1943, a military coup, in which Juan Perón played a major part, brought a group of army generals to power. A month later, Evita, shocked her colleagues in the rehearsal room at Radio Belgrano by demonstrating just how influential her stardom had made her. She picked up the phone and said to the other actresses: 'Hey, girls, listen to this.'

She dialled a number.

'Hello,' she said. 'Is that Government House? Give me, President Ramirez... Hello, Mr President. This is Eva Duarte... Yes, I'd love to have dinner with you tomorrow evening. At ten. Good. Until then. Chau, Pedro.'

As soon as the owner of Radio Belgrano heard about this, he upped her salary from 150 pesos a month to 5,000 pesos. It was a shrewd move. Evita was having an affair with Colonel Anibal Imbert, the Minister of Communications in the new administration, who controlled the country's radio stations.

Colonel Imbert moved his pretty young mistress out of the rough Boca district and into a comfortable apartment on Calle Posadas, a quiet, tree-lined street just off the fashionable Avenida Alvear. Her fellow actresses were jealous. They looked forward to the day when Imbert dropped her, as he surely would, and she would come crashing to the ground. But Evita was looking for an opportunity to move onwards and upwards.

On 15 January, 1944, an earthquake destroyed the Spanish colonial town of San Juan. Thousands were killed and a wave of sympathy swept across the country. Evita persuaded her lover to hold a huge benefit for the victims in Luna Park, the open-air boxing arena in the centre of Buenos Aires. Argentina's leading actors and actresses would turn out, and it would be broadcast nationwide on the country's radio stations.

On the night of the benefit, Evita spotted Libertad Lamarque – one of Argentina's loveliest actresses – on the arm of a tall, handsome army officer. Evita had done her homework. She knew that this was Colonel Juan Domingo Perón, the Minister of Labour, and rising strongman in the regime. She went over to Libertad Lamarque, who she knew slightly, and asked to be introduced. When it was Libertad's turn to do her bit at the microphone, Evita slipped into the empty chair beside him.

Perón was a ladies' man with a reputation for preferring young girls. He was then forty-eight; she was twenty-four. It took little to seduce him. In Evita's own words: 'I put myself at his side. Perhaps this drew his attention to me and when he had time to listen to me I spoke up as best I could: "If, as you say, the cause of the people is your own cause, however great the sacrifice I will never leave your side until I die."'

What dictator could resist? They went to bed that night. She soon learnt that Perón was involved with a number of other military men who were plotting to overthrow the civilian government. His plan was to put Fascism into practice, he said, without making the mistakes Mussolini had made. With her help, she was convinced power would be his.

A few days later, Evita marched around to Perón's apartment. At the time, he was living with a teenaged mistress, a girl from the northern provinces who Perón had nicknamed Piranha. Evita evicted her and, knowing his weakness for young women, persuaded him to move into an apartment in the same building as her own.

It was rare for an Argentinian man to marry his mistress and, with frequent coups and counter-coups, it was rare for a minister to hold his job for long. Evita realized that for them to stay together, he had to hold onto power.

The source of power in Argentina had traditionally been the gauchos (the cowboys from the Pampas), but they had largely migrated from their power base to the shanty towns that surrounded the major cities. Evita convinced Perón that he should mobilize their support. As Minister of Labour, he was in the perfect position to do just that. He brought in a minimum wage and gave workers four weeks holiday a year, sick leave and protected them from arbitrary dismissal. Most popular of all, he introduced the *agonaldo*, an extra month's wages to be handed to each worker just before Christmas. He developed a broad base of popular support and founded the *descamisados*, a civilian paramilitary organization similar to Mussolini's Blackshirts.

Evita continued her career as an actress but now, of course, she got the star parts. In *Circus Cavalcade*, she played opposite Libertad Lamarque who had not forgiven her for stealing Perón from her. To rub salt in the wounds, Evita got Perón to pick her up each evening from the studio. One day, Evita sat in Libertad's chair and Libertad slapped her across the face. The tension on set was palpable. The movie was a flop. Soon after, Libertad was forced into exile.

By 1945, Perón was Minister of War and Vice-president. Then there was another coup conducted by senior army officers alarmed by Perón's mobilization of the masses. When Perón was arrested, Evita organized a protest by the labour unions. Thousands gathered in public squares and he was released on 17 October, 1945. Together, Evita and Perón were taken to the presidential palace. From the balcony, he addressed a crowd of 300,000 people. A few days later, they married. Anti-Perónists spread the rumour that when he asked her to marry him, she was so shocked she nearly fell out of bed.

Evita cracked down on that sort of talk. Their love, she maintained, was not sexual, but pure. She did not consider herself the wife of Perón but 'an Argentine woman and an idealist who, confronting the responsibility of the fatherland, forgets everything'. When he wanted to reward her, she wrote, he did so with a kiss 'on the forehead'. Perón used his power to help conceal the sordid details of her past. The pornographic photographs she had posed for were collected and destroyed.

They contrived to give the impression that theirs was a sexless marriage, that they dedicated all their energy to the people. Certainly, Evita was Perón's greatest political asset. Despite her jewels, furs and regal manner, the people recognized her as one of them. Her beauty was said to personify Perónist femininity. Perónist posters portrayed her as the Virgin Mary, but political enemies still referred to her as 'the little whore'.

Years later, while travelling in an official car with an Italian admiral, jeering crowds taunted her.

'Do you hear that?' she said. 'They are calling me a whore.'

'I quite understand,' said the admiral. 'I haven't been to sea for fifteen years and they still call me an admiral.'

Even Argentine poet and leading opponent of the regime, Jorge Luis Borges, said: 'Perón's wife was a common prostitute. She had a brothel near Junín. And that must have embittered him, no? I mean, if a girl is a whore in a large city that doesn't mean too much, but in a small town in the Pampas, everybody knows everybody else. And being one of the whores is like being the barber or the surgeon. And that must have greatly embittered her. To be known and to be despised by everybody and to be used.'

Not content with being a back-seat First Lady, Evita wanted political power for herself. She tried to legalize prostitution and regulate Buenos Aires' red-light district, further exacerbating rumours about her past. She also promoted votes for women and organized workers. The Eva Perón Welfare Foundation pumped millions of pesos of government money into welfare programmes, though some of it was siphoned off into her Swiss bank account.

Through her sexual charisma, Evita controlled a web of men strategically placed throughout her husband's regime. She politically castrated many leading figures, and dealt more literally with others. Political opponents were tortured with electric shocks that left them impotent. She also took direct responsibility for the castration of rebel leaders, keeping her victims' testicles in a glass jar on her desk. This obviously made a considerable impression on the ministers, officials and union delegates who came to petition her.

Evita seems to have been faithful to her husband throughout her marriage – with one exception. During World War II, she met Aristotle Onassis, who was channelling food parcels through Argentina to Nazi-occupied Greece. When Evita was in Europe in 1947, they met again at a formal lunch and arranged a private meeting at her villa on the Italian Riviera. As soon as he arrived, they made love. Afterwards, he was hungry and she made him an omelette. In return, he donated $10,000 to her favourite charity. He said later that it was the most expensive omelette he ever had.

On that same trip, in Rome, thousands of people gathered outside her window at the embassy, screaming: 'Perón! Perón!' When she went out and waved to the crowd, they responded with a straight-armed Fascist salute, which had not been seen in Italy since the downfall of Mussolini. Fighting immediately broke out between Communists and Fascists. It took an hour for the riot police to clear the street and the embassy's flower beds had been trampled out of existence.

Evita died at the age of thirty-three from cancer of the uterus. Her death plunged Argentina into mourning and moves were made to have her canonized.

After Evita died, Juan Perón, who was already fifty-six, began to take an inordinate interest in the Union of Secondary School Students, especially its young female members. It had branches in every school. The girl recruits were sent to luxurious 'recreation centres' where they entertained high-ranking government officials. The centres had teams of doctors to handle unwanted pregnancies and venereal disease.

Perón had his private recreation centre where he would spend the afternoon with teenaged girls, watching them play basketball or swimming. One of them, Nellie Rivas, became his mistress.

The daughter of a worker in a candy factory, she was just thirteen, but Perón said he was not superstitious. She slept on a sofa at the foot of her parents' bed. One day at the Union of Secondary School Students at Olivos, she was told that she would be having lunch with the President. That lunch led to others.

Then she was assigned to take some papers from Olivos down to the presidential palace. She spent the afternoon there talking, then stayed the night. The next day she went to a sporting event with Perón. It finished late, so she stayed again. The third night there was a rain storm, so she could not go home. In fact, she never went home again.

Perón built her a luxurious love nest with mirrored walls and white bearskin rugs in the basement of one of his villas and showered her with jewels. But the relationship, though sexual, was caring. Perón would spend time teaching her the rudiments of culture. He even offered to send her to Europe to learn about the world, but she refused as she did not want to leave him.

'The very thought of leaving the residence brought me attacks of madness,' she wrote later.

Stories about Perón's teenaged mistress spread. Soon people were talking about sex orgies behind the high walls of the presidential mansion, with Perón running amok like a Roman emperor among slave girls. Although most of the tales were fanciful, many of his followers believed that Perón was defiling the memory of Evita. In 1955, amid economic ruin and having alienated a large section of his support, Perón was deposed. He was forced to seek sanctuary on a Paraguayan gunboat that had put into Buenos Aires harbour for repairs. Before it took him into exile, he scribbled a final note to Nellie Rivas. It read: 'My dear baby girl... I miss you every day, as I do my little dogs... Many kisses and many desires. Until I see you soon, Papi.'

Later, the torrid correspondence between Juan and Nellie was published, further besmirching his reputation. He was tried *in absentia* by a military court for his affair with Nellie Rivas and he was stripped of his rank of general for 'conduct unworthy of an officer and a gentleman'.

The judges wrote: 'It is superfluous to stress the horror of the court at the proof of such a crime committed by one who always claimed that the only privileged in the land were children.'

Nellie was heartbroken.

'He loved me,' she said. 'He could have been my grandfather, but he loved me. He always told me I was very pretty, but I'm not really, am I?'

Nellie was sent to a reformatory for eight months. Her parents went into exile in Montevideo. Later, she married an Argentine employee of the American embassy.

At the same time, Evita's remains were disinterred and removed from Argentina in an attempt to prevent them becoming an object of Perónist veneration. They were hidden in Italy.

Exiled in Spain, Perón met Isabel Martínez, an Argentine dancer. She quit her career to become his personal secretary. They married in 1961. In 1971, there was yet another coup in Argentina. This time the military promised to restore democracy and as a gesture to Perón, who still had a huge following, Evita's remains were returned to him in Madrid.

In 1973, Perón returned to Argentina and successfully stood in the presidential elections with Isabel Martínez as his running mate. When he took office in October 1973, he already knew he was dying. His widow succeeded him on 1 July, 1974. Politically, she suffered in comparison with Evita – or at least, the legend of Evita. In desperation, she brought Evita's remains back to Argentina and had them interred next to Juan Perón's in the crypt in the presidential palace.

It did no good. In 1976, she was seized by Air Force officers and held under house arrest for five years. In 1981, she was exiled to Spain, where she resigned as head of the Perónist party. She died there in 1985.

11

Shoe Fetishism in the Philippines

Ferdinand Marcos, the head of state of the Philippines from 1966 to 1986, was a master at fraudulently manipulating the electoral system. To keep himself in power, he declared martial law in 1973 and, again, in 1986. When he was forced to hold presidential elections in 1983, the opposition leader Benigno Aquino returned from exile in the U.S., only to be shot as he stepped off the plane.

Ferdinand managed to cling onto power for another three years until, in 1986, he and his wonderful wife Imelda went into exile in Hawaii, leaving behind her collection of over three thousand pairs of shoes.

As a child, Imelda had gone barefoot. Although she belonged to the influential Romualdez family on the Philippine island of Leyte, her branch of the family was poor. For a time, she and her mother lived in a car port; but by the time she was sixteen, she was a sought-after beauty.

In 1951, she fell in love with Victoriano Chan, the heir of a wealthy Chinese family who owned the Tacloban

Electric Plant. His parents considered her unsuitable and he broke it off. Soon she fell in love again, this time with Justo Zibala, a good-looking medical student from the island of Negros; but he was a Protestant and Imelda's father Orestes, a fervent Catholic, objected.

To escape another suitor, Dominador Pacho, a sawmill owner who had a reputation for getting what he wanted, Imelda fled to Manila with just five pesos in her purse. She got a job in a bank. In Manila, she was quickly noticed for her beauty. The editor of the Sunday supplement *This Week* used her picture on the cover of the Valentine Day's issue, which brought her instant stardom. At the home of her uncle, Congressman Daniel Romualdez, she was besieged by wealthy playboys of Manila's polo set. One of them picked her up, toyed with her, then dropped her. He was the young, up-and-coming politician Benigno Aquino.

Imelda decided that she had to make her way on her own merits, so she entered the Miss Manila competition. Her family were shocked. They assumed that the winner would have to sleep with the judges, but Imelda was above that. She lost to twenty-year-old Norma Jimenez from Pangasinan province.

Imelda did not give up that easily. She went to see Manila's Mayor Arsenio Lacson, the organizer of the competition. He was well known for his sexual proclivities. Every afternoon between three and four, he would retire to the Hotel Filipinas for 'Chinese tea' – he would spend an hour with a couple of Chinese girls supplied by his constituents. In his office, Imelda sobbed uncontrollably. He comforted her. When their meeting was over, Mayor Lacson disowned the decision of the judges and declared Imelda Miss Manila. The rumour immediately spread that Imelda was Lacson's latest conquest.

However, the judges insisted that their original decision stand, so Mayor Lacson was forced to name Imelda 'Muse of Manila' instead. It was a title he had made up himself. As the Muse of Manila, Imelda stood alongside the official Miss Manila in the Miss Philippines' contest. Neither girl won.

These shenanigans did not seem to damage Imelda's marriage prospects. She became involved with Ariston Nakpil, one of Manila's wealthiest men. He was the son of one of the city's oldest families and had studied architecture at Harvard and the Fontainebleau School of Fine Art in France. Imelda found him dashing and erudite. They spent the weekends together at his family farm in Bataganas and holidayed together in the mountain resort of Baguio. The only problem was that he was already married. Imelda's strict Catholic father came and took her home to Leyte.

But Imelda had tasted the good life and was no longer content with the sleepy ways of a backwater like Tacloban. She escaped back to Manila in the hope of resuming her year-long affair with Nakpil. It was then that she met Ferdinand Marcos, a politician who had already done the impossible – he had got himself elected to congress after being convicted of murder. In jail pending his appeal, he studied law and passed his bar examinations. He argued his own appeal in front of the Supreme Court, whose chief justice himself had been convicted of murder at the age of eighteen and had successfully represented himself to the Supreme Court. Marcos walked free.

Soon a rising politician, Marcos had given the address at Imelda's high-school graduation ceremony. He had also been a customer at the bank where she had worked. He had a reputation as a ladies' man and could not have failed to notice her there.

They met formally at an ice-cream party and he was smitten. He began to pester Imelda so persistently that she ran away to Baguio for Holy Week with three girlfriends as chaperones. Marcos set off in pursuit with a marriage licence, which he had already signed, and a justice of the peace, so the ceremony could take place just as soon as she gave in.

When she went to Mass each morning, he would sit beside her and tell her about the bright future they had in front of them. Then he took her and her girlfriends to the bank. In the vault, he showed her his safe deposit box which contained the best part of a million dollars in cash. Soon after, she signed the marriage contract. From meeting to marriage had taken just eleven days.

He bought a wedding ring of white gold with eleven diamonds set in it – one for each day of their courtship. The following day, a civil ceremony was performed by the justice of the peace. A few days later, they went to visit Imelda's father who, unexpectedly, took a liking to Marcos and forgave his daughter, provided they had a proper church wedding.

Marcos set up a glittering society affair at the Miguel Pro-Cathedral in Manila. Philippines President Ramon Magsaysay acted as co-sponsor. Imelda was dressed in a couture gown of tulle and white satin, embroidered with leaves of sequins, seed pearls and rhinestones. There were three thousand guests at the reception including a large number of congressmen and senators. It was held in Malacanany Park, across the Pasig river from the presidential palace. The cake was a replica of the Congress building.

'It was a very political wedding,' concluded Imelda's sister, Conchita.

The Marcoses had a very public honeymoon in Baguio. This was because Ferdinand already had a common-law wife, Carmen Ortega. She had met Marcos four years before when he had offered to sponsor her for the Miss Press Photography contest. Soon she became his full-time mistress and he moved her into the house he shared with his mother, Doña Josefa. A press announcement of their forthcoming wedding appeared, but they underwent neither a civil nor a church marriage. Nevertheless, Carmen Ortega was known around Manila as Mrs Marcos. Imelda must have known of her – once Marcos had taken Carmen to a bank where Imelda's sister, Loreta, worked to withdraw $50,000 for a spending spree in the U.S. and he had introduced Carmen as Mrs Marcos.

Doña Josefa considered Carmen to be her son's wife. As far as she was concerned, Imelda was simply his political mistress. Marcos was planning to run for the senate. The Romualdez family controlled over a million votes on the central island of Visayan; and Eduardo Romualdez was the chairman of Reconstruction Finance Corporation, which controlled millions of dollars-worth of foreign exchange credits. Although Imelda did not realize it at the time, marriage to her set the seal on his political and financial future.

By contrast, Carmen Ortega was without power or influence. While Ferdinand and Imelda honeymooned, Carmen and their three children were moved out of the

Marcos's home to a large house in the suburb of Green Hills. However, the memory of his mistress could not be erased so easily. The house Imelda was to share with her new husband and his mother was on Ortega Street. She tried to insist that they sell up immediately and move elsewhere, but Marcos and his mother refused.

If that was not painful enough, Imelda soon discovered that Marcos was continuing to see Carmen. So she screwed up all her courage and went over to Green Hills for a confrontation. Carmen must stop seeing her husband immediately, Imelda insisted, she was destroying her marriage and her happiness.

Carmen replied coolly that it was Imelda who was ruining her happiness. She was already pregnant with Ferdinand's fourth child – and, what's more, it had been conceived after his marriage to Imelda.

Imelda found herself completely powerless. After so public a wedding, she could not up and leave her husband. In a Catholic country like the Philippines, there was little hope of an annulment and no chance of a divorce; nor could she stop him seeing his mistress.

Imelda had a mental breakdown. Marcos sent her to New York for psychiatric help. After three months in Manhattan's Presbyterian Hospital, the dilemma she faced was just as stark – either leave her husband and face ruin, or bite the bullet and make the best of it.

Imelda decided to fight fire with fire. From New York, she flew to Portugal and, at the shrine of Our Lady of Fatima, she prayed for children. The following year, her prayers were answered and in the middle of Marcos's congressional campaign, Imelda gave birth to Imee, the first of their three children.

Her second child, Bong-Bong, was born two years later and her third, Irene, during Ferdinand's 1959 senate campaign. During these years, Imelda suffered from migraine and, on at least one occasion, took an overdose of medication. She sought psychiatric help again and, slowly, reconciled herself to her situation.

Although Ferdinand had succeeded in making her pregnant three times, he was far from attentive. He confided to one of his extramarital conquests that Imelda was frigid and that he had become impotent with her. In a public outburst, he claimed she suffered from 'virginitis'. However, their sex life may have been a little more active than Ferdinand made out. During the 1965 presidential campaign, a nude photograph of Imelda was circulated. It was said to have been filched from Ferdinand's private collection. The Marcos camp claimed that Imelda's head had been superimposed on another woman's nude body. When Imelda heard about it, she collapsed in a state of shock.

Her reaction was similarly dramatic later, when the governor of Negros, Alfredo Montelibano Jr, pulled a cruel trick on her. He installed a one-way mirror in the lavatory of his hacienda. During a party, he invited several guests into a back-room to watch while the Philippines' First Lady took a pee. A photograph of the act was circulated. Benigno Aquino had a print, which he kept in his wallet until shortly before he died.

Ferdinand Marcos's womanizing represented a political danger, and it was a danger particularly threatening to Imelda. Throughout his political career, he paraded his young wife. Their destinies were intertwined. Indeed, with a persistently unfaithful husband, she was

First Lady of the Philippines or she was nothing. In 1969, he began showing a great interest in Gretchen Cojuangco, wife of Eduardo Cojuangco who belonged to a family that controlled a billion-dollar sugar-producing organization. Losing Cojuangco family support would have destroyed Marcos's political base. Imelda sent Gretchen a note the content of which we know not, but after she had read it, Ferdinand said, Gretchen would 'no longer stop weeping'.

Eduardo Cojuangco knew what was going on and tried a more subtle approach. Marcos faced an election and needed a propaganda coup. Marcos had written a highly fanciful autobiography called *Rendezvous with Destiny*. In it, he claimed to have been a fearless fighter against the Japanese. He was rewarded for his valour with some twenty Philippine medals and the U.S. Medal of Honour. When, mysteriously, as President of the Philippines, he could not put his hand on his U.S. medal, the American government issued a new one. The Philippine army followed suit.

In fact, Marcos had fought on the Japanese side against the Americans during World War II, but at the height of the Cold War, why should the State Department bother with such details?

The idea was that Marcos's book be made into a feature film – it had already surfaced as a TV documentary. Eduardo Cojuangco had contacts in Hollywood. He set to work.

According to *Rendezvous with Destiny*, during his fictitious anti-Japanese guerrilla fighting days, Marcos had a Filipino–American lover called Evelyn, who had saved his life by stopping a Japanese bullet meant for him.

Cojuangco got a small-time producer at Universal Studios, Paul Mason, to recruit girls to audition for the part of Evelyn. He sent Joyce Reese and Dovie Beams.

When the two girls arrived, they were driven directly to a house in the Green Hills suburb for a party. They were taken to a half-finished house, to a room with a large bed in it. Ferdinand Marcos turned up a little later, introducing himself as 'Fred'. Dovie sang 'I Want To Be Bad'. 'Fred' got the message. After a few words in Tagalog (the Filipino language), the other men left the room, taking Joyce Reese with them.

Once they were alone, Marcos kissed Dovie on the back of the neck. She asked if he was a lawyer. He admitted that he did have something to do with the law. He was President of the Philippines. The next day, they became lovers.

He installed Dovie in the mansion in Green Hills which was being renovated with a swimming pool being built in the garden. He told her that he had been sexually estranged from Imelda for many years. They lived separate lives, he said. That may have been true, but Dovie soon found out that Marcos was still seeing Carmen Ortega; and, after Dovie had had a quarrel with Marcos, Carmen fell pregnant once again.

Dovie was told that she had got the part of Evelyn in the movie. He bought her a tape recorder to help teach her Tagalog, but sometimes he would break off from the lessons to make love to her. Soon Dovie had a library of very interesting tapes.

They also made love in the cottage on the palace golf course; and when Imelda was away, Marcos would sneak Dovie into the presidential palace. After they had made love and he had fallen asleep, she would quickly search through the papers on his desk and steal documents to stash away for a rainy day.

Marcos's aides were terrified by the affair. If they helped Ferdinand, Imelda might have them shot. If they didn't, Ferdinand might have them shot. It was a fine line to walk. When Imelda got suspicious and made them follow his car, somehow they would always manage to lose it.

One day, Dovie returned home to the house in Green Hills to discover that it had been closed up. Marcos told her that it was too dangerous to stay there. The place was being watched by spies. She would have to move to a hotel in Wack Wack. She soon discovered that her Green Hills home had been given to Carmen Ortega, which had been the plan all along. That was why it was being renovated.

Dovie continued surreptitiously recording their love-making sessions. Marcos wanted some souvenirs too. He bought a Polaroid camera and took a series of shots of Dovie in the nude, in explicit poses on the bed and in the bathroom. Then Dovie got lucky. Marcos asked for a lock of her pubic hair. She said she would give it to him in exchange for a lock of his. She sent that, the tapes and the documents she had filched to the U.S. for safe-keeping.

Marcos's affections were cooling fast. One night he told her that her movie was no good and she had been miscast. She packed her bags and headed back to Los Angeles.

Later, under the guise of making a travelogue about the Philippines, she returned. She was given $10,000 for her silence. She took it, but said that her silence was worth something more like $100,000. When that was refused, she upped her demand to $150,000. That night she was picked up by the secret police and taken to a safe house. Marcos turned up and there was a blazing row. It ended with Marcos trying to make up with her. She refused to kiss him though, and was taken to a room in the Savoy Hotel where she was beaten up and tortured.

When she was allowed to go to the bathroom, she escaped, found a phone and called a friend in Los Angeles. The friend contacted influential people Dovie knew in the U.S., one of whom was the Governor of California, Ronald Reagan. While the State Department alerted the American embassy in Manila, Dovie checked into the Manila Medical Centre under a false name.

By this time, Imelda had learned everything and her agents were combing the Philippines for Dovie. Dovie called the U.S. Embassy and talked to Consul Lawrence Harris. He and Ambassador Henry Byroade turned up at Dovie's bedside with an offer from Imelda – $100,000 tax free if she would keep quiet.

Dovie told the two diplomats of the incriminating evidence she held against Marcos. She believed her life was in danger. They arranged a press conference for her in the Bay View Hotel across Roxas Boulevard. There, she spilled the beans – but referred to Marcos only as 'Fred' so that the media could relay the facts without falling foul of reporting restrictions that prevented them from saying anything critical of the President of the Philippines. She even played one of her tapes that featured creaking bedsprings, murmurs, moans and Marcos singing an Ilocano love song which the whole of the Philippines knew was his favourite. Copies were soon changing hands at $500 a time.

Students at the University of the Philippines got hold of a copy. They commandeered the University radio station and played a looped section of the tape. In it, Marcos was begging Dovie to perform oral sex on him. Even the troops sent to re-take the radio station found it hard to keep a straight face. With his tongue buried firmly in his cheek, Senator Benigno Aquino called for a congressional investigation.

The U.S. authorities had to employ the strictest security to get Dovie out of the country. Imelda's secret agents were out to get her. Eventually, Dovie had to fly via Hong Kong, where an attempt was made on her life. The British secret service had to take her into protective custody for five days.

Dovie continued her campaign against Marcos from the U.S., publishing her accusations in the Manila-based journal *Graphic*, which was closed down, and a book called *Marcos' Lovie Dovie*, which included nude photographs. This mysteriously disappeared from bookshelves. Even the Library of Congress's copy has gone missing.

Meanwhile, Marcos was having an affair with the wife of a U.S. Navy officer and State Department cables were describing him as a 'ladies' man'. There were dangers for Filipino–American relations in this affair and Marcos soon moved on to Filipino singer Carmen Soriano. Imelda caught up with her in San Francisco in 1970. Going into her apartment with her financial adviser, Ernesto Villatuya, Imelda demanded that Carmen sign a declaration that she had never gone to bed with Ferdinand. When she refused, Imelda took a swing at her. She ducked and Imelda floored Villatuya. Soon after, he was made head of the Philippine National Bank, a position he held until 1972.

Imelda began extorting money and gold out of her husband over his affairs. At the same time she travelled the world as a roving representative of the Philippine head of state. She went to Libya and, afterwards, implied that Qaddafy had made a pass at her. But to friends, she confided that Qaddafy was gay. There were gay rumours about her too. Among the jetset the word was that Imelda and her constant companion Cristina Ford, wife of Henry Ford II, were lovers. Other gossip was that Imelda had gone to bed with actor George Hamilton.

It was Imelda's sexual jealousy that finally brought the Marcoses down. It was she who ordered that Benigno Aquino's feet should not touch Filipino soil again when he flew back from exile in 1983. Marcos watched in horror as his political rival was shot down on the aircraft steps at Manila airport in front of a plane-load of international journalists. He knew his time was up. Although Marcos managed to blame top military officials for the assassination and fixed the presidential elections, they had to flee the Philippines in 1986. The new president was Benigno Aquino's widow, Corazón. Marcos died of lupus in exile in Hawaii in 1989. Imelda went on to become the queen of the chat shows.

12

Eating Out in Africa

One of the most bloodthirsty dictators Africa has known was Idi Amin of Uganda. The son of a peasant witch doctor, he converted to Islam. His religion, however, did not stop him drinking. One morning, while he was still in the King's African Rifles, he awoke in a Mogadishu brothel with a fearsome hangover to hear the cry of the imam calling the faithful to morning prayer. Amin knelt at the brothel window and bowed his head, but his prayers were interrupted by the snores of the woman he had left in bed. So he walked over to her, pulled her out of bed by the hair, slapped her across the face and said in Swahili: 'Pray you Muslim bitch.'

After rising through the ranks of the Ugandan army to become a colonel, Amin staged a coup in 1971, and established his infamous dictatorship. Once in power Amin ruled both the country and his personal life with an awesome vindictiveness. To get any woman he wanted, he would simply order the execution of her husband or boyfriend. Edward Rugumayo, Amin's Minister of Education who defected in 1973, wrote a five-thousand-word condemnation of Amin, which he circulated around the OAU, UN and Commonwealth. In it, he charged Amin with being 'a racist, tribalist and dictator' and said that Amin 'would kill anyone without hesitation as long as it serves his interests, such as prolonging his stay in power or getting what he wants, such as a woman or money'.

Women who did not comply with Amin's orders would be brutally raped. Their breasts would be cut off. Some ended up in Amin's fridge. Sarah Amin, his fifth wife, said that she saw the head of a beautiful girl called Ruth in the icebox. She had been one of Amin's lovers and he suspected her of seeing other men.

Amin's first wife was Malyamu Kibedi, the daughter of a schoolteacher. He fell in love with her when he was a twenty-eight-year-old sergeant and army boxing champion. She was an intelligent six-footer. Her family opposed the match, but they lived together anyway.

They had several children, but did not get married formally until 1966 when they had already been together for thirteen years. Even then, there was no ceremony. Amin simply paid the bride price and the marriage was recognized. He did this because, as a Muslim, he was ready to take a second wife and he wanted Malyamu to be recognized as the senior of the two.

Three months after his marriage to Malyamu, he married Kay Adroa in a registry office. The daughter of a clergyman, Kay was a student at Makerere University and a striking ebony-skinned girl. She wore white for the wedding. Amin turned out in full dress uniform. The ceremony took place in Amin's home town, Arua, and there was a proper wedding reception. Kay called Malyamu 'Mama' in recognition of her status as senior wife.

Within a year, Amin married again. He had already risen to national prominence and was seen as a political threat by President Milton Obote. So he married Nora, a Langi from Obote's own region to allay his fears of tribal rivalry. She moved in with the other two wives and, by the late 1960s, Amin had fourteen or fifteen children.

Wife number four was Medina, a Baganda dancer. Her troupe, the Heartbeat of Africa, used to entertain foreign dignitaries at state functions. She was agile and sexy, and Amin used to sit and watch her spellbound. She was so attractive that she was picked to star in a Ugandan tourist film – though Amin had the footage of her cut out after they were married.

Their affair started in 1971 just after Amin had ousted Obote. In September 1972, people all over Uganda were tuning in to hear news of the ill-fated invasion Milton Obote had mounted from Tanzania. Instead, the news was dominated by the announcement of Amin's forthcoming marriage. Medina, Amin said, had been given to him by the grateful people of Buganda in recognition of all he had done for them since the coup. The only thing Amin had done for the people of Buganda was to murder them brutally in their thousands.

In March 1974, during the fighting that followed the mutiny of Brigadier Charles Arube, Amin had another incongruous announcement for his people. His first three wives, Malyamu, Kay and Nora were being divorced because, Amin said, they were involved in business. This was true. Amin himself had given them textile shops confiscated from the exiled Ugandan Asians. Malyamu, it was also intimated, was politically suspect. Her brother, Wanume Kibedi, the Minister of Foreign Affairs, had recently fled the country. Kay had to go because she was a cousin, the communiqué said, and this was too close a blood relationship to sustain a marriage.

The real reason was entirely different. With Medina and his mistresses, Amin had little time for his first three wives. He kept them locked up in one of the presidential lodges. Bored and frustrated, they took lovers. Kay became pregnant by Peter Mbalu-Mukasa, a doctor on the staff of Mulago Hospital and a married man with several children.

One night, the three women held a party for their lovers. Their guards were terrified that Amin would find out and phoned him directly. Furious, Amin got on the phone and told his wives that he was coming over to throw them out. They told him to keep Medina and go to hell. Then they locked the guards out and got on with their fun.

The following day, they heard about their divorces on the radio. Amin simply repudiated them three times, Muslim-style. Later he sent official letters of dismissal.

But, for Amin, this was not enough. A month later Malyamu was arrested for allegedly smuggling a bolt of cloth into Kenya. Refused bail, she was kept in prison for three weeks. In court, she was given a hefty fine and released.

The following year Malyamu was injured in an accident when one of Amin's bodyguards drove into her car. When Amin heard about the incident, he said: 'Is she dead?'

She was taken to hospital and lodged in a private ward at her own expense. An arm and a leg had been broken. She was put in traction and was in considerable pain when Amin turned up with a posse of journalists from the presidential press unit. He picked a fight with her in front everyone.

'You are a very unlucky woman. You cannot run your life properly,' he chided. He told her to go to a witch doctor whose magic would save her from future misfortune.

The next day, he ordered her removed from the private ward, even though she was paying for it herself, and put in a public ward.

In November 1975, she flew to London to seek medical help and never returned. She left her children with his other wives and her father took over her shop. Amin had the shop looted.

Kay's father, the Reverend Adroa, contacted Amin and persuaded him to take her back. Amin, who had no idea she was pregnant, agreed to build her a house in his home town Arua, but she did not want to live there. Amin visited her in her flat several times and they had blazing rows. After one of these confrontations she was arrested for the possession of a gun and ammunition. When he turned up at the police station, the row continued through the bars of her cell.

'You can't have me arrested for keeping a pistol which you yourself left in my apartment,' she screamed.

She was held overnight. In the morning, she explained to the magistrate that the gun belonged to her husband and she was released.

A few days later, her dismembered body was found in the trunk of her lover's car. He had killed himself and had tried to kill his family. There are indications that he had tried to perform an abortion on her which went wrong and she bled to death. Why the body was dismembered remains a mystery.

Amin had it sewn back together again to show to their children.

'Your mother was a bad woman,' Amin told them. 'See what happened to her.'

This humiliating harangue took place in front of reporters and the TV cameras. Amin did not attend Kay's funeral, nor did he send a representative. There were no further investigations by the police and her name was never mentioned again.

Amin's third wife Nora fared better and she continued running the business Amin had given her. This was probably for political reasons. She was a Langi, a section of the population he could not afford to alienate.

Medina was now the only wife and suffered for it. Their relationship was passionate – often violent. After one assassination attempt which he suspected she had had a hand in, he beat her so savagely that he fractured his own wrist.

He beat her up when she was pregnant, nearly causing her to miscarry. On another occasion, she was so badly beaten that she had to go to Libya for several weeks for medical treatment. When she returned she was still wearing dark glasses to hide the injuries around her eyes.

Amin's fifth wife was Sarah Kyolaba, the eighteen-year-old go-go dancer with the jazz band of the 'Suicide' Mechanized Unit, an army company named purely for dramatic effect. She was strikingly beautiful, but was living with the band leader, Jesse Gitta.

When she gave birth to a baby, Amin had her and the child transferred to a hospital in Kampala. Medina visited them there. The visit was covered on television and it was announced that President Amin had had another baby. There was no mention of who the mother was.

After she left hospital, Sarah went back to Gitta, who was the real father of the child, but periodically, Amin would send for her. When Gitta tried to stop her going, he disappeared. Sarah suspected that Amin had had him murdered, but there was nothing she could do.

At the next OAU meeting in Kampala, Amin promoted himself to Field Marshal and invited the visiting heads of state to witness his marriage to Sarah. Part of the celebration was Operation Cape Town, where the Ugandan Air Force were to bomb an island in Lake Victoria, showing what it could do to a South African city. Things did not go well. The bombs all missed their target and fell harmlessly in the water. The head of the Air Force, Smuts Guweddeko, was dismissed. Later he was found murdered.

The next day, Amin dressed up in his Field Marshal's uniform again to repeat the wedding ceremony, this time for the TV cameras. The resulting footage was broadcast to the nation every few days.

After Sarah married Amin, he forced her to write a satirical song about the disappearance of Jesse Gitta. Later she found Jesse's head in one of Amin's fridges. When he noticed that the fridge had been opened, he beat her.

There was little doubt that he ate his victims. One day in August 1975, Amin was talking to some officials who had been to Zaire where they had been served with monkey meat – something unacceptable to Ugandans. Seeing the audience were horrified, Amin shocked them further, saying: 'I have eaten human meat.'

Sensing he had gone too far, he added that for a soldier at war with no food, it is acceptable to kill a wounded comrade and eat his flesh to survive. Amin also freely admitted eating human flesh to his health minister, Henry Kyemba, who fled to Britain.

In exile, Amin again talked openly of eating human flesh and said he missed it. He could not remember whose heads he had kept in the fridge, but he thought that they might have been those of Chief Justice Ben Kiwanuka, Father Kiggundu and Archbishop Luwum, who he admitted he rather enjoyed killing.

He also claimed to be genocide champion of Africa, with half-a-million victims under his belt. He openly admired Hitler – though killing Jews, Amin thought, did not really count. Nevertheless, he renamed an area of south-eastern Uganda, Führer, in the mistaken belief that it was the site of a World War I battle that had, in fact, taken place hundreds of miles to the south in Tanzania.

Besides his five wives, he had as many as thirty mistresses at any one time. They lived in fear, watched over by spies and afraid to go out with other men. His sexual energy, Amin thought, was a symbol of his power and authority.

'He never tries to hide his lust,' said Henry Kyemba. 'His eyes lock onto any beautiful woman. His reputation for sexual performance is so startling that women often deliberately make themselves available, and his love affairs have included women of all colours and many nations, from schoolgirls to mature women, from street girls to university professors.'

He boasted that he had fathered the children of twelve women from different tribes. He said that he believed in having blood ties throughout East Africa.

Besides the official wives, there were at least ten unofficial ones. One, Sauda Amin, used his name. She bore him twins and had them named in a mosque. She fell out with him because of his womanizing. Others were afraid to cross him because of his murderous reputation. Henry Kyemba employed one of Amin's girlfriends – whose husband, a university professor, Amin had murdered – as a secretary. Amin also had the manager of the Tororo Hotel, a Mr Nshekanabo, killed when he took a fancy to his wife. Amin had the payment on Nshekanabo's life assurance policy rushed through to the widow. And the husband of a senior woman police officer was killed when Amin wanted his wife.

Amin considered nurses employed by the Ministry of Health his personal harem. A student nurse in Jinja fled to Kenya when he took an interest. Another girl at Mulago Hospital knew she was in trouble when Amin's bodyguards turned up at her parents' house with salt, sugar and 700 shillings in cash. When the girl's parents saw the gifts, they burst into tears. This girl, too, went into exile.

Amin was not a very liberated man when it came to other people's sexuality. Sexual promiscuity was frowned on and Amin warned students against venereal disease. There was some speculation that he was suffering from tertiary syphilis, which would have explained some of his bizarre behaviour. One former lover claimed to have been infected by him and rendered infertile. Amin denied this.

Amin had the author Denis Hills arrested after he wrote *The White Pumpkin* which passed comment on some of the excesses of the Amin regime. When British Prime Minister Jim Callaghan intervened to get him released, Amin denounced Hills as a sex maniac and drunkard who mixed with prostitutes in Uganda. Indeed, Hills' book gives useful tips on how to pick up Ugandan prostitutes in bars and how to make love to them. But Amin, himself, used prostitutes – as spies. Highly trained and hand-picked by Big Dada himself, they were sent out around the world to lure secrets out of foreigners.

Despite the fact that he had killed tens of thousands of his own people, Amin was seen merely as a buffoon. His curious turn of phrase made him good for a laugh. When Kenneth Kaunda of Zambia criticized him, Amin told him to cry into 'a twenty-five-year-old pair of the Queen's knickers'.

Amin's regime was brought down in 1979, when soldiers of his strayed over the Tanzanian border and raped a group of women. Tanzania could sit idly by no longer and invaded. Amin fled to Libya where he was treated well, and given his own villa.

Amin claimed to have married four Arab women to make up for the wives he had left behind. One of them was said to be Zurra Qaddafy, Colonel Qaddafy's daughter, though the rumour continued that she had left him because her father thought Amin was becoming an alcoholic. Even Colonel Qaddafy found this too much to bear and Amin moved on to Jeddah, where, he said, the

Saudi Arabian monarch had invited him to do some sunbathing. He died in Saudi Arabia in 2003.

* * *

Amin was a fan of another cannibal, Emperor Jean Bokassa, who Amin claimed had 'put the Central African Republic on the world map'. He certainly did that.

Born in Bobangui, Lobay, Jean Bedel Bokassa joined the French army at the age of eighteen in 1939. He moved steadily through the ranks, and when the republic gained its independence in 1963, he was made commander-in-chief of the army. Two years later he led a coup overthrowing President David Dacko, annulled the constitution and made himself life president.

On 4 December, 1977, Jean Bedel Bokassa followed in the footsteps of his hero Napoleon and crowned himself Emperor in a lavish ceremony in Bangui, capital of what had been, until then, the Central African Republic.

The coronation of Bokassa I cost a third of the newly renamed Central African Empire's $70-million annual budget. For several days before the ceremony an inner circle of six hundred of the two thousand five hundred invited guests were treated to meals at leading restaurants. They were put in the best hotels or in special housing provided by the South African government at the Emperor's expense.

On the day of the coronation, Bokassa rode to the 'coronation palace' – Bangui's stadium – in a brand new coach drawn by fourteen of the sixteen imported Normany horses that had survived the shock of the climate change.

Bokassa wore an ankle-length tunic, a thirty-foot crimson velvet, gold-embroidered, ermine-trimmed mantle which weighed over 70lb, and shoes made of pearls. He walked up to the red-velvet imperial throne, which was trimmed with gold. The back was a huge gold eagle. Another gold eagle perched on the heavy crown which he raised to his own head. A sword was buckled on and, with an ebony staff in his hand, he swore a solemn oath to continue the Central African Empire's democratic evolution.

Empress Catherine, dressed in gold, knelt at his feet as he crowned her. She was a white woman and the favourite of his nine wives, who had between them presented him with fifty-four legitimate children. He had several illegitimate children too. While he was a sergeant in the French army, he had served in Indochina. As head of state, he sent word to Vietnam that the children he had had with local girls there should come to the Central African Republic. When a bunch of Vietnamese orphans turned up, Bokassa discovered that they probably were not his at all and they disappeared.

After the coronation, Emperor Bokassa and Empress Catherine rode in state to Notre Dame de Bangui where the archbishop consecrated the coronation with a High Mass. He bestowed the 'kiss of peace' on the newly crowned Emperor and the papal nuncio read personal greetings from the pope. After the Te Deum, Bokassa gave a banquet for four thousand guests, with French food of course. The language of the imperial court was French, rather than Sango, the local language. A French Navy band played waltzes. Bokassa I, in the uniform of a Marshal, and Empress Catherine, in a Parisian gown, opened the dancing.

At the end of the evening, the Emperor retired to his imperial abode at Berengo, about fifty kilometres from Bangui. But this was no Versailles. It looked more like a cheap motel in an army compound.

Two years later, there were widespread protests against imperial rule. Bokassa responded by killing a hundred schoolchildren and on 21 September, 1979, French troops deposed him and installed the former president, David Dacko, as head of state.

A search of Kologa Palace led to the discovery of human corpses stuffed with rice and prepared for eating.

Bokassa fled to his delightful eighteenth-century château near Paris. Stories in the French press about Bokassa's generous gift of diamonds worth £250,000 to President Valéry Giscard d'Estaing helped to lose him the presidential election in 1981.

Meanwhile, in Bokassa's absence, charges were made against him in the Central African Republic. These included conducting cannibalistic rites, procuring bodies for cannibalistic purposes, personally murdering seven out of as many as two hundred schoolchildren who went, missing following protests against him, and ordering the killing of numerous fellow ministers, politicians, officials and army officers.

Once Giscard d'Estaing was out of office, the French authorities revoked his asylum and Bokassa moved to the Ivory Coast. Fed up with living in exile, he adopted the pseudonym 'M. Christian Sole' and, wearing a white cassock and carrying a cross given to him by Pope John Paul II, went home to be tried.

He lost the case and was condemned to death, but the sentence was unaccountably commuted to ten years imprisonment. Released after seven in 1993, he now lives in straitened circumstances in Bangui.

Meanwhile, the French are chasing him for £300,000 in back taxes. To raise the money, he has had to sell his château to the National Fighters' Circle, a group of ultra-right-wing veterans of French colonial wars. The National Fighters' Circle, which is associated with Jean-Marie Le Pen's anti-immigration party, had been renting the château since Bokassa left France in 1986.

* * *

Fortunately things are not always so gruesome in Africa. In April 1995, Omar Bongo, President of the west African state of Gabon since 1967, was implicated in a good old-fashioned sex scandal when a routine Parisian court case involving allegations of prostitution erupted into an affair of international dimensions. Bongo, the court was told, was regularly supplied with prostitutes by the Italian couturier who also supplied his made-to-measure suits.

The trial of Francesco Smalto, the Paris-based menswear designer, became the setting for bizarre and extravagant allegations about the ferocious competition in the fashion world for free-spending celebrity clients. It also presented a wounding portrait of Bongo, a debonair autocrat who is reputed to be one of the wealthiest men in Africa.

According to evidence presented to a Paris tribunal, prostitutes were terrified of having sex with Bongo because he refused to wear a condom. Bongo was not represented in court, but his Paris lawyer and doctor denied the allegations.

Police interest in Smalto's activities stemmed from an investigation started two years earlier into a Paris network of les call-girls de luxe. The local vice squad found a link with a small fashion-related business run by a young woman named Laure Moerman, who supposedly supplied models for shows.

Several of the young women employed by Moerman told police that Smalto had hired them to take shipments of suits to Libreville, the Gabonese capital, where their duties apparently had more to do with removing Bongo's clothes.

In testimony read to the court by the presiding judge, a girl named Monica explained what happened on one trip: 'It went very badly that evening. Bongo didn't want to wear a condom, and as he had a friend who had died from Aids, I refused to make love to him.'

Another girl, Chantal, testified that she had been told the going rate with Bongo was £6,000 without a contraceptive and £1,200 if he had to wear one.

Having previously denied all knowledge of the affair, Smalto told the court that Bongo had been his best customer, spending £300,000 a year on suits and other clothes, and he had been frightened of losing him to a rival.

'We knew that President Bongo was sensitive to a feminine presence, and that is why I sent a girl on every trip,' Smalto said. 'I suspected that he kept her to sleep with, but I wasn't sure.'

Omar Bongo's appetite for luxury is legendary and this was not the first case in which his name has surfaced in the French courts. When Chaumet, the French society jeweller, ran into financial difficulties, Bongo was named in the firm's accounts as owing £500,000.

The case inflicted lasting damage on Smalto's reputation as 'the king of tailors and tailor to kings' after the transcript of a recorded telephone conversation between two prostitutes named Ariane and Sarah was read out.

'Marika telephoned me, she has to go to Libreville. I told her that's dramatic. His [Bongo's] friend died of the thing,' said Ariane.

'Aids? That's disgusting,' said Sarah.

'Yes, the worst is, a great couturier proposed it,' Ariane replied.

Gasps were heard in the Parisian court-room.

13

Atatürk – Father of a New Turkey

Kemal Atatürk is seen by many as a liberator. Certainly he was more liberal that the Sultan's regime that he overthrew in 1920. But Atatürk believed in modernization at all costs and this required a one-party state. When he did flirt with the idea of creating an opposition party in 1930, it proved so successful that he immediately crushed it. Opposition by ethnic minorities, such as the Kurds, was suppressed even more ruthlessly.

Besides, Atatürk openly acknowledged that he was a dictator. He was proud of it. When a French journalist wrote that Turkey was governed by one drunk (Atatürk was famous for liking a drink), one deaf man (Atatürk's prime minister) and three-hundred deaf-mutes (the chamber of deputies), Atatürk said: 'The man is mistaken. Turkey is governed by one drunk.'

At the age of twelve, Mustafa Kemal was sent to the military academy in the then Ottoman city of Salonika. He already loved uniforms and became one of a group of flashy dressers. Although he had entered a practically all-male world, he managed a small romance with a girl named Emine. She was the eight-year-old daughter of an official at the school. Years later she recalled how fastidiously he dressed and how, in her schoolgirl's eyes, she believed he was destined to become sultan. However, they were kept apart by Muslim custom and barely did anything beyond look at each other longingly through the window of her house as he passed by.

Kemal was incredibly jealous when his widowed mother remarried. He searched for a pistol to scare her new husband but, fortunately, did not find one until they were safely out of reach. He did not see her again until he finished his military training.

At fourteen, he moved on to an academy at Monastir. Before he went, a friend gave him a knife to defend himself against the sexual interest of other men. Women were still behind the veil and pretty young boys like Kemal were much in demand. Occasionally, he would travel back to Salonika to see Emine. Her sister recalled that they planned to marry, but nothing came of it.

On his vacations in Salonika, he enjoyed visiting the European quarter where women were unveiled and sang and danced and sat at tables with men. He enjoyed drinking and the women there found this handsome young soldier irresistible.

Later he was posted to Istanbul, where he became a regular visitor at the home of Madame Corinne, an Italian widow who lived in Pera, a Westernized district of the city. When he went to Sofia as military attaché, he wrote to her constantly, assuring her that there were no pretty women there. However, his letters are strewn with mentions of women he had met – each and every one, he stressed, was not beautiful. One woman he did not mention was a German nurse called Hildegarde. When he moved on, he began corresponding with Hildegarde too.

In Sofia, he became the favourite of society hostess Sultane Rasha Petroff. One night, at a masked ball, he met Dimitriana 'Miti' Kovachev, daughter of the Bulgarian Minister of War. They danced and talked all night. Soon Kemal was a regular visitor to the Kovachev household where Turkish was often spoken. He was also allowed to take Miti out on the town without a chaperone. In Turkey at that time, no young lady from a good family would be allowed out with a young man.

Miti was Kemal's ideal European bride, but there was the problem of religion. Kemal consulted his friend Fethi, who was wooing the daughter of General Ratcho Petroff. When the question of marriage came up, General Petroff said: 'I would rather cut my head off than have my daughter marry a Turk.'

General Kovachev also put his foot down. Marriage was out of the question. Miti was a Christian; Kemal a Muslim. To make his feelings abundantly plain, General Kovachev even refused to attend a diplomatic ball at the Ottoman embassy.

The beginning of World War I saw Kemal recalled to Istanbul. After showing great bravery at Gallipoli, Kemal returned to Sofia. He and Miti were plainly still in love, but convention demanded they be no more than polite to each other. Four years later, she tried to visit him in Istanbul, but the collapse of the Bulgarian front made the journey impossible. She married a Bulgarian deputy, but continued to follow the astonishing career of her young Turk.

Kemal had a reconciliation with his mother after she split from her second husband. After his death, her husband's young sister, Fikriye, came to live with her, and Kemal took her as his mistress. Kemal's mother disapproved heartily. Fikriye was not nearly good enough for her son.

Although she was technically married to an Egyptian, she lived with Kemal in the Sisli district of Istanbul. This did not prevent him from continuing his relationship with Corinne. After the British occupied Istanbul, Corinne's house was searched for weapons. Kemal had fled to Anatolia, where began the struggle for independence.

Fikriye followed him there, where she lived openly as his mistress. She wanted to be his wife, but although he loved her dearly he would not hear of it. He wanted a Western-style marriage to a woman who could stand beside him. Although she kept her face unveiled, Fikriye was an oriental woman who would always walk behind. Besides, as a Pasha, his first wife should be a virgin. The dark, slender Fikriye was already, technically, married. Nevertheless, she would do for the present. Having her with him on the campaign would keep him away from the promiscuous women who hung around the garrison with whom he had entertained himself before.

The campaign to liberate Turkey ended with the burning of Smyrna. While Atatürk was there, a young woman came to his headquarters and asked to see him. He refused, then thought he might take a look. When he saw her, he dismissed his orderly and asked her to sit down.

Her name was Latife and she was the daughter of Ushakizade Muammer, a rich Smyrniot with interests in shipping and international commerce. Although Latife was a Turk with olive skin and large dark eyes, she had studied law in Europe and spoke French like a Frenchwoman. Her parents were spending the summer in Biarritz, but she had returned to Turkey to help his cause. Like many Turkish women, she wore his picture in a locket around her neck. In Atatürk's mind, this fuelled the fantasy that she was in love with him.

She lived in a large house outside the city and invited Kemal and his staff to stay there. She even threw a formal reception for him. But she would not go to bed with him. This puzzled Kemal who, as a liberator of his country, was used to willing, eager women. But Latife was determined to become his wife, not just his mistress. When he left Smyrna for Ankara at the end of the month, she still had not succumbed.

Kemal wrote to Latife. Now he was head of state, he needed a wife, he said, and she seemed to fit the bill. She visited Ankara. Kemal's ailing mother died while she was there, but, nevertheless, Kemal asked Latife to marry him at once. The following day, they married in European style in her father's house. In an Islamic marriage, the bride and groom do not see each other until after the ceremony. Kemal and Latife broke with tradition and took their vows seated together at a table.

Kemal took his new wife on a honeymoon tour, using her as an example in his campaign to emancipate Turkish women. This was how women should be treated, he said, indicating Latife standing beside him in breeches. When women offered to put her up, he insisted that his wife stay with him. There was to be an end to the harem and the separation of the sexes.

Flaunting his new wife in such an unseemly manner provided ammunition for the traditionalists among his opponents – especially when Latife appeared in low-cut gowns at gala events.

At the time of the wedding, Fikriye was away in Germany in a sanatorium. The hardships of his military campaign had left her with tuberculosis. The first she heard of the marriage was in the newspaper. She returned to Turkey and stayed with Kemal and his new bride at Chankaya for four days in the summer of 1923. Then she returned to Ankara and checked into a hotel. A few days later, she went to see Kemal at the presidential palace, but was refused admission. She drove back to her hotel and shot herself with a pistol she had bought in Germany. The shot did not kill her immediately, but she died soon after in hospital.

The guilt that Kemal felt over Fikriye's death made married life impossible. Kemal and Latife clung together for the next two years, but on 5 August, 1925, the marriage was dissolved. Latife went to live in Istanbul, though would be discreetly out of town if Kemal visited the city. In 1933, he was given the name Atatürk – Father of the Turks – by the National Assembly. He continued his heavy drinking and died of cirrhosis of the liver in 1938. Latife outlived him by thirty-eight years.

14

Playboy of the Western World

King Farouk of Egypt was a failed dictator, though his reputation was worse than many who succeeded. He was an ally of the Nazis, a war profiteer, an insatiable glutton, a ruthless seducer, a profligate gambler, a kleptomaniac and a wastrel. If there were seven deadly sins, it was said, Farouk would find an eighth.

After ascending the Egyptian throne in 1936 at the age of sixteen, he was kept in power by the British. He detested this arrangement. Not only did Farouk like to see himself as an all-powerful king with Egypt the dominant force in the Arab world, but also, ultimately, as the caliph of all Islam. In 1941, he made little secret of the fact that he hoped the Germans would invade and kick the British out. However, when the British finally withdrew their support from his regime in 1952, his anti-British army officers Gamal Abdel Nasser and Anwar Sadat – who had spent three years in jail during World War II for plotting a pro-Nazi take-over – ousted Farouk in an effortless coup.

Even before he was ousted, Farouk could not exert any real power. All he could do was indulge his whims. He once issued a decree banning any of his subjects from owning a red car. Then he had his hundred or so royal cars sprayed red.

In 1938, at the age of eighteen, Farouk married the beautiful seventeen-year-old Safinez Zulficar. It was a marriage made in hell. Farouk was a virgin who had been cossetted in the harem by his mother, Queen Nazli, whereas Safinez was a manhunter. Queen Nazli had no shortage of fun herself. At the time of Farouk's wedding, she began a celebrated affair with her son's tutor, Ahmed Mohammed Hasanein, a famous soldier, scholar and explorer. Then she took up with a young diplomat, a Coptic Christian named Riad Ghali, who she married off to her daughter, Farouk's little sister. The three of them moved to Beverley Hills, where they lived together. It all became too much for Farouk when mother and daughter converted from Islam to Catholicism. He confiscated their lands and banished them from Egypt forever.

Still a naive young romantic, Farouk changed his new bride's name legally to Farida, which means 'the only one'. She did not return the compliment and began taking lovers.

Hurt by his wife's infidelity, Farouk began taking lovers too. One of the first was Fatima Toussoun, the wife of Farouk's cousin, Prince Hassan Toussoun, who threw herself at the young king. He could not resist the fair-skinned Circassian. They met for moonlit trysts at a small palace on the Nile at Halwan. Give me a son, he told Fatima, and I will marry you.

229

Farouk began suffering bouts of impotence from the age of twenty-three, and was believed to have under-developed genitals. To conceal this fact, he created for himself the image of a virile and insatiable lover. He invoked the *droit du roi* over the most beautiful wives and daughters of his subjects and claimed to have in-timate contact with over five thousand women in his lifetime. He gave Farida a present every morning, but that did not compensate for what he was unable to do at night.

He consulted hormone specialists and became a con-noisseur of aphrodisiacs. Love potions used in the time of the pharaohs were concocted. He tried ampheta-mines, hash mixed with honey, caffeine tablets and powdered rhino horn. He consumed vast quantities of oysters and eggs. Pigeons and mangoes were also cures for impotence, he believed. He put on pounds. Every morning in his bathroom, which was decorated with a mosaic showing naked slave girls, he was massaged vigor-ously by his chambermaids in an attempt to shed some weight.

Meanwhile, he flirted with attractive women. Those who would not succumb, he kidnapped. They were taken to one of his 'harems' in the five palaces he owned around the country. Married women were more of a problem. Husbands often caused trouble if he kid-napped their wives. Instead he would resort to blackmail to get them into bed.

He would go through phases, collecting different types of women – the same way he collected stamps and antiquities. His aide, Antonio Pulli, would be sent out to find him European chorus girls who may be in need of the 'diamond' bracelets he liked to bestow on his conquests. Or Pulli would be sent to comb the upper-class brothels for fair-skinned girls. Farouk went through a belly dancer phase, going through the top stars in the country.

One of the most attractive of his consorts at this time was an Alexandrian Jewess, Irene Guinle. Farouk never let race, religion or politics stand in the way of pleasure. They met when they were both twenty-one. Farouk was still slim and handsome then. Their affair lasted two years.

The daughter of a cotton broker, Irene spoke six languages. At seventeen, she had been discovered by a scout for MGM at the Alexandria Sporting Club. She took part in a lot of sport and had an athletic body with an especially well-developed bosom. But her mother would not hear of her becoming an actress. She considered them little better than whores. Instead, Irene was married off to Loris Najjar, an English-educated Alexandrian Jew who was about twenty-nine.

Unfortunately, Najjar had picked up certain predilections from his English public school. On their wedding night, he opened an attaché case and produced a cane and a pair of black patent-leather high-heeled shoes. Irene ran from their Cairo hotel in horror. He found her cowering behind the pyramids and dragged her back to their room. He forced her to beat him until he bled, then scrape the high heels down his cuts. She had to do it three times a day.

'Everybody does it this way,' he told his young bride.

The whole thing sickened her. She became ill and her hair began to fall out. Irene was naive and believed that marriage was for life. It was only four years later that she discovered she could get a divorce. After Najjar, Farouk came as a welcome relief.

They met at a charity ball in aid of the war effort in 1941, when the German forces were posted on the Libyan border and seemed unstoppable. Although the assignation had been arranged by a mutual friend who knew how unhappy Farouk's fairy-tale marriage had become, Irene avoided him.

'I was allergic to anyone pro-German,' she said.

Eventually, he cornered her by the gambling tables. Suddenly Irene found that she was winning every bet. Then she felt as if someone was looking down her dress. She turned around and there was Farouk, grinning like a Cheshire cat. Attendants quickly brought a gilded throne for him to sit on. He gave it to Irene and sat on a small chair beside her.

He asked her to come for a moonlight dip. She refused and got up to go, but as she made her way to the door, she was approached by the British Ambassador, Sir Miles Lampson. With British control of Egypt and the Suez canal in jeopardy, it was vital that they kept the pro-Nazi King Farouk under their wing.

'Of course you must go swimming with him at the palace,' Lampson said. 'You must.'

She only consented because she hated the Germans – and still she played hard to get. She sent Farouk's Rolls-Royce to her home to fetch her swim-suit. On the long beach at Montazah, Irene changed into her swimming costume and plunged into the warm sea. Farouk, in full military regalia, sat on the sand in the jasmine-scented air and watched. Afterwards she went to the bathhouse in the Palladian temple to change. She had left her

sandals on the beach and sent Farouk back for them.
After that, the Rolls took her home.

He called her at ten o'clock the next morning and
asked if he could see her. She refused, saying she did not
like men with beards. This was a deliberate ploy on her
part. Farouk's newly grown beard allied him with the
militant Muslim Brotherhood, who also wanted the British out of Egypt.

The fact that Irene was Jewish did not bother Farouk.
In fact, it rather counted in her favour. His father, Fuad,
had a Jewish mistress, Mrs Suarez, for twenty years. She
even arranged his first marriage for him to his nineteen-
year-old cousin, Princess Shivekar. The princess was one
of the wealthiest women in Egypt. Fuad had crippling
gambling debts and Mrs Suarez steered the princess's
money into investments with her Jewish friends, who
turned an already great fortune into a vast one. Mrs
Suarez also pressured the British into putting Fuad on
the throne, even though he was not, strictly speaking,
next in line of succession. She died in his arms, waltzing
at a ball, and he spent the rest of his life mourning
her.

After months of pressure from both Farouk and
Lampson, Irene eventually consented to go out on a
date with him. She wore a black dress that was so
complicated to undo that she was confident the king
would not get anywhere near her.

They ate a ten-course dinner, featuring oysters, pi-
geon and sea bass cooked by a French chef. It was served
by four Sudanese waiters in his huge bedroom over-
looking the sea. From the conversation, she soon realized that Farouk had had his spies checking up on her.
He knew every intimate detail of her marriage. She also

realized that he was like a child and she could control him.

She reached home around 12.30 a.m. Ten minutes later he called. He wanted to see her again. For two months, they saw each other regularly, but nothing happened.

He invited her to stay the weekend with him at the Abdine Palace. When she arrived, his servants took her suitcase to his bedroom. They were to sleep in the same bed. She asked him if it was all right if she slept naked. It was too hot to wear a nightgown. He said he did not mind if she did not. Then he kissed her goodnight chastely on the cheek and the two of them slept together naked.

Next day they went swimming in the palace's indoor pool, naked. But there was no sex. After her nightmare marriage, Irene was rather relieved.

Farouk told Irene that he loved her. Fatima Toussoun had just given birth to a baby girl at the time and Irene asked about their relationship. Farouk said that he had sent her a pearl necklace in hospital, but had not gone to visit her.

Farouk began to take Irene out publicly and she became his official mistress. But he refused to accompany her to pro-British events.

Eventually she became his mistress in the physical sense and he shaved his beard off for her. In return, he wanted her to convert to Islam and gave her a jewelled Koran, which she studied. In the street, people would shout 'Long live Irene' at her and Irene became queen of Egypt in all but name. Farida was wheeled out only on state occasions. Otherwise Irene would be seen everywhere with him. The only person who disapproved was

Irene's mother, who asked her to move out of the family's apartment.

Irene spent most of her time in the Abdine Palace, which had five hundred rooms. Farida and Farouk's other women were kept in the harem, but Irene stayed with Farouk in his apartment.

While Irene kept Farouk entertained, pro-German demonstrations on the streets reached fever pitch. The pro-British Egyptian prime minister was forced to resign but Lampson was determined to pick his successor. He surrounded the Abdine Palace with tanks, shot the locks off the palace gates and led troops up the grand staircase to Farouk's study. There he presented the king with articles of abdication. Farouk could either sign them, or approve Lampson's new prime minister. He had no choice.

By 1943, the German threat had receded and their affair rather lost its urgency. Farouk and Irene went to Farouk's hunting lodge at an oasis south of Cairo, with Humphrey Barker – who Irene believed to be the 'bastard son of the king of England' – and his attractive companion, Barbara Skelton. One evening, Irene saw Humphrey drinking alone. She went upstairs to Farouk's bedroom and found the door locked. She pounded on it until Farouk opened the door. Inside, Irene saw Barbara in their giant bed.

'I hope you find my bed comfortable,' Irene said.

The next morning, Farouk, Irene and Barbara had breakfast together. When a second round of croissants was brought out, Irene said to Barbara: 'What a shame you won't have time to finish. You have just been called back to Cairo.'

Irene had ordered the servants to pack Barbara's bag and she was hustled off into the car.

'What have you done?' Farouk complained. 'She was an incredible woman, fantastic.'

Irene refused to speak to him for the rest of the day. Back in Cairo, she went to stay with a friend. As she departed, Farouk promised to make her queen of Egypt. She would have his son and heir.

Soon after, she met Percival Bailey, a British officer, and they embarked on a whirlwind romance. Farouk would follow them around like a wounded puppy. If they went out to dinner or dancing, he would leave his pith helmet or his walking stick on their table, so they would know he had been there. After six weeks they married. This gave Irene a British passport. With an Egyptian passport alone, she would never have been able to get out of the country.

Before she left for England, Farouk's aide, Antonio Pulli, came to see her. He told her that she was the only woman that Farouk had ever loved. Now she was leaving, he was afraid that the king was dying. He did not eat and did nothing but lay in bed all day.

She went to see him one last time and found him in a rage. If she left Egypt, he said, he would never allow her to return. He threatened to declare war on the Jews.

'I'll lose my hair. I'll lose my eyesight. I'll only go with whores. I'll spend the rest of my life gambling,' he ranted. And that is very much what he did.

She left for England and went to live in Sutton Place, the home of her husband's aunt, the Duchess of Sutherland. Later, it was the home of oil-billionaire J. Paul Getty. After divorcing Bailey, Irene Guinle went on to marry a Brazilian millionaire.

Although Irene thought that she had seen off Barbara Skelton, the affair was more enduring. Barbara first saw King Farouk in Marseilles when he was sixteen. She was on her way to India with her Uncle Dudley. During World War II, she was sent to Egypt as a Foreign Office cypher clerk. She caught his eye one evening in a night club. Next day an equerry visited her with an invitation to go to Fayoum for the weekend. After that she began seeing him once a week.

Irene was his official mistress at this time and Barbara conceded that she was a great beauty. But Barbara continued seeing Farouk because he was so much more interesting than the British officers she was surrounded by.

Later, when Barbara Skelton became a novelist, she wrote a thinly fictionalized account of her time in the Abdine Palace. She talks of roof-top champagne parties with nude belly dancers who had their pubis shaved, the king going off to his bedroom with the pick of the pretty girls, and of the king beating her with a dressing gown cord. In her diaries, she admits she would have preferred a splayed cane.

She accompanied him to balls in haute couture gowns that he provided. The British authorities thought that she and the king were getting a little too close and feared that he might be pumping her for secret information. So they posted her home.

Barbara later married the writer Cyril Connolly and publisher George Weidenfeld. Her other lovers included poet Peter Quennell, critic Kenneth Tynan, cartoonist Charles Addams, film producer John Sutro, editor Robert Silvers, Françoise Sagan and Bernard Frank.

* * *

Eleven years of marriage to Farida had produced three daughters. Despite her own infidelity, Farida became increasingly distressed by women scampering up the backstairs to entertain the king until dawn. When a famous French opera singer was seen leaving his bedroom, Farida asked for a divorce. He consented. He wanted the chance to have a son.

In 1949, Princess Patricia 'Honeychile' Wilder Hohenlohe, a genuine American princess, turned up in Egypt. Born in Georgia, she was a former star of the *Bob Hope Show*. Her ex-husband was Austrian Prince Alexander Hohenlohe, but Honeychile had kept the title – and a lot else besides – after the divorce. She boasted of Hollywood romances with Clark Gable and Tyrone Power, both of whom she threw over for her riding teacher. She also claimed to have had sex with John F. Kennedy in a dank air-raid shelter in London early in World War II. Now, despite the presence of her current, polo-playing, Argentinian husband, she was to have Farouk too.

They met in a Cairo club and Honeychile flirted with him simply to pique her philandering husband. It worked. Soon her Argentine consort went big game hunting in India, while Honeychile moved into the Abdine Palace with the king.

Honeychile had delusions that she could exchange her 'Princess' for 'Queen', but Farouk had already decided to marry a plump little commoner. He had met sixteen-year-old Narriman Sadek in a jewellers shop where she had been choosing an engagement ring with her former fiancé. When Farouk flattered her with his

238

attentions she realized that she had hit the jackpot and unceremoniously dumped her beau.

Before the wedding, Farouk set out on a three-month bachelor party. Prostitutes from across Europe flocked to join his ever-swelling entourage. Barbara Skelton joined him at Biarritz. Later, she introduced her husband Cyril Connolly to him in Rome, but they did not get on.

Narriman's royal wedding was so opulent that it could have come straight out of the Arabian Nights. It was followed by a four-month honeymoon in Europe – probably one of the most lavish and expensive honeymoons in history. He overwhelmed her with gourmet food, couture clothes, expensive jewels and priceless art. They stayed at the Royal Monçeau in Paris, the Danieli in Venice and the Carlton in Cannes. When they went out on the royal yacht, he dressed the entire party of sixty in identical blue blazers, white flannels and yachting caps. Ashore they were ferried around in a fleet of Rolls-Royces. One can only wonder what Narriman, a peasant girl, made of all this.

Farouk was no more faithful to Narriman than he had been to his first wife. He had the entire top floor of the Mossat Hospital in Alexandria turned into the ultimate bachelor pad, staffed with beautiful nurses.

However, Narriman did provide the son he craved and followed him into exile in 1952. He left behind a vast collection of pornography – blue films, magazines, books, cards and watches and clocks whose moving parts were decorated with, well, moving parts. The new regime sold it off, along with his stamp collection, and raised more than a million dollars.

Ex-King Farouk established himself in Rome and squandered his dwindling fortune on the life of the ultimate playboy. He was the darling of the paparazzi and the papers were filled with his lurid escapades and jet-set lovers. But despite his dissolute lifestyle, he still had one great love left in him.

He met sixteen-year-old aspiring actress Irma Minutolo at Canzone del Mare, the Capri beach club owned by Gracie Fields, the British music-hall star. She had big eyes, big lips and big breasts, which were shown off to great advantage in the bikini she was wearing.

Farouk spotted her emerging from the water. His eyes locked onto her. Abandoning his companions, he sauntered over to her, wearing a white terry cloth robe with the Egyptian crown emblazoned on it.

He took off the dark glasses that had become his trademark, stroked her reddish-blonde hair and complimented her on her figure. She immediately fell under the spell of his blue-green eyes. His huge girth, his balding head and his glasses, she recalled, suited him as a king. They made him less of a boy.

That night, Irma won the Miss Capri contest. The next morning Farouk had a hundred and fifty roses delivered to the hotel where she was staying with her mother. They had planned to stay the whole month but when the roses arrived, Signora Capece Minutolo grabbed her teenaged daughter and high-tailed it back to Naples.

Farouk was not to be put off so easily. He had her address traced and began sending her huge bouquets of flowers every day. Irma's mother forbade her to answer the phone, but one day it rang while Mama was out in the garden and she answered it. It was Farouk. How had she liked the flowers, he asked. What flowers, she said. So Farouk got right to the point. He told her that he was in love with her and that she was the only ray of light in the darkness of his exile.

Suddenly the phonecalls and the flowers stopped. Irma was heartbroken. Her mother had made her so ashamed of the flirtation that she did not even dare tell her schoolfriends.

About a month later, Irma came out of school to find that the car that normally took her home was not waiting for her. Down the street, she spotted an emerald-green Rolls-Royce with the Egyptian flag flying from the antenna. A man in a dark suit came up to her. He was King Farouk's secretary, he said. Would she follow him?

He led her to the Rolls-Royce. In the backseat was Farouk, wearing an elegant pin-striped suit. Where was her driver, she asked. That was all taken care off, Farouk said. He would be back in fifteen minutes.

Farouk reached over and stroked her hair, and he told her again that he loved her. What about the thousands of women he had had, she said, repeating what her mother had told her. Farouk laughed. They meant nothing to him, he said. She was the only one who had won his heart. Would she be his third Queen?

Irma burst into tears. She flung open the car door and ran. A little way down the street, she found her car and begged her driver to take her home. They struck a deal. If he said nothing, neither would she.

Irma heard no more for two weeks. Then, during school break, the caretaker told her that there was a call for her in his office. It was Farouk. He told her that the following day a dozen roses would arrive for her. She must examine them closely. He gave her the number of

the Villa Dusmet at Grottaferrata in the Alban Hills
outside Rome where he was staying.

The next day, the caretaker called Irma into his office.
The roses had arrived. She examined them carefully and
found that one of them was imitation. She opened it and
inside was a ruby ring, encrusted with diamonds.

With a shaking hand she called the number she had
been given. She was passed through three secretaries
before she got to speak to Farouk himself. She told him
that he should not have bought her such an expensive
gift. Of course he should, he said.

'But why me?' Irma wanted to know.

'Because you are different,' he said. 'Because you are
a child. Because you are pure. Because I adore you.'

Then he asked her to promise that she would think of
him for an hour every day until he returned to Naples in
a fortnight. Not only did she think of him for an hour
every day, she thought about him twenty-four hours a
day. She devoured everything about him in the Italian
newspapers and magazines, though it hurt her to see
pictures of him out in nightclubs with actresses and
Swedish blondes.

Around this time, Farouk was seeing the voluptuous
eighteen-year-old Swede Brigitta Stenberg, former lover
of Lucky Luciano, the American mobster who had been
deported back to Italy in 1946. Luciano and Farouk also
met at Gracie Fields' Canzone del Mare. They had a lot
in common – both were in exile, both had known great
power, and both loved beautiful women. Luciano provided Farouk with protection on numerous occasions
when Nasser, ever fearful that the Western powers
would try to re-install Farouk on the throne, was out to
kill him. Luciano knew every hit man in Italy. No plot

could be hatched without him knowing about it and he thwarted Nasser at every turn.

Luciano met Brigitta just as she was picked up by a Sicilian–American who said he had a job for her in New York. The man gave her a ticket to New York with a stopover in Buenos Aires and took her passport for safekeeping. Luciano told her that the man was a white slaver; the stop-over would be a permanent one. He got her passport back.

Farouk had seen Brigitta out with Luciano a couple of times when he spotted her in a restaurant in Rome with a young friend from the U.S. embassy. He introduced himself and they spent an hour talking before he dropped her off home in his bullet-proof Mercedes. Farouk made a deal with Luciano to take her off his hands.

Brigitta liked Farouk because of his 'sweet eyes' and because he had the power of life and death over twenty million people. He liked her, he said, because she reminded him of Narriman.

Despite Farouk's attempts to keep pictures of himself and Brigitta out of the papers, the paparazzi always got through. Brigitta loved seeing the pictures in the papers. Irma did not.

Irma also had to worry about Farouk's wife who was always there in the background, but the stories about Narriman gave her hope. When Farouk had met Narriman, she too had been a commoner, sixteen, blonde and a virgin.

When Farouk returned to Naples, Irma left school early and took a train to the fishing port of Posilipo. They met in the private room of a restaurant there. When they parted, Farouk gave her a letter. In it, he poured out his heart. She took it home and read it over and over again.

After that, there was another long period of silence. Then, in March 1953, the newspapers broke the story that Narriman had left Farouk. She planned to fly back to Cairo, obtain an Islamic divorce and sue for custody of their fourteen-month-old son, Fuad.

Farouk blamed the new regime in Egypt for the break-up of his marriage. They had used 'that most powerful of all weapons, the mother-in-law,' he told the press. Narriman's mother, he described publicly as 'the most terrible woman in the world'.

The break-up of Farouk's marriage would certainly have been to the advantage of Egypt's revolutionary regime. Farouk had been deposed, but the monarchy had not yet been abolished. So little Fuad was techni-cally King of Egypt and the Sudan. Under Islamic law, a child should live with its mother until it is seven years old.

A few weeks later, Irma got another call from Farouk in the caretaker's office. He asked her to come and live with him. To Irma, this was tantamount to a proposal.

To her old-world father, it was an outrageous sugges-tion, but her mother's opposition to Farouk began to wane. She could see how lovesick her daughter was. She was impressed by the ruby ring he had given her and, although Farouk now claimed to be poor, he was known to be one of the richest men in the world.

That summer, Signora Capece Minutolo told her husband that Irma should go away to a language school in Rome to brush up her French. Signor Capece Minu-tolo said Irma's French did not need improving. So

Signora Capece Minutolo said perhaps Irma would benefit from a summer with the Sisters of the Sacred Heart in their Convent near the Spanish steps in Rome. Her husband agreed.

He was busy the day that Irma left, so he could not take her to the railway station in Naples. She was picked up there by Farouk's Rolls-Royce and whisked back to his villa at Grottaferrata.

She was given a wing to herself with a huge marble bathroom remodelled to look like one in a Rita Hayworth movie that Irma had once casually remarked that she had seen. She was taught deportment, music, literature and how to ride. Top couturiers and furriers were summoned to dress Irma for her forthcoming 'début'. This was to take place on Rome's Via Veneto, the home of la dolce vita where Farouk and Irma soon became king and queen of the nightclub crowd.

Farouk was constantly surrounded by beautiful women, but Irma smothered her jealousy and he never left her wanting for attention. At dawn the whole entourage would return to the Villa Dusmet. He would kiss her chastely on the hand and she would retire to her wing, not to see him until nine o'clock the next evening when the whole thing would start all over again.

With this sort of lifestyle, Irma was bound to attract attention, especially wearing the décolleté gowns he bought her. Soon the Italians were calling her 'Irma Capace de Totalo' – 'Irma, Capable of Anything'.

Within a month, she was on the front page of every scandal sheet in Italy. Her father was furious. Farouk, gallantly, went to Naples to see her family. Why hadn't Farouk asked permission before taking his daughter away, asked her father. Because you would have locked her in a convent forever, Farouk replied.

Now that Irma was Farouk's official mistress, Brigitta Stenberg decided to make the break. She did not want to be his backstreet mistress permanently. As a going away present, Brigitta offered him the current Miss Universe, a Finnish girl named Armi Kuusia who had worked for her aunt. Brigitta said she would write to Armi to find out if she was interested.

Brigitta Stenberg returned to Sweden where she used her early experiences with Luciano and Farouk as a springboard to launch a successful career as a novelist.

Farouk took Irma away on a year-and-a-half tour of Europe, introducing her to stars, socialites and royalty. They even dined with Honeychile Hohenlohe in Kitzbühel, though Farouk walked out because he believed that the English woman sat next to him was an agent of Nasser's out to poison him.

His demands on Irma were minimal. When they travelled, they would always stay in separate suites. Back in Rome, he rented her an apartment in his block, but only saw her once or twice a week. When she expressed an interest in becoming an opera singer, he paid for her singing lessons and he staged a triumphant début for her in Naples. But he stopped taking her to clubs and never took her gambling.

He did not stop going out himself of course. The novelist Gore Vidal remembers one night out with Farouk on the Via Veneto. The fat ex-king was sucking the nipple of a prostitute when a thief on a motor scooter snatched her purse. Farouk laughed, went on sucking her nipple, then gave her enough money to make up for what she had lost.

Through the newspapers and magazines, Irma knew he was seeing other women – Vidal dubbed them 'chubby chasers'. But Farouk refused to discuss his other women and Irma remained convinced that she was the only one he really loved. He was more jealous than Othello, she said. When she took the Rolls for a drive down to the beach at Anzio without telling him, she discovered that half the police in Italy were looking for her. Another time a chauffeur made eyes at her. He was swiftly sacked.

Although he continued his philandering ways, they remained friends until his death, at the age of 45. The grossly overweight Farouk was in a restaurant with his latest girlfriend, the voluptuous blonde Annamaria Gatti, the night he died. He had collected her himself that night from her tenement flat on the Via Ostiense. Bodyguards were a thing of the past. He was driving a Fiat 2300 with diplomatic plates. The Rolls had been sold. They drove to a roadhouse called the Ile de France out on the Via Aurilia Antica for a midnight supper. Farouk consumed a dozen raw oysters with tabasco sauce, a lobster thermidor, a roast baby lamb with roast potatoes, a creamy chestnut Monte Bianco, two oranges and two large bottles of mineral water with a Coca-Cola chaser. He lit a Havana cigar – another of his trade marks – then suddenly clutched his throat and collapsed over the table. Everyone thought he was playing one of his famous practical jokes. When they realized that he wasn't, it was too late. He was dead before he reached the hospital.

Many royalist expatriates believe he was poisoned, but, at nearly twenty-two stone, he was grossly overweight and suffered from high blood pressure. The death certificate said the cause of death was a cerebral haemorrhage. There was no autopsy and no inquest.

When he died, Farouk was carrying two U.S. thousand-dollar bills, a wad of 10,000-lire notes, a gold pill-box containing his blood-pressure tablets and a 6.35 Biretta that he carried to protect himself from assassination attempts. Soon after, his companion Annamaria Gatti disappeared.

At the funeral in 1965, Irma was allowed to walk behind the coffin with his first wife Farida and their daughters. After thirteen years as his official mistress, Irma had been accepted as the third queen. She went on to achieve fame as the oversexed opera singer in Franco Zeffirelli's 1988 movie *Young Toscanini*, playing opposite Elizabeth Taylor.

15

The Peacock Throne

The last Shah of Iran learnt many of his tricks from his father, Reza Khan. Reza Khan's first wife, Taj al-Moluk, was a strong woman who put up with his extramarital affairs. She presented him with twins – the Shah and his sister Ashraf.

In 1922, Reza Khan was having a very public affair with Aziz Khanom, the darling of wealthy Tehranis in the 1920s. He soon realized that this affair could damage him politically, and took advantage of Islamic law to make Aziz his second wife. Even though Aziz looked up to her as the senior wife, Taj al-Moluk refused to have her under the same roof.

To make things worse, later that year Reza Khan took a third wife, Turan Khanom, the daughter of the Qatar prince Majd ad-Dowleh, who bore him a son. But he divorced her after barely a year.

The following year, he fulfilled his Islamic quota with a fourth wife, sixteen-year-old Esmat Khanom, another Qatar princess. Reza Khan borrowed money from his in-laws to build a new home, and towards the end of 1923, he moved in with Esmat, visiting Taj al-Moluk, his first wife, for just two nights a week. This was not a formula for marital accord.

'To think, I wasted my youth and beauty on you,' she would say; but there was little she could do. By all accounts, Esmat was Reza Khan's true love. She bore him four sons and one daughter. But Taj al-Moluk was the mother of his first-born son and heir. Divorce was unthinkable.

In 1925, Reza Khan seized power and was named Shahanshah – King of Kings. In 1939, he made the mistake of siding with Hitler. Tehran was on a vital supply route to Russia, so the British deposed Reza Khan and put his son on the throne instead.

The Shah's first marriage had been arranged for him by his father. The girl in question was Fawziah, the seventeen-year-old sister of King Farouk. She was a great beauty. Educated in Switzerland, she had been presented at most of the courts of Europe, including that of St James's. The idea of going to a comparatively backward country like Iran did not please her. Farouk, however, was delighted at the prospect of making a diplomatic alliance with Persia in the age-old fashion. He was already negotiating to marry his other two sisters off to King Faisal of Iraq and Crown Prince Talal of Jordan, with the aim of building a pan-Arabic alliance.

The couple only met once before the wedding in the Abdine Palace in Cairo. Then they had to wait until after a second ceremony in Tehran before they could consummate it. Just getting Fawziah to Tehran was an ordeal. She had over two hundred items of luggage, taking with her two hundred dresses, one hundred and sixty pairs of shoes, seven fur coats and vast quantities of jewellery. Her wedding dress alone cost £10,000.

The following year, Fawziah gave birth to a baby daughter, Shahnaz. However, the marriage was not a happy one. Fawziah was quickly bored with Tehran. She would linger in bed until noon, spend a couple of hours dressing, then while away the rest of the day playing cards or going for a drive. After 1942, she lived in a separate apartment and seldom spent the night with her husband. The Shah complained that she constantly found excuses to shirk what he called her 'marital duty' and members of the court called her 'the frigid Venus'.

The Shah began to court other women, and when Fawziah received anonymous notes telling her this, she responded in kind. There were rumours that the Shah's half brother, Prince Gholam-Reza, was in love with Fawziah. Then word spread that she was seeing Taqi Emami, a local tennis pro. Emami soon found himself banished from the court and forbidden to leave the country.

One of the Shah's closest aides brought the matter to a head. One evening, he took the Queen to a small villa in the palace grounds where she found the Shah in a compromising position with society beauty Pari Khanom. The Shah made a half-hearted attempt to give an innocent account of the scene. Fawziah ran back to her apartments, locked the door and cried for hours.

In 1945, Fawziah returned to Cairo. The Shah granted her a divorce in 1948, but cited her infidelity rather than admitting his own. Five months later, Fawziah married Esma'il Shirin, the nephew of Farouk's favourite mistress.

For more than a year, members of the Shah's family scoured the world in search of a new bride. His twin sister Ashraf came up with a girl called Nina Bakhtiar; but two of his other sisters, the Princesses Shams and Fatemah, had plans of their own. Both were eager to get back into favour. Princess Shams had been banished after divorcing her husband and marrying the son of an army musician, and Fatemah had married an American adventurer named Patrick Hilliyer against the Shah's expressed orders. They found an eighteen-year-old girl called Soraya in London. She was living in a bedsit in Kensington and attending a private English language school. Her photograph was sent to Tehran and the Shah decided to have her checked out.

Soraya was the daughter of Khalil Esfandi, a minor tribal chief, and Eva Karl, who had been born in Moscow of German and Baltic extraction. They met and married in Berlin and went to live in Iran where Soraya was born. When she was fifteen, the family returned to Europe, where Soraya completed her schooling and her father ran up huge debts in the casinos.

When no embarrassing skeletons were found in the closet, Princess Shams returned to Tehran in triumph with Soraya in tow. A dinner was organized by the Shah's mother to introduce her to his brothers and sisters. Shams and Fatemah managed to insinuate their husbands into the gathering. When the Shah himself turned up unannounced in one of his flashiest uniforms, Soraya slipped into a state of shock. Nevertheless, the Shah was impressed by her, especially by her beautiful, green, almond-shaped eyes. Shams was told to ask Soraya for her hand in marriage on his behalf. He wanted an answer that night.

'In that case, my answer is yes,' Soraya said.

A wedding date was set, but Soraya came down with typhoid. There was an epidemic in Tehran at the time. The situation was grave. The doctors gave up on her. In desperation, the Shah let a personal friend, Lieutenant-Colonel Karim Ayadi – an army vet – try his hand at saving his young fiancée from what everyone agreed was certain death.

Ayadi miraculously succeeded in saving her, with the help of a new drug called aureomycin which he had read about in a French magazine. It had to be flown in from America. He was rewarded by being appointed the Shah's personal physician. It was not until four years later that he qualified as a doctor.

For the wedding, a Christian Dior gown was flown in from Paris, but it was too heavy for the weakened Soraya to wear, so Ayadi and the Shah lopped ten yards off the train to the horror of the French couturier. For warmth, Soraya was told to wear thick woollen army socks and a cardigan, which she wore over her Dior gown and under her fur coat. The Iranians were pleased with the wedding pictures. They were happy that the Shah was marrying someone pleasantly fat.

However, Soraya soon became unpopular – and not just because she was thin. She never mastered Persian and her childish ways upset the courtiers. The Shah, on the other hand, found her childishness alluring and indulged her every whim. He would whisk her off to romantic hideaways. They were very much in love.

But after five years of marriage, she had not had a child and the Shah still had no son. Soraya was such a jealous person, he could only visit his daughter from his first marriage in secret. People began talking about 'the German cow' and 'the barren one'. The mullahs began to put pressure on him. Under Islamic law, he could take a second wife. Although the Shah resisted the suggestion, Soraya believed he would change his mind.

Then at a ball, Soraya caught the Shah dancing with a beautiful blonde, and gave an ultimatum. Either he abdicate and live with her in exile, or keep his crown and lose her. That night she flew out of Tehran. She settled in St Moritz and the Shah repudiated her under Islamic law. He gave her $80,000. She kept the jewels she had collected over the years and he conferred the title Imperial Majesty on her. They continued to exchange letters and, on one occasion, agreed to meet informally. But both thought better of it.

So by the early 1950s, the Shah needed a wife again. His mother Taj al-Moluk interviewed a stream of débutantes. Each week a new list of possible brides for the Shah was published and journalists would receive hefty bribes from the families of eligible girls to mention their daughters as possible candidates.

Meanwhile the Shah had a number of brief affairs. He was seen with twenty-two-year-old Dokhi, nineteen-year-old Safieh and a German film actress named Helga Anderson. Things got serious with Princess Maria-Gabriella of Savoy, the daughter of ex-King Umberto of Italy. They met in Switzerland, fell in love and considered marriage. The problem was that Maria-Gabriella was neither a Persian nor a Muslim. Her nationality could be fixed easily enough with an imperial decree. The Iranian embassy in Paris began the ground work. They paid huge sums to French genealogists to prove that Maria-Gabriella was a descendant of Princess Zelidah, the daughter of Muhammad II, the eleventh century Moorish ruler of Seville. The press announced that the Shah's intended was a woman of impeccable Islamic background.

Maria-Gabriella would still have to become a Muslim, of course. Otherwise there would be hell to pay with the ayatollahs. The problem was that ex-King Umberto prided himself on being a good Catholic and he vehemently opposed his daughter's planned conversion to Islam. Large sums of money were offered and ex-King Umberto slowly came round. He said he would stifle his objections if the pope gave his benediction to the marriage. In February 1959, the Shah paid a brief visit to Pope John XXIII, who said he could not sanction the marriage unless the Shah converted to Catholicism. This was impossible. Three months later the Iranian government announced that rumours regarding His Imperial Majesty's marriage to a foreign subject were greatly exaggerated. The Shah would not think of taking a non-Muslim wife.

A few months later, the Shah's sister Princess Shahnaz and her husband, Ardeshir Zahedi, found a new bridal candidate, eighteen-year-old Farah Diba. She had returned home for the summer holidays from the Ecole des Beaux Arts in Paris where she was studying architecture. They found her charming and decided to introduce her to the Shah. He had, in fact, already met her at an official reception for Iranian students at the Iranian embassy in Paris. But the meeting had left little impression on him.

'How could you forget having met me?' she would chide later. 'Was it not love at first sight?'

255

Farah remembered the incident all too well. She had broken with two of her friends, who were Communists, to attend. Then she had been shoved aside by royalists who mobbed the King of Kings. To restore order, the students were presented one by one. When it was Farah's turn, the Shah expressed surprise that a woman should want to become an architect.

'He had such sad eyes, beautiful and sad eyes,' she wrote to her mother.

She was still in Paris when she heard of the break-up of the Shah's second marriage. Again she wrote to her mother.

'I have just heard that His Majesty and Soraya have parted. What a shame!' she wrote.

The Shah's search for a new bride filled the French press that summer and fellow students teased her about it. At one student party, everyone signed a paper saying that she should be queen.

When she arrived home for the holidays, her family urged her to visit Hessarak, Zahedi's residence. She was presented to Princess Shahnaz. The two women met a number of times and it was clear to Farah that she was under scrutiny.

Shahnaz introduced her to the family. At one tea party at Hessarak, the Shah turned up. Farah quickly recovered from her shock and reminded him of the previous time they had met. The Shah showed a polite interest, nothing more.

Farah had an athletic body and the black eyes cherished by Persians, but she was a brunette and it was well known that the Shah preferred blondes.

By the time Farah was to return to Paris, nothing had been said. Shahnaz asked her to delay her departure for a couple of days, and at one final party at Hessarak, the Shah indicated that everyone except Farah should leave.

'I wish to have a private talk with you,' he said. 'I hope you don't mind.'

He explained how his first two marriages had ended in divorce and the responsibilities – and possible dangers – of being his queen. Then he asked her to marry him.

Although he was more than twice her age, she did not hesitate.

'I would be honoured, Your Majesty,' she said. Then he took her hand for the first time.

Later she asked him why he had chosen her. He replied: 'I liked your simplicity, your purity.'

But why had she accepted – did she love the man or the monarch?

'The two are one,' she said. 'And I knew that I loved the man who was asking me to marry him.'

Ten months after their wedding, the Shah personally drove his wife to the maternity hospital, where she gave birth to a boy. This made her extremely popular with the Iranians. She was a full-blooded Persian and now she had delivered an heir. In celebration, the Shah released ninety-eight political prisoners and slashed income tax by twenty per cent.

During the first years of her marriage, Farah received a number of anonymous letters, warning her of her husband's inability to remain faithful to a single woman. Her sole function, she was told, was to produce babies while he sought carnal pleasures elsewhere. In five years, she produced three children.

Although he had her crowned as his queen, it was true that the Shah could not remain faithful. Anyone on the make in Persia knew that women were the Shah's weakness and would use this to their advantage.

'You had to pimp to progress,' said one courtier.

General Muhammad Khatam and Amir-Assadollah Alam made huge personal profits providing the Shah with courtesans. The Shah's personal physician, now General Abdul-Karim Ayadi, scouted Western European circles for 'companions'. Mainly they were blondes with big mouths. Lufthansa hostesses were in great demand.

It was rumoured that he had a love child in France and that one of his mistresses sent a huge bill for couture dresses to the Iranian embassy in Paris. But there were conquests closer to home. The Shah once insisted on making love to one of his ministers daughters in a helicopter hovering over Isfahan.

Former Italian prime minister Giulio Andreotti recalled that when the Shah arrived at the Venice Film Festival, he shocked the local prefect by asking for a woman for the night. The prefect replied: 'That is a job for the police!'

Diplomats reported that the Iranian imperial court reeked of sex. Everyone gossiped about the Shah's latest favourite. He made no effort to hide his infidelities from his wife. She appears to be the only one in the whole court who was chaste. Most notorious was the Shah's sister, Princess Ashraf. She was said to have been photographed naked with a U.S. senator. A 1976 CIA report said that she had a 'near legendary reputation for financial corruption and for successfully pursuing young men', many of them securing government positions in recognition of services rendered.

The Shah also had a full-time pimp, Amir-Hushang Davalloo, who bore the title 'His Majesty's Special Butler'. Empress Farah dismissed Davalloo as 'the court jester – he made the Shah laugh'.

In the imperial court, Davalloo was the only person who could go and see the Shah whenever he wanted. He could even enter the Shah's private quarters without an appointment.

In fact, Davalloo had begun his career as a procurer in Paris in the 1940s. He fixed Nazi officers up with 'escorts'. At one time, he numbered Herman Göring among his clients. He maintained links with the Parisian maison of Madame Claude which included among its customers King Hassan of Morocco. Madame Claude recruited amateur call-girls, many of whom went on to make good marriages. During the years when the Shah was kept in power by his vicious secret police, SAVAK, she kept him well supplied with women. One of Claude's girls, a tall well-built blonde who called herself Ange, spoke out.

She said that she had spent several months in Tehran in 1969. She flew there first class and was met at the airport by a young man from the Ministry of the Court. He drove her to the Hilton in a Mercedes with tinted windows. They were given adjoining suites and he tried to seduce her, but Madame Claude had warned her that if she succumbed she would be on the next plane home, forfeiting a lucrative fee. She was there for the pleasure of the Shah alone.

For three days she did nothing but fend off her minder's advances and learn how to curtsy – the Shah insisted that women curtsy, she was told. On the fourth day, she was driven to a villa in northern Tehran. It was heavily guarded. She was shown into a room where there was a table laden with food. She noticed a bottle of brandy and took a swig to calm her nerves. By the time the Shah turned up three hours later, she was completely drunk. She tried to curtsy and fell over. The Shah shook her hand.

'But I have to curtsy,' she said, trying it again.

Madame Claude had told her that the Shah liked to drink and to dance. So she poured him some brandy and did the tango. Then she dragged him upstairs. He was hours late for a meeting with the Empress at the airport and there was a huge row.

The Shah enjoyed her company so much that he insisted that she stay on in Tehran. She was closeted in the hotel and he saw her twice a week.

'He was always very nice to me,' she said, 'kind, gentle and generous – not at all like the Arabs.'

They used to play games in the bedroom. His favourite was tag, which is called chat, or cat, in French. She used to chase him around the bed shouting: 'Chat, Shah, chat, Shah.'

He laughed a lot, but those around him did not and Ange sensed that he was a deeply sad man.

Ange soon tired of being a prisoner in the hotel. Everybody knew what she was there for and kept an eye on her. She could not even go to the pool without a guard. The only person she was allowed to be alone with was the man from the Ministry. He was a good-looking man and continued to try to seduce her. He would invite her to his suite for dinner, then emerge from the shower with his dressing gown undone.

'No one will know, I promise,' he would say. But she resisted.

American businessmen in the hotel offered her thousands of dollars, but she turned them down too.

'I was there for the Shah,' she said.

After six months Ange had had enough.

'You cannot leave,' said the man from the Ministry. 'You please His Majesty.'

But she went anyway.

When the Shah came to Paris for de Gaulle's funeral in 1970, he tried to contact her, but she was going on a fishing trip with her boyfriend and refused to change her plans. Madame Claude was furious. She had to find someone else for the Shah. Over the years, hundreds of young women from Madame Claude's found their way to Tehran.

Farah turned a blind eye to such things as best she could. Only once did her husband's womanizing cause a serious rift. In the early 1970s, it was rumoured that the Shah had fallen in love with a nineteen-year-old Iranian girl with bleached blonde hair named Gilda. Worse, he was said to have married her and installed her in a cottage in the palace grounds. At the end of 1972, Farah abruptly left for Europe. A CIA report noted: 'This sparked rumours of a rift between the Shah and Farah. Although there were suggestions that Ashraf may have had a hand in the affair it seems more likely that the Shah's dalliance with another woman was the real cause.'

Queen Farah returned and demanded that the Shah get rid of Gilda. He was rescued by his brother-in-law General Khatami, the husband of his sister Princess Fatemah. Khatami kindly agreed to take Gilda as his own mistress. The Shah was said to have been very grateful at the time.

In 1973, an intrepid Italian journalist, Oriana Fallaci, had the audacity to ask the Shah whether it was true that he had taken another wife.

'That is a stupid, vile, disgusting libel,' railed the Shah.

'But, Your Majesty, you're a Muslim. Your religion allows you to take another wife without repudiating Empress Farah,' Fallaci said.

'Yes, certainly. According to my religion, I could, so long as my wife grants her consent,' he pointed out, softening. 'And, to be honest, one must admit there are cases where...when a wife falls ill, for instance, or when she refuses to perform her wifely duties, thereby causing her husband unhappiness... Let's face it. One has to be a hypocrite or an innocent to believe that a husband will tolerate that kind of thing. In your society, when something like that occurs, doesn't a man take a mistress, or even more than one? Well, in our society, instead, a man can take another wife.'

In January 1979, Farah accompanied the Shah into exile. They ended up in Panama after General Noriega assured the Shah that every man in the country had a mistress as well as a wife. Noriega even procured for him. One evening, he booked a suite in the Panama Hotel and arranged for a young woman to come for dinner. Noriega insisted that she was from a good family, not a whore. The Shah had dinner with the woman, then they retired for the night. This may have been the last time the Shah made love. He died in June 1979, with his loyal Queen Farah by his side.

16

The Bawdy Saudis

King Fahd and the House of Saud rule Saudi Arabia with a rod of iron. And although drinking, gambling, pornography and promiscuous behaviour are out of the question for most of the subjects of the desert kingdom, the royal family can do more or less what they like.

Ibn Saud was the founder of the kingdom and father of the last three kings. He ruled from 1953 to 1964. His attitude to women was simple. They were baby-making machines. During his reign, there were no schools for girls in Saudi Arabia. What was the point? Learning did not become them. He never even ate a meal with a woman and he kept his harem in a windowless basement.

'Windows let lovers in,' he said.

Not that he was an overly jealous man. When he divorced one of his wives, Hassa Al Sudeiri, she married his brother. When Saud decided that he wanted her back, he persuaded his brother to divorce her and remarried her himself. She then produced seven sons, including the present King Fahd.

But sex was not just about making babies. It was also an instrument of policy. He tried to unify Arabia by marrying into over thirty tribes. At any one time he would have four wives, four concubines and four slaves on hand to satisfy him. Saud was related to most of Saudi Arabia by marriage.

Saud was also a show-off. When a tribe spread rumours that his virility was flagging, he paid them a surprise visit and 'shamed' them by deflowering one of their virgins.

He would mention in passing that he had deflowered seven-hundred virgins. Once he had deflowered them, he would give them away. British double-agent Kim Philby was one of the lucky recipients.

Once when Saud went to Egypt, he was heard to remark: 'This country is full of pretty women and I would like to buy some of them to take back home. How about £100,000 worth of them.'

Saud also boasted that he never saw the faces of the women he slept with. Towards the end of his reign, some ten per cent of the doctors in the country were dedicating their time to finding ways to keep the old king virile.

Saud's sons followed in their father's footsteps. They would marry dozens of women every time he went away. They were also big drinkers. Prince Nasir once killed four guests with the homebrew he had distilled. His father forgave him. Things were a little more problematic with Prince Mishari, who shot the British Vice-consul in Jeddah when he would not give him any more whisky. The Vice-consul's widow was given £70,000 and Prince Mishari was given a few months in jail. At this time, flogging if not public execution was the standard punishment for the possession of alcohol.

The young princes also went abroad for fun. They believed that any young woman in a bikini was for sale – their father had told them so. One was particularly fascinated by a restaurant where diners could watch a woman swimming underwater. They slept with expensive prostitutes, left behind stacks of unpaid bills and gave everyone they came into contact with a gold watch with their father's picture on the face. In one year, they gave away 35,000 watches while their playboy bills were picked up by American oil companies, eager to curry favour with the future rulers of the world's most oil-rich country.

When Ibn Saud died in 1953 his son, also named Ibn Saud, succeeded him. Saud eventually became ill, and spent much of his time abroad seeking medical assistance. In 1964, while he was away, his brother Faisal, with the support of his brothers, took over.

At the behest of his wife, Faisal opened a girls' school, but he did nothing more to improve the lot of the country's women. Years later, he was asked when he was going to grant women rights. He replied: 'When we grant them to men.'

In 1975, Faisal was assassinated by his nephew. His brother Khalid took over, and when he died in 1982, Fahd became king. But the situation on women's rights did not improve. Women are still not even allowed to drive cars. In 1991, a number of female college professors conducted a group drive in protest. They were arrested, tried, imprisoned and lost their jobs.

Education has done the women in the royal family little good – they are supposed to sit at home and do nothing, not even social work. They have become adept at telephone sex; they carry scraps of paper with their telephone numbers on when they go shopping in case they see any attractive men. Many take lovers, while others pay for sex.

The price of such misadventures can be ruinously high, as the ATV film *Death of a Princess* demonstrated. Princess Mishaal made the fatal mistake of falling in love. She had been educated in Beirut and exposed to Western ways. When she returned to Saudi Arabia at the age of seventeen, she was given away to a royal cousin. He ignored her and, when she protested, he divorced her.

During a trip to Europe, she met a young Lebanese man named Muhammad Al Shaer, who had good Saudi connections. His uncle was in the Saudi government.

Princess Mishaal went back to Saudi to ask her family's permission to marry him. They refused. She tried to escape the country dressed as a boy, but was apprehended. Meanwhile, her lover managed to get into the country. They met in a hotel in Jeddah, where they were arrested.

Princess Mishaal had the misfortune to be the granddaughter of Muhammad 'Twin-Evils', another of Ibn Saud's sons. The twin evils that gave him his name were alcohol and violence. His alcoholic outbursts were so ferocious that even the three of his brothers who have occupied the throne were afraid of him. In a rare moment of lucidity, in 1964, he renounced his right to the throne.

He had his granddaughter, Princess Mishaal, and her lover imprisoned. He demanded that his brother King Khalid sentence them to death. When he demurred, Twin-Evils went to the imam. He thought there should be a proper court of enquiry. This would take too long, so Twin-Evils issued the sentence of death himself. The public executioner was doubtful about the procedure, so Twin-Evils ordered his own guards to do the job.

In July 1977, Princess Mishaal and Muhammad Al Shaer were dragged out into a dusty square on the outskirts of Jeddah. Against all precedent, Mishaal was shot while Muhammad looked on. He was then be-headed and his body dismembered. Two days later, the story was released that Princess Mishaal had died in a drowning accident.

Unfortunately, Princess Mishaal's German nurse, Rosemary Beacheau, knew the whole story. It was leaked to a TV producer in Britain who made *Death of a Princess*. There was huge pressure not to have it shown. Mobil Oil suspended its sponsorship of the Public Broadcasting System in America, fearing the film's effect on the Saudi–American relationship; Saudi tourists to London dropped by 70 per cent; and the Saudi government spent $500 million on a damage-limitation exercise.

Princess Mishaal was not the only one to suffer such a fate. Eight months after the airing of *Death of a Princess*, another prince asked King Khalid to execute his adulterous daughter. Nervous of another international scandal, the King suggested that his brother handle the situation himself. He did. He took his daughter to the swimming pool in his palace and drowned her. Again the announcement was made that it was an accident. The father had been married thirty-six times.

17

The Mother of All Mothers

There can be little doubt that Saddam Hussein is a monster, but there are, apparently, a number of women who find a bushy macho moustache, olive green fatigues, an iron fist and a carelessness with the lives of others, irresistibly sexy.

Saddam's sex life began conventionally enough. After taking part in the assassination of President Qassem of Iraq – he only provided covering fire for the assassins though his semi-official biography says that he did the deed single-handed – he escaped to Syria, then moved on to Egypt where he enrolled as a law student at the University of Cairo.

While he was there, he decided to marry his cousin Sajidah Talfah. They had known each other since childhood and had been brought up as brother and sister. Following tradition, he wrote requesting her hand in marriage. It was granted. The couple were engaged in Egypt and married shortly after their return to Iraq in 1963. A year later, their first son Udai was born.

Sadly, Saddam Hussein did not have time to finish his law studies in Cairo. Not a man to be disappointed, in 1972 he strode into Baghdad University with a pistol in his belt, surrounded by bodyguards, and was awarded a law degree. Four years later, he got his M.A. the same way.

There have been numerous reports of Saddam Hussein's marital infidelity. One report states that the wife of an Armenian merchant was his mistress for a while. Another says that his girlfriend was the daughter of a former Iraqi ambassador. There were rumours that Saddam's trusted bodyguard and presidential food taster, Kamel Hanna Jejjo, fixed him up with women. Usually this was handled discreetly, but as Saddam became increasingly bored with his wife, he began to be seen around Baghdad with Samira Shahbandar, the ex-wife of the Chairman of Iraqi Airways – though the opposition suggested that Samira was not actually a member of the respected Shahbandar family at all, but the family cook who had borrowed the name.

Samira became pregnant, rocking Saddam Hussein's marriage and damaging his carefully nurtured 'family man' image. For a time, the story went, Saddam was considering either divorcing Sajidah or taking Samira as a second wife, which is acceptable under Islamic law but against Ba'ath Party policy.

A son was born. The opposition say he was named Ali. This would mean that Saddam was 'Abu Ali', literally 'father of Ali' but also an Arabic idiom for a trickster.

Saddam's first son, Udai, had grown up to be fiercely protective of his mother and not a man to take things lying down. He had already killed an army colonel who tried to prevent him seducing his teenaged daughter, and an officer who took exception to the pass Udai had made at his wife in a Baghdad disco.

Udai knew that the presidential food-taster Jejjo had introduced Samira to his father and had acted as go-between during the affair. In a drunken rage, Udai beat Jejjo to death. There followed the mother of all family rows. Saddam had Udai thrown in jail. Sajidah immediately jumped to her son's defence.

'Why arrest him?' she asked her husband. 'After all, it is not the first time he has killed. Nor is he the only one in the family who has killed.'

Saddam relented and Udai was sent into luxurious exile in Switzerland. This was done at the request of the Jejjo family, Saddam announced publicly. They had accepted that what had happened was 'the will of Allah', he said.

In 1995, the deep divisions in the family surfaced again, when Saddam's two daughters and their husbands ran off to Jordan. In 1996, they returned to Iraq. Within hours of crossing the border, Saddam's sons-in-law were murdered by Udai. That helped confirm Saddam's position as a bloodthirsty dictator.

Despite the trouble it caused in the family and the fact that taking more than one wife was expressly forbidden by the Ba'ath Party, Saddam eventually married Samira, taking her as his second wife. He placated his first wife Sajida by making her 'Lady of the Ladies', while Samira became 'First Lady'. But that did not stop him fooling around.

'He particularly enjoyed having affairs with married women because it was a way of humiliating their husbands,' said one former palace official.

If he liked a woman, she would be taken against her

will from her home while her husband was out and brought to a special house in the Mansour district of Baghdad. And once the assignation was over, she would be returned home the same night.

His appetite for young, blonde women, it was said, had remained undiminished over the years. If he saw one he liked on television, for example, he would send his bodyguard to bring her to him. When he had finished with her, they would be told to pay her handsomely – unless she had failed to please him, in which case she would be taken out and shot.

The search for weapons of mass destruction that dragged on throughout the 1990s was made all the more difficult because of the large number of palaces Saddam built for his wives and mistresses. At the height of the Monica Lewinsky scandal, President Clinton threatened Iraq, but Saddam quickly dubbed America's aggressive overtures as 'the war of Clinton's penis'.

Then, as the debate over weapons of mass destruction heated up the UN in 2002, a mysterious blonde named Parisoula Lampsos, who claimed to have been Saddam's lover for thirty years, appeared. Parisoula was the daughter of a wealthy Greek engineer who worked on Iraq's oil pipelines. She was born and brought up in pre-civil war Beirut, then known as 'the Paris of the Middle East'. 'At eighteen,' she said, 'I was gorgeous.' And that youthful beauty became an obsession for Saddam.

In 1968, Parisoula was visiting Baghdad when she was invited to a party thrown by a textile magnate called Harout and was introduced to a young military officer rising rapidly in the Ba'ath Party – Saddam Hussein. He squeezed her hand and stared deep into her eyes.

Harout was serving fish and Saddam said: 'You are going to be the fisherman's bite tonight.'

She was bowled over by this smooth chat.

'He was young, good-looking, well dressed and in power,' she said. 'I wasn't aware he was such a criminal. How could I have been?'

Saddam called her simply *Shaqraa* – 'the blonde' and was immediately jealous of her. He told one of his brothers who was at the party: 'Do not touch her, Barzan. She's mine.'

Parisoula admits that she succumbed that night.

Their ongoing affair was conducted discreetly, mainly at Harout's home. But when Parisoula's family found out, they took her back to Beirut. Thinking her affair with Saddam Hussein was behind her, Parisoula married a wealthy Iraqi businessman in 1970 and produced two daughters. The family settled in Baghdad. However, by 1972 Saddam had risen to become Iraq's de facto leader. He threw her husband in jail and seized his assets, leaving Parisoula and her daughters penniless. She had no choice but to turn to her husband's jailer for help.

Saddam's lawyer told her to divorce her husband and convert to Islam. For the next two years she and Saddam were lovers again. According to Parisoula, Saddam found her a second husband, a crony who was ordered to go through with the ceremony but not to consummate the marriage. However, Saddam's plan did not work out. In 1974, she fell pregnant by her new husband and fled to Greece.

In 1978, with Saddam on the brink of the bloody putsch which brought him supreme power, she returned to Baghdad and resumed the relationship. According to Parisoula, Saddam's two wives, Sajidah and Samira, knew of the affair but were forced to accept it.

When the Iran-Iraq War began in 1980, like foreign spouses of Iraqis, she was ordered to take Iraqi citizenship. Unwilling to relinquish her Greek passport, Parisoula left for Greece and stayed away six years.

By 1986 she had fallen on hard times and approached the Iraqi embassy in Athens who organised for her to travel to Baghdad without a passport. Two days after she arrived, she was driven to the presidential palace.

'When we met, I went to shake his hand, but he held me close and hugged me,' said Parisoula. 'That day we had sex again in the palace.'

But she was in for a shock.

'After he finished he slapped me round the face and shouted at me, saying, "I'm never weak in my life, except when I'm with you."'

Parisoula and her two young daughters, who had inherited their mother's beauty, moved into a villa in the palace grounds and lived a life of luxury. She was given a job working for Saddam's son Udai, who took a shine to one of her daughters.

One weekend in 1987, he took Parisoula's daughters to a party at Habaniya, a popular lakeside resort used by Baghdad's elite. There, like hundreds of other young Iraqi girls in Iraq before and since, Udai raped the fifteen-year-old girl. She returned bruised and bloody, and Parisoula took her to the Baghdad hospital used by the regime's upper echelon.

Parisoula blamed herself. She should have protected her daughter. Instead, she was working as Udai's private secretary and sleeping with his father. But she knew neither she nor her daughter could speak out. Indeed, her daughter continued to see Udai, fearful of the consequences if she did not. The relationship ended only in 1996, after an assassination attempt left Udai paralysed. She eventually escaped to Europe.

'No mother should have to endure what I've gone through,' said Parisoula. 'But then, in a sense, every Iraqi mother has.'

Parisoula went on seeing Saddam. Though he was a tough man, she said he wept when he was forced to withdraw from Kuwait, but he did not fear America and regarded the UN weapons inspectors with contempt.

As the years went by, their passion cooled.

'After the rape of my daughter, I felt hatred for him, and when I slept with him, I felt I was being raped too,' she said. 'I admit it was balanced by the good life. I was turned into the palace whore.'

But gradually the once affectionate Saddam became cruel. He beat her. She said she wanted out, but she realised she would never be allowed to leave.

'I asked him why.' She begged him to let her go, saying: 'I don't have anything to give you any more. You can have any woman. What do you need of me?'

Parisoula said that Saddam then 'looked at me very, very, very strongly. He said, "You belong to me. You are going to die here in Baghdad."'

She tried to break off the relationship many times. Then early in 2002 she managed to slip across the border into Jordan. There she was picked up by agents of the opposition Iraqi National Congress. They protected her and in September organised an interview with ABC News correspondent Claire Shipman in Beirut.

'She's a bubbly, vivacious woman who can make a man feel very comfortable and very masculine,' said

274

Shipman. 'She's captivating. There's something about her that draws people to her.'

Parisoula told Shipman that Saddam had a 'collection' of women that included three wives and five other mistresses. She claimed she was his favourite mistress, and was friendly with his wives. She saw Saddam two or three times a week, and had it all – jewels, cars, her own home and a private villa in the grounds of Saddam's palace with an entire room just for her designer clothes. But though she was plied with expensive gifts, she found herself living in a world where women were treated as mere possessions. She lived, she said, in a gilded prison.

She also described the Iraqi dictator as a twisted sadist who had a fetish for Hitler – 'I am Saddam… heil Hitler!' he would say.

'His goal is for his name to live for a thousand years,' she said, 'as the new Arab hero, the second Saladin.'

When relaxing Saddam never read books, but loved watching the movie *The Godfather*. Of an evening, Saddam would smoke cigars and drink whisky – in contravention of Islamic law – don a cowboy hat and listen to the gay anthem "Strangers in the Night" by Frank Sinatra while watching videos of his enemies being tortured in his regime's torture chambers. These torture videos, she said, made him 'happy, happy, happy'.

She also claimed that Saddam supported Osama bin Laden and saw him in Hussein's palace in the 1980s. She also believes Saddam ordered the assassination of Udai. When the assassination attempt failed, leaving Udai paralysed, she recalled him saying: 'I didn't want it this way. I wanted him to die. It was better for him.'

In their relationship, at first, she said, 'He was tender. He was warm. He was nice. He was another person.' But as Saddam grew older, he began to worry about his flagging prowess. He dyed his hair, used a relaxation mask to reduce wrinkles, and sometimes used Viagra to sex up their encounters. Apparently he was having trouble with his biological weapon.

Later he suffered a stroke.

'If you see him in some photos, his mouth is not normal,' she said. 'It droops.'

Eventually, sex became coercive.

'Saddam, he don't need to force anybody,' she said. 'You are afraid. You are afraid to say no. I was with him because I was afraid of him.'

Even in exile she moves constantly between safe houses and hides her face behind a veil.

'Here you have a decent woman from a good family who lost everything, despite submitting to Saddam's every whim,' said her INC minder. 'Like so many other Iraqi families, Shaqraa's life and her family's was destroyed by the dictator.'

Once the Anglo-American invasion of Iraq had started, Saddam Hussein was caught with his pants down – literally – when the Kuwaiti secret police revealed that they had a shocking 1968 hardcore gay porn film which showed the flamboyant Iraqi strongman involved in hot man-on-man action. The quality of the grainy 16 mm film was poor, but experts who studied at the hairy-chested stud performing raunchy homosexual acts were '100 per cent certain' it was a younger, trimmer Saddam, according to US supermarket tabloid *Weekly World News*.

'There is no doubt in my mind that this is Saddam,' said biographer Sadiq al-Sabah after reviewing the footage first hand. 'There's no mistaking those eyes and that distinctive nose.'

Sadiq admits that it is hard to believe that the ruthless dictator who took over one of the most powerful nations in the Middle East once acted in blue movies, 'but to anyone familiar with how reckless and sexually promiscuous Saddam was in his youth, this will come as no surprise. It's also a known fact that the young, desperate soldier did anything for money.' When a struggling law student, Saddam may have acted in porn to make ends meet but, Sadiq said, he also did it because he was addicted to gay sex. Indeed, earlier developments revealed that he was addicted to Greeks and he and his men do have moustaches that would not look out of place on Castro Street.

According to one researcher Saddam appeared in as many as eighty-five porn films under a variety of stage names, most frequently 'Omar Studdif'. Still photographs from the XXX-rated movie *La'iba al-Waladaani* – 'The Two Boys Played' – were leaked to a Kuwaiti news magazine after authorities found it among a stash of illicit porn in the vault of a recently deceased sheikh. Release of the pictures has resulted in howls of protest from Baghdad, who condemned them as 'CIA propaganda'.

'President Hussein is the manliest of men,' said an Iraqi spokesman. 'He would never behave in such a repugnant manner.'

However, rumours that Saddam appeared in gay porn films had dogged him for decades and almost toppled his political career when he was a rising star in the ruling Ba'ath Party.

'He was able to squelch the rumours in the past,' said a State Department analyst. 'But now it looks like the Kuwaitis have found the smoking gun.' Though what part in the plot that played has not been revealed.

In the newly uncovered eighty-six-minute prison flick, a slim thirty-four-year-old Saddam plays a naïve young peasant boy who is wrongly convicted and sent to jail. There he is initiated into a wide variety of homosexual practices by a series of older and more experienced men.

'Saddam's acting in the picture is actually quite good,' Sadiq says. 'In one scene, he buries his face in a pillow and cries – it is so touching you almost can forget you're watching a low-budget sexploitation film.'

There were more revelations about Saddam's sex life once the invasion was over and US troops threw open the doors on what they called Saddam's Baghdad 'love shack'. It was a split-level, one-bedroom town house in a Ba'ath Party enclave in an upmarket neighbourhood where generals and senior party officials lived. Upstairs they found a king-size bed in a mirrored alcove. On the wall there was a painting of a near naked pneumatic blonde with a green demon behind her, pointing a finger at a moustachioed hero. From the tip of her finger came a giant serpent, which had wrapped itself around the macho warrior. Another 1960s-style fantasy painting showed a buxom woman chained to a barren desert mountain ledge, with a huge dragon diving down to kill her with its sharp talons.

The town house also boasted lamps shaped like naked women, a well-stocked bar and other items direct from the world of Austin Powers. And one of the soldiers who discovered the love nest described it simply as 'Shagadelic'. Indeed, the carpet was a navy blue shag.

Index

Adroa, Kay, 207-8, 210-11
Al Shaer, Muhammad, 266-7
Aleksandrovna, Eugenia, 75
Alekseeka, Nina, 74
Alexander I, Czar, 39
Amin, Idi, 206-16
Amin, Medina, 208, 209, 211, 212
Amin, Nora, 208, 211
Amin, Sarah, 207, 211-12
Amin, Sauda, 214
Andreotti, Guilio, 258
Aquino, Benigno, 193, 194, 199, 204, 205
Armand, Elisabeth d'Herbenville (Inessa), 53-8
Armand, Vladimir, 53-4
Arvad, Ingrid, 115
Ashraf, Princess, 249, 252, 258-9, 261
Atatürk, Kemal, 222-7
Audisio, 90-1
Ayadi, Karim, 253, 258
Aziz Khanom, Empress of Iran, 249

Bailey, Percival, 236
Balabanoff, Angelica, 54, 57, 77
Balart, Rafael Dmaz, 152, 154
Barker, Humphrey, 235
Barras, Paul, 13-14, 15-16, 17, 19, 20-1
Basquette, Linda, 110
Bazhanov, 59
Beams, Dovie, 201-4
Beaucheau, Rosemary, 267
Beauharnais Bonaparte,

Eugène de, 12, 14, 20, 26, 27
Beauharnais Bonaparte, Hortensede, 27, 28, 42
Bechstein, Helene, 100, 101, 102
Bellanger, Marguérite, 44
Beneni, Giulia, 44
Beria, Laventry, 69-75
Beria, Nino, 69-71
Beria, Sergo, 74
Berman, Jakub, 68
Bernadotte, Jean Baptiste, 10
Blangini, Félix, 42
Bloch, Eduard, 97
Bokassa, Empress Catherine, 217
Bokassa, Emperor Jean, 216-19
Bonaparte, Caroline, 30, 31
Bonaparte, Jerome, 11
Bonaparte, Joseph, 34
Bonaparte, Louis, 28
Bonaparte, Lucien, 28
Bonaparte, Pauline, 11, 39-42
Bongo, Omar, 219-21
Borghese, Count Camillo, 41
Braun, Eva, 115-22
Büchner, Elisabeth, 103
Bullitt, William, 68
Burgos, Pedro, 172

Callaghan, Jim, 215
Canourville, Armand Joules de, 42
Canova, Antonio, 42
Castiglione, Contessa di, 45

Castro, Angel, 152
Castro, Fidel, 151-65
Castro, Fidelito, 153, 156-7, 165
Castro, Mirta, 152-4, 156, 158
Casuso, Teresa, 154-5
Caulaincourt, General Louis de, 34, 38
Ceausescu, Elena, 4-5
Ceausescu, Nicholae, 5
Ceausescu, Nicholae-Andruta, 5
Ceausescu, Nicu, 5
Chan, Victoriano, 193-4
Charles, Hippolyte, 21-2, 23, 24-5, 27, 28, 34
Chernyshevsky, 54-5
Chiang Ch'in, 128-37
Chung Hye-sung, 146-7
Clary, Désirée (Eugénie), 9
Claude, Madame, 259, 260, 261
Cojuangco, Eduardo, 200-1
Cojuangco, Gretchen, 200
Connolly, Cyril, 237, 239
Cora Pearl, 44
Coraboeuf, Magda (Fontanges), 83
Cordal, Carmencita, 168
Corinne, Madame, 223, 225
Cucciate, Elene Curti, 89
Curti, Angela, 84, 89
Custodio, Isabel, 155-6

Dacko, David, 216, 218
Dalser, Ida, 81-2
Davalloo, Amir-Hushang, 259
Decoud, Carlos, 168

Denuelle, Eléonore, 31, 36
Dior, Christian, 253
du Colombier, Caroline, 7
du Colombier, Madam, 7
Dûchatel, Marie
    Antoinette, 30-1, 37
Duchesnois, Mademoiselle,
    33

Ehrenburg, Ilya, 47
Emami, Taqi, 251
Esmat Khanom, Empress
    of Iran, 249-50

Fahd, King of Saudi
    Arabia, 263, 265
Faisal, King of Iraq, 250
Faisal, King of Saudi
    Arabia, 265
Fallaci, Oriana, 262
Farah, Empress of Iran,
    255-9, 261, 262
Farida, Queen of Egypt,
    229, 230, 234, 235, 238,
    248
Farouk, King of Egypt,
    228-48, 250
Fatemah, Princess, 252, 261
Fawziah, Empress of Iran,
    250-1
Fegelein, Hermann, 121,
    122
Fernandez, Alina, 154, 158
Fesch, Cardinal, 30
Fleischer, Tillie, 114, 122
Fontenay, Thérèse de, 13
Forbin, Louis Philippe
    Auguste de, 41
Ford, Cristina, 205
Forster, Edmund, 100
Fourés, Lieutenant, 26
Fourés, Pauline, 26-7
Franco, Francisco, 1-2
Franco, Nunca, 2-3
Franco, Ramón, 2
Frank, Bernard, 237
Frederick Louis, Prince,
    36-7
Fréron, Louis, 40-1
Fuad, King of Egypt, 233

Gable, Clark, 238
Gaitán, Gloria, 158
Gao Gang, 133
Gardner, Ava, 160-1
Garmendia, Pancha, 167-8
Gatti, Annamaria, 247,
    248
Ghali, Riad, 229
Gholam-Reza, Prince, 251
Giscard d'Estaing, Valéry,
    218
Gitta, Jesse, 212
Goebbels, Josef, 110, 112,
    113, 114, 122
Goebbels, Magda, 110-11,
    123
Göring, Herman, 93, 112,
    121, 123, 259
Gorky, Maxim, 67
Gourgard, Gaspard, 39
La Grissini, 29
Guidi, Anna, 78
Guidi, Augusta, 78
Guinle, Irene, 231-7
Guweddeko, Smuts, 212

Hamilton, George, 205
Hanfstaengl, Putzi, 113
Harris, Lawrence, 203
Hasanein, Ahmed
    Mohammed, 229
Hassa Al Sudeiri, 263
Hassan, King of Morocco,
    259
Hess, Rudolf, 93
Hilliyer, Patrick, 252
Hills, Denis, 215
Himmler, Heinrich, 100,
    107, 108, 121
Hitler, Adolf, 66-7, 92-123,
    213, 250, 275
Hitler, Alois, 94-7
Hitler, Klara, 95-8
Hitler, Patrick, 107
Hitler, Paula, 96, 102
Ho Tzu-chen, 126-7, 128,
    130-1
Hoche, General, 12, 16
Hoffmann, Heinrich, 106,
    115, 118

Hoffmann, Henriette, 105,
    106
Hohenlohe, Prince
    Alexander, 238
Hohenlohe, Princess
    Patricia 'Honeychile'
    Wilder, 238, 246
Hong Il-chon, 145
Hong Yung-hui, 146
Hoser, Gisela, 122-3
Howard, Elizabeth, 43
Hussein, Saddam, 268-78
Hussein, Sajidah, 268, 269,
    270
Hussein, Udai, 268, 269-70

Ibn Saud, King of Saudi
    Arabia, 263-5
Imbert, Colonel Anibal,
    185
Isabella, Queen of Spain,
    171
Isabella of Brazil, Princess,
    176

Jantsen, Stefanie, 98
Jejjo, Kamel Hanna, 269,
    270
Jiménez, Marcos Peréz,
    163-4
John XXIII, Pope, 255
John Paul II, Pope, 218
Johnson, Lyndon B., 115
Joséphine, Empress, 12-39

K, Elizabeth de, 48-53
Kaganovich, Lazar, 61
Kang Sheng, 132-3
Kapler, Aleksei, 63
Kaunda, Kenneth, 215
Kennedy, John F., 115, 238
Key, Ellen, 53
Khalid, King of Saudi
    Arabia, 265, 266, 267
Khatam, General
    Muhammad, 258
Khatami, General, 261-2
Kibedi, Malyamu, 207,
    208-10
Kim Chong-il, 144-9

INDEX

Kim Il-sung, 144, 145, 147, 149-50
Kim Jong-suk, 144-5, 147
Kim Pyong-il, 145
Kim Song-ae, 145
Kissinger, Henry, 1
Kovachev, Dimitriana 'Miti', 224
Kovachev, General, 224
Krupskaya, Nadezhda Konstantina *see* Krupskaya Nadya
Krupskaya, Nadya, 46-8, 54-8
Krushchev, Nikita, 73
Kubizek, Gustl, 98-9
Kuusia, Armi, 246
Kyemba, Henry, 213-14

Lacson, Arsenio, 194-5
Lakoba, Nesto, 71-2
Lamarque, Libertad, 185, 187
Lampson, Sir Miles, 232, 233, 235
Langer, Henry A., 94
Laugier de Bellecour, Pierre François, 6
Le Pen, Jean-Marie, 219
Leclerc, Victor, 40-1
Lenin, 46-59
Li Pyong, 145
Li-Sang-jin, 146
Liptauer, Susi, 103
López, Benigno, 171
López, Carlos Antonio, 166, 167, 168, 171-3, 174, 175
López, Francisco, Solano, 166-79
López, Juan Francisco, 173, 179
Lorentz, Marita, 159-64
Luciano, Lucky, 242-3, 246
Lynch, Eliza, 169-80

Mao Tse-tun, 124-43
Marchand, Louis, 39
Marcos, Ferdinand, 193, 195-205

Marcos, Imelda, 193-205
Maria-Gabriella, Princess of Savoy, 254-5
Marie Louise, Empress, 37-8
Matzelberger, Franziska, 95
Maurice, Emil, 102, 106, 107
Méneval, 39
Minutolo, Irma, 240-2, 243-6, 247, 248
Mishaal, Princess of Saudi Arabia, 266-7
Mishari, Prince of Saudi Arabia, 264
Mitford, Diana, 111-12
Mitford, Unity, 111-12, 118
Moerman, Laure, 220
Mohammed Reza Khan, Shah of Iran, 249, 250-62
Molotov, V.M., 68
Montansier, Mademoiselle de, 10
Montelibano, Alfredo Jr, 199
Montijo, Eugénie de, 43-4
Morrell, Theo, 119
Muammer, Latife, 225-7
Muammer, Ushakizade, 225
Muhammed 'Twin-Evil', Prince of Saudi Arabia, 266-7
Mütter, Renate, 109-10
Murat, Joachim, 31
Mussolini, Benito, 76-91, 115, 121, 181, 187
Mussolini, Rachele, 78-9, 81, 87-8

Najjat, Lovis, 231-2
Nakpil, Ariston, 195
Napoleon I, 6-42
Napoleon III (Louis Bonaparte), 28, 42-5, 168-9
Narriman, Queen of Egypt, 238-9, 243, 244
Nasir, Prince of Saudi Arabia, 264

Nasser, Gamal Abdel, 1, 228, 242-2, 246
Nazli, Queen of Egypt, 229
Neipperg, Count von, 38
Nicholas II, Czar, 66
Noriega, General, 262

Obote, Milton, 208
Onassis, Aristotle, 189
Ortega, Carmen, 197-8, 201, 202

Pacho, Dominador, 194
Palacios, Father, 173, 175-6
Pari Khanom, 251
Pauker, K.V., 67-8
Peng Dehuai, 141-2
Permon, Albert, 11
Permon, Laure, 11
Permon, Madame, 11
Perón, Evita, 182-90, 191, 192
Perón, Isabel, 192
Perón, Juan Domingo, 181-2, 185-92
Pesoa, Juana, 172
Petacci, Clara, 83-91
Petroff, Sultane Rasha, 224
Petroff, Ratcho, 224
Philby, Kim, 264
Pinochet, General, 1
Pius VII, Pope, 30
Pol Pot, 3
Polo y Martínes Valdés, María del Carmen, 2-3
Polzl, Klara, 95, 96, 97, 98
Potocka, Countess Anna, 40
Power, Tyrone, 238
Pulli, Antonio, 230-1, 236

Qaddafy, Colonel, 205, 215
Qaddafy, Zurra, 215
Qassem, President, 268
Quatrefages, Xavier, 169
Quennell, Peter, 237

Randolf, Dr, 105, 106
Rafanelli, Leda, 82
Raubal, Angela, 103, 104, 105, 106

SEX LIVES OF THE GREAT DICTATORS

Raubal, Geli, 103-9, 116
Reagan, Ronald, 203
Redesdale, Lady, 111, 112
Redesdale, Lord, 111
Reese, Joyce, 201
Reiter, Mitzi, 103
Rémusat, Claire de, 29-30, 32
Revuelta, Natalia, 153-4, 157, 158
Reza Khan, Shah of Iran, 249-50
Riefenstahl, Leni, 93, 112-15, 122
Ritossa, Zita, 85
Rivas, Nellie, 190-2
Röhm, Ernst, 93, 108
Rolandeau, Louise, 29
Romualdez, Eduardo, 197
Rosengoltz, Arkaday, 71
Rosengoltz, Yelena, 71-2
Rugumayo, Edward, 206-7
Rumyantsev, Mihkail, 48, 49
Ruz, Lina, 152

Sadat, Anwar, 228
Sagan, Françoise, 237
Salote-Croix, Chevalier de, 39
Sanchéz, Celia, 157, 160, 164
Sanger, Yurike, 4
Sarfatti, Margherita, 81, 82-3, 84
Schwartz, Franz Xavier, 106
Ségur, General de, 38
Shahbandar, Samira, 269, 270
Shahnaz, Princess, 255, 256-7
Shams, Princess, 252
Shirin, Esma'il, 251
Shivekar, Princess, 233
Silvers, Robert, 237

Skelton, Barbara, 235-6, 237, 239
Slezak, Margaret, 111
Smalto, Francesco, 219-21
Son Nui-rim, 146
Sorya, Empress of Iran, 252-4, 256
Soriano, Carmen, 204
Soto Del Vaile Jorge, Dalia, 164-5
Stalin, Ekaterina, 59-60
Stalin, Joseph, 59-75
Stalin, Nadya, 60-2, 75
Stalin, Svetlana, 61, 62-4
Stalin, Vasily, 64
Stalin, Yakov, 63-4
Stempfle, Father, 106
Stenberg, Brigitta, 242, 243, 246
Stendhal, 33
Strasser, Gregor, 104, 107-8
Strasser, Otto, 104, 105, 107
Suarez, Mrs, 233
Subirán, Sofia, 2
Sukarno, Dewi, 4
Sukarno, Fatmawati, 4
Sukarno, Inggit, President, 3-4
Sun Hye-rim, 145-6
Sutro, John, 237
Svanidze, Alexandr, 59

Taisey-Chatenoy, Marquise, 44
Taj al-Moluk, Empress of Iran, 249, 250, 254
Talal, Crown Prince of Jordan, 250
Tallien, Thérèse, 16
Talma, François, 42
Tao Szu-yung, 125-6
Tascher-Beauharnais, Hortense, 17, 20, 28-9, 42

Ting Ling, 128
Tito, Marshal, 68
Tizon, Aurelia, 181
Toussoun, Fatima, 229, 234
Trenker, Luis, 111, 113, 114, 116
Trotsky, Leon, 61
Tsai Chang, 125
Turan Khanom, Empress of Iran, 249
Tynan, Kenneth, 237

Ulynov, Vladimir Ilych, 46
see Lenin
Umberto II, King of Italy, 254, 255

Vergeot, Alexandrine, 43
Vidal, Gore, 246
Villatuya, Ernesto, 204-5
Volkogonov, Dimitri, 74

Wagner, Winifred, 102, 106, 118
Walewska, Countess Marie, 35-6, 38
Walewski, Count Alexandre, 35, 36, 38
Weymer, Marguérite, 31-2
Whitlin, Thaddeus, 69
Wu, Lily, 128, 131
Wu In-hui, 147

Yakubova, Apollinaria, 46-7
Yang Kai-hui, 126, 127, 128
Ye Zilong, 133
Yu Qiwei, 129
Yu Shan, 132

Zahedi, Ardeshir, 255
Zeisler, Alfred, 109
Zhang Yufeng, 142
Zibala, Justo, 194